ENCYCLOPAEDIA OF MOLECULAR BIOLOGY
Vol. II
MOLECULAR BIOLOGY OF GENETICS

By

Dr. M. Prakash

DISCOVERY PUBLISHING HOUSE
NEW DELHI-110002

First Published-2007

ISBN 81-8356-210-8 (Set)

Published by

DISCOVERY PUBLISHING HOUSE

4831/24, Ansari Road, Prahlad Street,
Darya Ganj, New Delhi-110002 (India)
Phone: 23279245 • Fax: 91-11-23253475
E-mail:dphtemp@indiatimes.com

Printed at:

Sachin Printers, Delhi

Preface

The present title **Encyclopaedia of Molecular Biology** is a fast growing area of research from majors or carrers in physics, chemistry, mathematics and engineering as well as animal, plant, cell biology and medicine. The overall objective of this publication is to provide a professional level reference work with comprehensive coverage of the molecular basis of life and the application of that knowledge in genetics, evolution, medicine, and agriculture. It deals with the life processes at a molecular level genetic disease diagnosis and genetic therapy; the theory and techniques for understanding manipulating, and synthesizing biological molecules and their aggregates; and the application of biological processes to make or modify products to improve plants or animals or to develop microorganisms for specific uses.

Teachers and professors in schools and universities will use this publication for course preparation, and members of the press will find useful background information on new development in biotechnology and genetic medicine. Efforts have been made to prevent a concise treatment of their field of expertise at a level useful to both colleagues and researchers who are experts in related fields, as well as to university students requiring an introduction to a specific molecular biology discipline.

There can be no claim to originality except in the manner of treatment and much of the information has been obtained from the books and scientific journals available in the different libraries.

The author express his thanks to his friends and colleagues whose continue inspirations have initiated him to bring out this book.

The author expresses his gratitude to Mr. Wasan and staff of M/s Discovery Publishing House for their whole hearted co-operation in the publication of this book.

Author

CONTENTS

Genes, Cumulative or Quantitative Genes, Modifying Factors, Pleiotropy, Expressivity, Atavism.

mRNA Alternative Conformations, General Transcriptional Termination Hypothesis, Histidine Operon Control, Post-translational Control via Noncovalent Binding of Signal Molecules, Regulated Steps of a Biochemical Pathway, Effects of Noncovalent Interactions with Signal Molecules, Post-translational Control via Covalent Modification, Glutamine Synthetase of E. coli, Chemotaxis in E. coli.

1

INTRODUCTION

Earth originated about 5 billion years ago and life originated about 3 billion years ago and that too in water on this earth. All life that has appeared on earth is descended from organisms that were originally very simple. The physical and chemical evolution on earth that preceded the appearance of organisms (prebiotic evolution) was followed by an organismal evolution over the last 4 billion years which culminated in organisms of extraordinary complexity, such as ourselves. Note that present-day organisms—those in existence the past few thousand years—would occupy much less horizontal space in figure than the vertical line marking the interval at 0, for even if 1000 vertical lines could be drawn between 0 and –1, each thin line would represent 1000 thousand (that is, 1 million) years!

It has been reported in this latest thin line of time a great variety of organisms—plant and animal, microscopic to mammoth, incredibly diverse—making up some 2 million kinds, or species. These organisms range from viruses and bacteria through protozoans, sponges, corals and jellyfish, flat, round, and segmented worms, shellfish and starfish, spiders and insects, finned fishes, amphibians, reptiles, birds, mammals, algae and fungi, mosses, ferns, and seed plants in a bewildering tangle of forms of life.

By collecting information about these various organisms and by organizing such information—that is, by developing the science of biology—we can group facts about organisms, and establish principles and generalities that apply to many species. Such common threads among species are revealed by studying their structe, form, function and composition.

All organisms have a common origin, and all of them require one or more *cells* and many cell products for their structure and function. Cells vary in size and complexity from the tiny and relatively simple cell of a bacterium, about 100 of which can fit across the dot of an *i*, to the giant and relatively complex yolk, which is the single cell of a chicken or an ostrich egg.

Features of a typical cell can be suggested by imagining a plastic bag containing a very porous sponge which is saturated with a thick vegetable soap. This sponge, in turn, surrounds a smaller plastic bag containing noodle soup. The outer plastic bag represents the *cell membrane*, or the outside limit of the cell. The inner plastic bag represents the *nuclear membrane*, the outside limit o the *nucleus*. The sponge represents the *endoplasmic reticulum*, which is a network of membranes (forming channels often interconnected) that also connect the other two membranes. The soups and membranes make up *protoplasm*, which is called *cytoplasm* outside the nucleus. The vegetables in the cytoplasm include various types of bodies (membrane-bound bodies are called *organelles*), such as *ribosomes*, *Mitochondria* and, in green cells, *chloroplasts*. The noodles of the nucleus represent the *chromosomes*. One or a few chromosomes are also present in each mitochondrion and chloroplast. Nucleus-containing cells are *eukaryotic* cells, and organisms composed of such cells are *eukaryotes*. The cells of bacteria and blue-green algae, on the other hand, can be likened to a single plastic bag, the size of a mitochondrion or smaller, containing soup with relatively few vegetables and only a noodle or two. Such cells consists largely of a small mass of protoplasm bounded by a cell membrane, containing ribosomes and one or a few chromosomes. Lacking a nucleus the cells are said to be *prokaryotic*; the cells also lack an endoplasmic reticulum, mitochondria, and chloroplasts. Although all *prokaryotes* are single-celled organisms, eukaryotes may also be composed of single cells, as are protozoans such as amebae or of as many as trillions of cells, as in each human being.

The common features of cell structure and form are accompanied by common features of cell function. The thousands of chemical reactions and physical changes that occur in protoplasm comprise the cell's *metabolism*. Metabolism occurs primarily at sites and surfaces provided by membranes, organelles, and large molecules (including chromosomes). The reactions that synthesize more energy-containing substances or protoplasm are *anabolic*; the reactions which degrade energy-providing substances or protoplasm are *catabolic*. By drawing raw materials and energy from the environment and processing them through metabolism, cells are able to maintain themselves, grow, and divide to produce more cells. All of today's organisms are characterized functionally, therefore, by their capacity for two basic functions; (1) *self-maintenance*, which involves growth, replacement, and/or repair of parts of an organism; and (2) *self-reproduction*, which involves making more of the same kind of organisms.

Requirements for Genetic Material

The genetic material is of central importance to cell function and therefore must fulfil a number of basic requirements:

1. It must contain the information for cell structure, function, and reproduction in a stable form. This information is encoded in the sequence of basic building blocks of the genetic material.
2. It must be possible to replicate the genetic material accurately such that the same genetic information is present in descendant cells and in successive generations.
3. The information coded in the genetic material must be able to be decoded to produce the molecules essential for the structure and function of cells.
4. The genetic material must be capable of (infrequent) variation. Specifically, mutation and recombination of the genetic material are the foundations for the evolutionary process.

The nucleic acids, *deoxyribonucleic acid* (DNA) and ribonucleic acid (RNA), meet all these requirements.

Presence of Genetic Material

Organisms have unique requirements at the structural level, at the functional level and at the macromolecular level. Each organism must possess a facility or factor that (1) persists during the entire existence of the organism, (2) is repeated in each of its progeny, (3) is different in different organisms, and (4) contains the information needed for synthesizing characteristic proteins and nucleic acids. For purposes of scientific investigation, we assume that we are dealing with a material factor rather than a spiritual one. Since this material factor must contain the instructions for the creation, or genesis, of an organism, we can call it *genetic material*. All the different organisms that have appeared on earth are likely to have had a single ancestor, (1) there is only one basic tye of genetic material, and (2) the genetic material can be changed yet still be reproduced. The single most important feature of all organism is, with this view, genetic material.

This material is characterized by being preserved, replicated, capable of replicating its modifications, and contains the information for unique protein and nucleic acid. The study of the properties and functions of genetic material thus comprises the core of the study of all organisms, that is, of the science of biology.

Some mature viruses, or *virions*, are composed only of nucleic acid and protein in combination. Clearly, their genetic material must be one or the other or some combination of these two types of macromolecule. A determination can be made through the infection experiments described in the next section.

GENETIC VIEW

The concept of the gene has been the focus of some hundred years of work to establish the basis of heredity. A gene is a sequence of DNA that carries the information representing a protein. Until very recently this would have been an adequate (if incomplete) bio-chemical description. The sequence of DNA could be identified as a continuous stretch of nucleotides, related to the protein sequence by a colinear read-out. But now it is clear that the sequence representing protein is not always continuous; it may be interrupted by sequences not concerned with specifying the protein. So genes may be in pieces that are put together during the process of gene expression. The large number or genes that make up the genome of any species are organizd into a comparatively small number of chromosomes. The genetic material of each chromosome consists of an extremely long stretch of DNA, containing many genes in a linear order. How many genes are present in total has been a puzzle for a long time.

Recently the view that each gene may reside by itself as a unique entity has been superseded by the realization that, in many cases, there may be clusters of related genes that constitute small families. The genome generally has been viewed as rather stable, subject to changes in overall constitution and organization only on an extraordinarily slow evolutionary time scale. This contrasts with recent evidence that in some instances there may be rearrangements that occur regularly; and there may be components of the genome that are relatively mobile. The concept of the gene has therefore undergone an evolution in which, although many of its traditional properties remain, exceptions have been found to show that none constitutes an absolute rule. Starting from the discovery of the gene as a fixed unit of inheritance, its properties were defined in terms of its residence at a definite position on the chromosome, this in turn leading to the view that the genetic material of the chromosome is a continuous length of DNA representing many genes.

A gene may exist in alternative forms that result in the expression of a different characteristic (such as red versus white flower colour). These forms are called *alleles*. The law of independent segregation states that these alleles do not affect each other when present in the same plant, but segregate unchanged by passing into different gametes when the next generation forms. In a true-breeding organism, a *homozygote*, both alleles are the same. But a mating between two parents each of which is homozygous for a different allele generates a hybrid or *heterozygote*. If one allele is *dominant* and the other is *recessive*, the organism will have the appearance or *phenotype* only of the dominant type (so the heterozygote is indistinguishable from the true-breeding dominant parent). But Mendel's first law recognizes that the genetic constitution or *genotype* of the hybrid comprises the presence of both alleles. This is revealed, when the hybrid is crossed with another hybrid to form the second generation. The critical point is that the alleles do not mix, but are physical entities whose interaction is at the level of expression.

Alleles may exhibit *incomplete (partial) dominance* or no dominance (sometimes known as *codominance*). In the latter case the heterozygote is distinguished from the homozygotes by properties that are intermediate between them. In the snap-dragon, for example, a cross between red and white generates hybrids with pink flowers. Although there is no dominance, the same rule is observed that the first hybrid (F_1) generation is uniform; and the same ratios are generated in a further hybrid cross, although three phenotypes can be distinguished instead of two.

INDEPENDENCE OF DIFFERENT GENES

Mendel's second law which is the independent assortment summarizes of different genes. When a plant that is dominant for two different characters is crossed with a parent that is recessive for both, as before the F_1 consists of plants uniformly of the dominant type. But in the next hybrid cross, two classes of plants are seen. One consists of the two *parental types*. The other consists of new phenotypes, representing plants with the dominant feature of one parent and the recessive feature of the other. These are called *recombinant types*; and they occur in both possible (*reciprocal*) combinations. The ratios in which these occur can be explained by supposing that gamete formation involves an entirely random association of one of the alleles for the first character with one of the alleles for the other. All four possible types of gamete are formed in equal proportion, and associate at random in forming the zygotes of the next generation. Once again, the characteristic ratio of phenotypes conceals a greater variety of genotypes, which can be confirmed by the *backcross* to the recessive parent. Essentially the backcross provides a method for looking directly at the genotype of the organism that is being examined.

The law of independent assortment therefore says that the behaviour of any pair (or greater number) of genes can be predicted overall by the rules of mathematical combination. Thus the assortment of one gene does not influence the assortment of the other. Implicit in this concept is the view that assortment is a matter of statistical probability and not an exact result. The ratios of progeny types will approximate increasingly closely to the predicted numbers as a greater number of crosses are performed.

CHROMOSOMES IN HEREDITY

When the chromosomal theory of inheritance was simultaneously proposed by Sutton and by Boveri, it resolved the discussion that had been continuing for some time on the role of chromosomes. They had already been implicated in heredity, although in a somewhat hazy manner, in 1903 it was realized that their properties corresponded exactly with those ascribed to Mendel's particulates units of inheritance. The cell theory established in the middle of the nineteenth century proposed that all organisms are composed of cells, and that these can arise only from preexisting cells.

Early cytology showed that a "typical" cell consists of a dense nucleus separated by a membrane from the less-dense surrounding cytoplasm. Within the nucleus, the granular region of *chromatin* could be recognized by its reaction with certain stains. Not long after Mendel's work, it was found that the chromatin consists of a discrete number of thread-like particles, the *chromosomes*. Chromosomes can be visualized in most cells only during the process of cell division.

The two types of division in sexually reproducing organisms explain both the perpetuation of the genetic material and the process of inheritance as predicted by Mendel's laws. During growth of the organism, the *cell cycle* falls into two parts. The long period of *interphase* represents the time during which the cell engages in its synthetic activities and reproduces its components. Then the short period of *mitosis* is an interlude during which the actual process of division into two daughter cells is accomplished. The products of the series of mitotic divisions that generate the entire organism are called the *somatic cells*. At the end of mitosis, each daughter cell can be seen to start its life with two copies of each chromosome. These are called *homologous*.

The total number of chromosomes in what is known as the *diploid set* can therefore be described as *2n*. The typical somatic cell exists in the diploid state. During interphase, a growing cell duplicates its chromosomal material. This is not evident at the time and becomes apparent only during the subsequent mitosis. During mitosis, each chromosome appears to split longitudinally to generate two copies. These are called *sister chromatids*. At this point, the cell contains *4n* chromosomes, organized as *2n* pairs of sister chromatids. In other words, there are two (homologous) copies of each sister chromatid pair. The series of events, by which mitotic division is accomplished. Essentially the sister chromatids are pulled toward opposite poles of the cell, so that each daughter cell receives one member of each sister chromatid pair. Now these are chromosoems in their own right. The *4n* chromosomes present at the start of division have been divided into two sets of *2n* chromosomes. This process is repeated in the next cell cycle. Thus mitotic division ensures the constancy of the chromosomal complement in the somatic cells.

Meiosis generates cells that contain the *haploid* chromosome number, *n*. This involves two, successive divisions. Once again, the chromosomes have been duplicated previously, so that the cell enters division with *4n*. At the time of first division, the homologous pairs of sister chromatids *synapse* or *pair* to form *bivalents*. Each bivalent contains all four of the cell's copies of one homologue. The first division causes each bivalent to segregate into its two component sister chromatid pairs. This generates two sets of *2n* chromosomes, each set consisting of *n* sister chromatid pairs.

Now the second meiotic division follows, in which both of the sets of *2n* divide again. This division resembles the mitotic division, since one member of each sister chromatid pair segregates to a different daughter cell. The overall result of meiosis is to divide the starting number of *4n* chromosomes into four haploid cells. These may then give rise to mature eggs or sperm. In forming these gametes, homologous of paternal and maternal origin are separated, so that each gametes gains only one of the two homologues of its parent.

A critical feature in relating this process to the predictions of Mendel's laws was the realization that nonhomologous chromosomes undergo segregation independently, so that either member of one homologous pair enters the gamete at random with either member of a different homologous pair.

Genes occur in allelic pairs, one member of each pair having been contributed by each parent; the diploid set of chromosomes results from the contribution of a haploid set by each parent. The assortment of nonallelic genes into gametes should be independent of origin, nonhomologous chromosomes undergo independent segregation. The critical provision is that each gamete obtains a complete haploid set, and this is fulfilled whether viewed in terms of factors or chromosomes.

ARRANGEMENT OF GENES

Linear

The proof that genes reside on chromosomes required a demonstration that a particular gene is always present on a particular chromosome. This was provided by the properties displayed by a variant of the fruit fly *Drosophila melanogaster* obtained by Morgan in 1910. This white-eyed male appeared spontaneously in a line of flies of the usual red eye colour.

The red eye colour is the *wild type* of character. The white eye is the *mutant* phenotype. The event responsible for generating the mutant phenotype is a genetic change called a *mutation*. Most mutations prevent the gene in which they occur from functioning properly or at all; and so the study of mutation is for the most part the study of inactive alleles.

Sometimes it is possible for a mutation to be reversed by a genetic change that restores the original state of the genetic material. This is called a *reversion* to the wild type. The white mutation could be located on a particular chromosome because of its association with sexual type.

In many sexually reproducing organisms there is an exception to the rule that chromosomes occur in homologous pairs whose separation (disjunction) at meiosis produces identicai haploid sets. Male and female sets may differ visibly in chromosome constitution, the most common form of difference being the replacement of one member of a homologue pair with a different chromosome in one of the sexes. This pair is referred to as the *sex chromosomes*, and the remaining homologous pairs are called the *autosomes*.

The chromosome complements of the two sexes can be described as 2A + XX and 2A + XY, where the haploid set of autosomes is denoted A and the two sex chromosomes are X and Y. The sex with the complement of 2A + XX is called *homogametic*; if forms gametes only of the type A + X. The sex with the complement of 2A + XY is called *heterogametic*; it forms equal proportions of gametes of the types A + X and A + Y. The random union of gametes from one sex with gametes from the other sex perpetuates the equal sex ratio at zygote formation. In *Drosophila* the females are homogametic.

A critical prediction of Mendel's laws is that the results of a genetic cross should be the same regardless of orientation— that is, irrespective of which parent introduces which allele. But the reciprocal crosses with white eye in *Drosophila* give different results.

The cross of white male × red female gives the entirely red F_1 expected if red is dominant and white is recessive. But in the F_2 all the white-eye flies that reappear are males. In the reciprocal cross of red male × white female, all the F_1 males are white-eyed and all the females are red eyed. Crossing these gives an F_2 with equal proportions of white and red eyes in each sex. This pattern of inheritance exactly follows that of the sex chromosomes. If the alleles for red and white eyes are carried on the X chromosome, with no locus for eye colour present on the Y chromosome, the phenotype of a male will be determined by the single allele present on its X chromosome. This allele will be transmitted to all of its daughters and none of its sons. This is the typical pattern of *sex linkage*.

The separation of chromosomes seen at meiosis explains the independent assortment of genes that are carried on different chromosomes. But the number of genetic factors is much greater than the number of chromosomes. Each chromosome may bear as many as 1000 to 10000 genes. The quickening pace of genetics after the turn of the century was shown by the passage of only three years between the report of the first eye-colour mutant and Stretevant's study in 1913 of the pattern of inheritance of six sex-linked mutations. Morgan had shown in 1911 that each of these factors shows the same sex-linked pattern as white/red eye colour. By the same logic each must therefore be carried by the X chromosome.

Morgan proposed that the cause of genetic linkage is the simple mechanical result of the location of the factors in the chromosomes. He suggested that the production of genetic recombinant classes can be equated with the process of *crossing over* that is visible during meiosis. Early in meiosis, at a stage when there are four copies of each chromosome organized in a bivalent, pairwise exchanges of material occur between the closely associated (synapsed) homologue pairs. This exchange is called a *chiasma*.

In maize and in *Drosophila*, suitable *translocations* had occurred in which a part of one chromosome had broken off and become attached to another. This allows the translocation chromosome to be distinguished by its appearance from the normal chromosome. In suitable crosses, it is then possible to show that the formation of genetic recombinants occurs only when there has been a physical crossing-over between the appropriate chromosome regions. As the distance between the genes increases, the probability of crossing-over between them will increase. Thus if crossing-over is responsible for recombination, genes lying near each other will be tightly linked, and genetic linkage will decrease with physical distance apart. Reversing the argument, genetic linkage can be taken to be measure of physical distance.

The concept that genes on the same chromosome are linked was extended by Sturtevant with the proposal that the extent of recombination between them can be used as a *map distance* to measure their relative locations. This is expressed as the percent recombination; that is,

$$\text{Map distance} = \frac{\text{Number of recombinants} \times 100}{\text{Total number of progeny}}$$

Distance is given in terms of *map units*, defined by 1 map unit (or centiMorgan) equal 1% recombination.

Thus if two genes A and B are 10 units apart, and it is 5 units from B to a further gene C, the direct measure of distance between A and C will be close to 15. The genes can therefore be placed in *linear order*. A crucial point in the construction of maps is that the distance between genes does not depend on the *alleles* that are used, but only on the gene *loci*. The locus defines the *position* on the chromosome at which the gene for a particular trait resides; the various alternative forms of the gene—that is, the alleles used in mapping—all reside at the *same* location.

The genetic mapping is concerned with identifying the locations of gene loci, which are fixed and in a linear order. In a mapping experiment the same result is obtained irrespective of the particular combination of alleles. Sturtevant concluded that his results "form a new argument in favour of the chromosome view of inheritance, since they strongly indicate that the factors investigated are arranged in a linear series, at least mathematically."

This last qualification is interesting. Although a genetic map can be constructed that represents a chromosome as a linear array of genes, this does not prove that the genetic content of the chromosome is *physically* a continuous array of genes. Many other models were considered before it became clear that a chromosome contains a single thread of genetic material. Linkage is not displayed between all pairs of genes located on a single chromosome.

The maximum recombination that occurs in the 50% predicted by Mendel's second law. (Although there is a high probability that recombination will occur between two genes lying far apart on a chromosome, each individual recombination event involves only two of the four associated chromosomes, thus generating 50% crossover between the genetic factors).

The factors that are well separated may show no direct linkage, in spite of their presence on the same chromosome. However, each can be linked via intermediate factors, and so a genetic map can be extended beyond the limit of 50 map units directly measurable between any pair of genes.

In fact, because of the distortion of linkage measured directly between markers that are not closely linked, map distances usually are based on measurements between fairly close factors, and may be subject to corrections from the simple percent recombination. The *linkage group* includes all those genes that can be connected either directly or indirectly by linkage relationships. Those close together show direct linkage; those more than 50 map units apart in practice assort independently.

As linkage relationships are extended, each gene identified in an organism can be placed into linkage with a group of previously mapped genes. Thus the genes fall into a discrete number of linkage groups. Genes in one linkage group always show independent assortment with regard to genes located in other linkage groups. The number of linkage groups is the same as the number of chromosomes.

The relative lengths of the linkage groups are similar to the actual relative sizes of the chromosomes. The example of *Drosophila* (where it happens to be particularly easy to measure the chromosome lengths). Mendel's concept of the gene as a discrete particulate factor can therefore be extended into the concept that the chromosome constitutes a linear unit divided into many genes, whose physical arrangement may underlie their genetic behaviour.

IDENTIFICATION OF DNA AS THE GENETIC MATERIAL

Two classic experiments led to the identification of DNA as the genetic material and, in so doing, laid the foundation for molecular genetics. These experiments are described in the following section.

Transformation Experiments

The development of the current idea that DNA is the genetic material began with an observation in 1928 by Fred Griffith, who was studying the bacterium responsible for human pneumonia—i.e., *Streptococcus pneumoniae* or *Pneumonoccus*. The virulence of this bacterium was known to be dependent on a surrounding polysaccharide capsule that protects it from the dense systems of the body. This capsule also causes the bacterium to produce smooth-edged (S) colonies on an agar surface. It was known that mice were normally killed by S

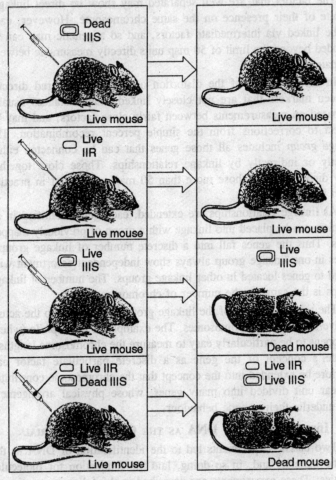

Fig. 1.1. Griffith's demonstration of transformation in pneumococcus.

bacteria. Griffith then isolated a rough-edged (R) colony mutant, which proved to be both nonencapsulated and nonlethal. He subsequently made a significant observation—namely, whereas both R and heat-killed S were nonlethal, a mixture of live R and heat-killed S was lethal. Furthermore, the bacteria isolated from a mouse that had died from such a mixed infection were only S—i.e., the live R had somehow been replaced by or *transformed* to S bacteria. Several years later it was shown that the mouse itself was not needed to mediate this transformation because when a mixture of R and heat-killed S was grown in a culture fluid, living S cells were produced. A possible explanation for this surprising phenomenon was that the R cells restored the viability of the dead S cells; but this idea was eliminated by the observation that living S cells grew even when the heat-killed S culture in the mixture was replaced by a cell extract prepared from broken S cells, which had been freed from both intact cells and the capsular polysaccharide by centrifugation. Hence, it was concluded that the cell extract contained a *transforming principle*, the nature of which was unknown.

15 years later when Oswald Avery, Colin MacLeod, and Maclyn McCarty partially purified the transforming principle from the cell extract and demonstrated that it was DNA. These workers modified known schemes for isolating DNA and prepared samples of DNA from S bacteria. They added this DNA to a live R bacterial culture; after a period of time they placed a sample of the S-containing R bacterial culture on an agar surface and allowed it to grow to form colonies. Some of the colonies (about 1 in 10^4) that grew were S type.

To show that this was a permanent genetic change, they dispersed many of the newly formed S colonies and placed them on a second agar surface. The resulting colonies were again S type. If an R colony arising from the original mixture was dispersed, only R bacteria grew in subsequent generations. Hence the R colonies retained the R character, whereas the transformed S colonies bred true as S. Because S and R colonies differed by a polysaccharide coat around each S bacterium, the ability of purified polysaccharide to transform was also tested, but no transformation was observed. Since the procedures for isolating DNA then in use produced DNA containing many impurities, it was necessary to provide evidence that the transformation was actually caused by the DNA alone.

This evidence was provided by the following four procedures.

1. Chemical analysis showed that the major component was a deoxyribose-containing nucleic acid.

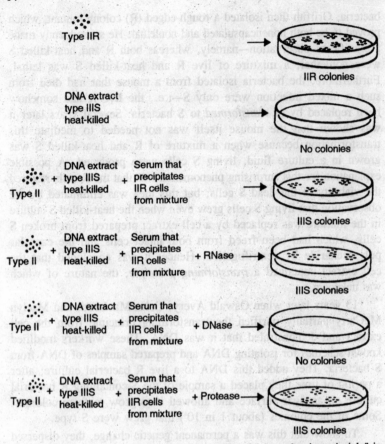

Fig. 1.2. Avery, MacLeod, and McCarty's proof that the "transforming principle" is DNA

2. Physical measurements showed that the sample contained a highly viscous substance having the properties of DNA.

3. Experiments demonstrated that transforming activity is not lost by reaction with either (a) purified proteolytic (protein-hydrolyzing) enzymes—trypsin, chymotrypsin, or a mixture of both—or (b) ribonuclease (an enzyme that depolymerizes RNA).

4. It was demonstrated that treatment with materials known to contain DNA-depolymerizing activity (DNase) inactivated the trans-forming principle.

The transformation experiment was not accepted by the scientific community as proof that DNA is the genetic material, because it was widely believed that DNA was a simple tetranucleotide incapable of carrying the information required of a genetic substance.

The tetranucleotide hypothesis was based on chemical analyses that indicated that DNA consists of equimolar amounts of the four bases; this conclusion was based on inadequate chemical procedures for analyzing base composition and on the use of higher organisms as sources of DNA; in these organisms the base composition is not far from being equimolar. However, as techniques improved and a greater range of organisms was examined, it was found that the base composition varies widely from one species to the next and that DNA is not a simple small molecule. With these results, the idea that DNA is the genetic material became acceptable. The following experiment provided the final proof.

The Blendor Experiment

An elegant confirmation of the genetic nature of DNA came from an experiment with *E. coli* phage T2. This experiment, known as the *blendor experiment* because a kitchen blendor was used as a major piece of apparatus, was performed by Alfred Hershey and Martha Chase, who demonstrated that the DNA injected by a phage particle

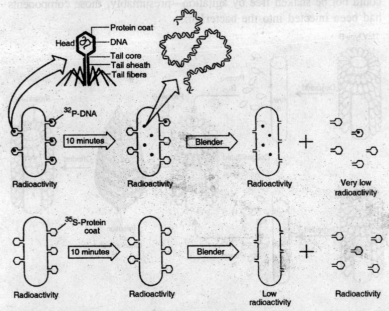

Fig. 1.3. The "Hershey-Chase experiment"—evidence that DNA is the genetic material in bacteriophage T2.

into a bacterium contains all of the information required to synthesize progeny phage particles. A single particle of phage T2 consists of DNA (now known to be a single molecule) encased in a protein shell.

The DNA is the only phosphorus-containing substance in the phage particle; the proteins of the shell, which contain the amino acids methionine and cysteine, have the only sulfur atoms. Thus, by growing phage in a nutrient medium in which radioactive phosphate ($^{32}PO_4^{3-}$) is the sole source of phosphorus, phage containing radioactive DNA can be prepared. If instead the growth medium contains radioactive sulfur as $^{35}SO_4^{3-}$, phage containing radioactive proteins are obtained. If these two kinds of labeled phage are used in an infection of a bacterial host, the phage DNA and the protein molecules can always be located by their radioactivity. Hershey and Chase used these phage to show that ^{32}P but not ^{35}S is injected into the bacterium. Each phage T2 particle has a long tail by which it attaches to sensitive bacteria.

Hershey and Chase showed that an attached phage can be torn from a bacterial cell wall by violent agitation of the infected cells in a kitchen blendor. Thus, it was possible to separate an adsorbed phage from a bacterium and determine the component(s) of the phage that could not be shaken free by agitation—presumably, those components had been injected into the bacterium.

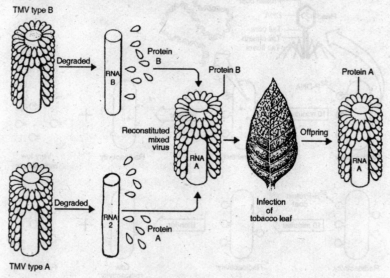

Fig. 1.4. Proof that the genetic material of tobacco mosaic virus (TMV) is RNA, not protein.

In the first experiment ^{35}S-labeled phage particles were adsorbed to bacteria for a few minutes. The bacteria were separated from unadsorbed phage and phage fragments by centrifuging the mixture and collecting the sediment (the pellet), which consisted of the phage-bacterium complexes. These complexes were resuspended in liquid and blended. The suspension was again centrifuged, and the pellet, which now consisted almost entirely of bacteria, and the supernatant were collected. It was found that 80 percent of the ^{35}S label was in the supernatant and 20 percent was in the pellet. The 20 percent of the ^{35}S that remains associated with the bacteria was shown some years later to consist mostly of phage tail fragments that adhered too tightly to the bacterial surface to be removed by the blending. A very different result was observed when the phage population was labeled with [32]P. In this case 70 percent of the ^{32}P remained associated with the bacteria in the pellet after blending and only 30 percent was in the supernatant.

Of the radioactivity in the supernatant roughly one-third could be accounted for by breakage of the bacteria during the blending. (The remainder was shown some years later to be a result of defective phage particles that could not inject their DNA.) when the pellet material was resuspended in growth medium and reincubated, it was found to be capable of phage production. Thus, the ability of a bacterium to synthesize progeny phage is associated with transfer of ^{32}P, and hence of DNA, from parental phage to the bacteria.

Transfer Experiments

Another series of experiments, known as *transfer experiments*, supported the interpretation that genetic material contains ^{32}P but not [35]S. In these experiments progeny phage were isolated, after blending, from cells that had been infected with either [35]S- or [35]P-containing phage and the progeny were then assayed for radioactivity, the idea being that some parental genetic material should be found in the progeny. It was found that no ^{35}S but about half of the injected ^{32}P was transferred to the progeny. This result indicated that though ^{35}S might be residually associated with the phage-infected bacteria, it was not part of the phage genetic material. The interpretation (now known to be correct) of the transfer of only half of the ^{32}P was that progeny DNA is selected at random for packaging into protein coats and that all progeny DNA is not successfully packaged.

PROPERTIES OF A GENETIC MATERIAL

To comprise the genes, DNA must carry the information to control the synthesis of the enzymes and proteins within a cell or organism, self-replicate with high fidelity yet show a low level of mutation, and be located in the chromosomes.

Control of the Enzymes

The growth, development, and functioning of a cell are controlled by the proteins within it, primarily its enzymes. Thus the nature of a cell's phenotype is controlled by the protein synthesis within that cell. The genetic material must determine the presence and effective amounts of the enzymes in a cell. For example, given inorganic salts and glucose, an *E. coli* cell can synthesize, through its enzyme-controlled biochemical pathways, all of the compounds it needs for growth, survival, and reproduction.

An enzyme is a protein that acts as a catalyst of a specific metabolic process without itself being markedly altered by the reaction. Most reactions that are catalyzed by enzymes could occur anyway, but only under conditions too extreme for them to take place within living systems. For example, many oxidations occur naturally at high temperatures. Enzymes allow these reactions to occur within the cell by lowering what is called the *activation energy* (ΔG) of a particular reaction. Most metabolic processes, such as the biosynthesis or degradation of molecules, occur in pathways in which an enzyme facilitates each step in the pathway.

Each reaction product in the pathway is altered by an enzyme that converts it to the next product. The enzyme threonine dehydratase, for example, converts threonine into a-ketobutyric acid. Enzymes are composed of folded polymers of amino acids; the sequence of amino acids determines the final structure of an enzyme. The genetic material determines the sequence of the amino acids.

The three-dimensional structure of enzymes permits them to perform their function. An enzyme combines with its substrate or substrates (the molecules it works on) at a part of the enzyme called the *active site*. The substrates "fit" into the active site, which has a shape that allows only the specific substrates to enter. This view of the way an enzyme interacts with its substrates is called the *lock-and-key model* of enzyme functioning. When the substrates are in their proper position in the active site of the enzyme, the particular reaction that the enzyme catalyzes takes place. The reaction products then separate from the enzyme and leave it free to repeat the process.

Enzymes can work at phenomenal speeds. Some can catalyze as many as a million reactions per minute. Not all of the cell's proteins function as catalysts. Some are structural proteins, such as keratin, the main component of hair. Other proteins are regulatory—they control the rate of production of other enzymes. Still others are involved in different functions; albumins, for example, help regulate the osmotic pressure of blood.

Replication

The genetic material must replicate itself precisely so that every daughter cell receives an exact copy. Some *mutability*, or the ability to change, is also required because we know that the genetic material has changed, or evolved, in the history of life on earth. In their 1953 paper, Watson and Crick had already worked out the replication process based on the structure of DNA. Mutability is also a natural derivative of this process.

Location

It has been known since the turn of the century that genes, the discrete functional units of genetic material, are located in chromosomes within the nuclei of eukaryotic cells: The behaviour of chromosomes during the cellular division stages of mitosis and meiosis mimics the behaviour of genes. Thus the genetic material in eukaryotes must be a part of the chromosomes.

For a long time, proteins were considered the most probable cell components to be genetic material because they have the necessary molecular complexity. Amino acids can be combined in an almost unlimited variety, creating thousands and thousands of different proteins. The first proof that the genetic material is deoxyribonucleic acid (DNA) was provided in 1944 by Oswald Avery and his colleagues. The Watson and Crick model in 1953 ended a period when DNA was thought to be the genetic material, but its structure was unknown.

Storage and Transmission of Genetic Information by DNA

The information possessed and conveyed by the DNA of a cell is of several types:

1. The sequence of amino acids in every protein synthesized by the cell.
2. A start and a stop signal for the synthesis of each protein.
3. A set of signals that determine whether a particular protein is to be made and how many molecules are to be made per unit time.

This information is contained in the sequence of DNA bases. The amino acid sequence and the start and stop signals are not obtained directly from the DNA base sequence but via RNA intermediates. That is, DNA serves as a template for synthesis of specific RNA molecules called messenger RNA. The base sequence of the mRNA is complementary to that of one of the DNA strands and it is form the mRNA sequence that the amino acid sequence is translated. In particular, the base sequence is "read" in order in groups of three bases called *triplets* or *codons* and each group corresponds to a particular amino acid or to a start or stop codon.

The two-stage process has the advantage that the DNA molecule neither has to be used very often nor has to enter the protein-synthetic mechanism. Since protein synthesis occurs continually, one can appreciate why DNA evolved with bases having groups capable of forming hydrogen bonds. First, by specific patterns of hydrogen-bonding—that is, base-pairing—the base sequence of DNA is easily transcribed into an RNA molecule by means of an enzymatic system that adds a base to the polymerizing end of an RNA molecule only if that base can hydrogen-bond with the base being copied. The use cf hydrogen-bonding enables the cell to use less genetic material to hold information than if van der Waals forces had been selected in the course of evolution; this is because van der Waals forces are so weak that the error frequency in transmitting information would be much greater than with hydrogen bonds unless more bases (or other molecules) were used for complementary binding.

Transmission from Parent to Progeny

When a cell divides, each daughter cell must contain identical genetic information; that is, each DNA molecule must become two identical molecules, each carrying the information that was contained in the parent molecule. This duplication process is called *replication*. Once again, the value of bases capable of hydrogen-bonding is apparent. That is, to make a replica, the replication system need only require that the base being added to the growing end of a new chain be capable of hydrogen-bonding to the base being copied.

Chemical Stability of DNA

In long-lived organisms a single DNA molecule may have to last one hundred years or more. Furthermore, the information contained in the molecule is passed on to successive generations for millions of years with only small changes. Thus, DNA molecules must have great stability. The sugar-phosphate backbone of DNA is extremely stable. The C—C bonds in the sugar are resistant to chemical attack under all conditions other than strong acid at very high temperatures.

The phosphodiester bond is a little less stable and can be hydrolyzed at room temperature at pH 2, but this is not a physiological condition.

In considering the stability of the phosphodiester bond, one can see immediately why 2´-deoxyribose rather than ribose is the constituent sugar in DNA. The phosphodiester bond in RNA is rapidly broken in alkali. The chemical mechanism for this breakage requires the OH group on the 2´ carbon of the sugar. In DNA, because deoxyribose is used, there is no 2´-OH group, so the molecule is exceedingly resistant to alkaline hydrolysis. The N-glycosylic bond is also very stable, though it would not be so if the bases were not rings. An alteration in the chemical structure of a base definitely means loss of genetic information.

In a cell there are certainly a large number of chemical compounds that can attack a free base. In considering this problem one can see immediately the value of the double helix. One aspect of this is that the molecule isredundant in the sense that identical information is contained in both strands; that is, the base sequence of one strand is complementary to that of the other strand. In fact, there exist in cells elegant repair systems that can remove an altered base and then by reading the sequence on the complementary strand, can replace the correct base. The more important aspect of this double-helical structure is that the nature of the bases and the duplex structure of DNA provides extreme protection against chemical attack.

The bases are hydrophobic rings having charged groups that contain the genetic information. It is therefore the charged groups that need protection. The hydrophobic nature of the base causes the bases to stack so extensively that water is almost completely excluded from the stacked array. This has the effect that water-soluble compounds are often unable to come into close contact with the "dry" stack of bases. The bases themselves, with the exception of cytosine, are very stable. At a very low rate, however, cytosine is deaminated to form uracil.

Deamination is a disastrous change because the deamination product, uracil, pairs with adenine rather than with guanine. This has two effects: (1) an incorrect base will appear in mRNA and (2) an adenine instead of a guanine will occur in newly replicated DNA strands. There exists an intracellular system, for removing uracil from DNA and replacing it with thymine. The necessity for eliminating a uracil formed by deamination explains why DNA utilizes thymine and not uracil as the base complementary to adenine. If uracil were the normal DNA base, there would be no way to distinguish a correct uracil from an incorrect uracil produced by deamination of cytosine. By using thymine, the cell follows the rule: Always remove a uracil from DNA because it is unwanted.

It is not obvious why RNA uses uracil and not thymine nor why DNA evolved with cytosine rather than with some base that would not deaminate. This may have been an evolutionary accident. It is possible, though, that the original DNA and RNA molecules both contained cytosine and uracil because these were the only pyrimidines available in the primordial sea. Cells then gained the ability to methylate uracil to form thymine because this provides a cell with a criterion for eliminating the result of a cytosine→uracil conversion. It is significant that the final step in the synthesis of thymidylic acid is the methylation of deoxyuridylic acid. The thymidylic acid is then converted to the triphosphate needed for incorporation into DNA.

Mutation

The process by which a base sequence changes is called *mutation*. There are two main mechanisms of mutation:

1. A *chemical alteration* of the base that gives it new hydrogen-bonding properties and causes a new base to be present in a newly replicated daughter molecule.
2. A *replication error* by which an incorrect base or an extra base is accidentally inserted in the daughter molecules.

On the average, mutational changes are deleterious and lead to cell death. Therefore, it is important that not too many mutations occur in a single DNA molecule because otherwise the rare advantageous alteration would always occur in a cell destined to die by virtue of lethal mutations. Thus, the mutation rate must be low or controlled. This is accomplished in two ways. First, the hydrophobic, water-free core of the DNA molecule reduces the accessibility of the DNA to attacking molecules, as we discussed earlier. Second, the cell has evolved several repair mechanisms for correcting alterations and replication errors. These repair systems are not entirely efficient though and allow mutations to occur at a rate that is very low but useful in the long run.

The mutations are usually deleterious, so that it is important that the parental information is not lost. Such loss is prevented in two ways: (1) The other members of the species retain the parental base sequence and (2) a double-stranded molecule is redundant. Normally only one strand is altered, and DNA replicates in such a way that after cell division the DNA molecule in each daughter cell receives only one of the parental single strands. Thus, it is possible for one of the daughter DNA molecules to be normal and the other to be mutant; the mutant may not be able to survive but the cell with the parental base sequence will. If the mutant is better equipped to survive and multiply than the parent organisms or any other member of the species, then after a great many generations, Darwin's principle of survival of the fitest will lead to ultimate replacement of the parental genotype by the mutant phenotype in nature.

RNA AS GENETIC MATERIAL IN SMALL VIRUSES

As more and more viruses were identified and studied, it became clear that many of them contain RNA and proteins, but no DNA. In all cases so far studied, it is clear that these "RNA viruses" store their genetic information in nucleic acids rather than in proteins just like all other organisms, although in these viruses the nucleic acid in RNA. One of the first experiments that established RNA as the genetic material in RNA viruses was the so-called reconstitution experiment of H. Fraenkel-Conrat and B. Singer, published in 1957. Fraenkel-Conrat and Singer's simple, but definitive, experiment was done with tobacco mosaic virus (TMV), a small virus composed of a single molecule of RNA encapsulated in a protein coat. Different strains of TMV can be identified on the basis of differences in the chemical composition of their protein coats.

By using the appropriate chemical treatments, one can separate the protein coats of TMV from the RNA. Moreover, this process is reversible; by mixing the proteins and the RNA under appropriate conditions, "reconstitution" wall occur, yielding complete, infective TMV particles. Raenkel-Contrat and Singer took two different strains of TMV, separated the RNAs from the protein coats, and reconstituted "mixed" viruses by mixing the proteins of one strain with the RNA of the second strain, and vice versa. When these mixed viruses were used to infect tobacco leaves, the progeny viruses produced were always found to be phenotypically and genotypically identical to the parent strain from which the RNA had been obtained. Thus, the genetic information of TMV is stored in RNA, not protein.

2

NUCLEAR MATERIAL

PROKARYOTIC CHROMOSOMES

Most textbooks in biology have until very recently presented a very erroneous picture of the chromosomes of prokaryotes. They have characterized prokaryotic chromosomes as "naked molecules of DNA," in contrast to eukaryotic chromosomes with their associated proteins and complex morphology. This misconception has resulted, at least in part, because (1) the pictures of prokaryotic chromosomes most often published have been autoradiographs and electron micrographs of isolated DNA molecules, *not metabolically active or functional chromosomes,* while (2) the most common pictures of eukaryotic chromosomes have been of highly condensed meiotic or mitotic chromosomes—again, *metabolically inactive chromosomal states.* We now know that functional bacterial chromosomes or "nucleoids" ("nucleoids" rather than "nuclei" since they are not bounded by a nuclear membrane) bear little resemblance to the structures seen in Cairns' autoradiographs just as the metabolically active interphase chromosomes of eukaryotes have little morphological resemblance to mitotic or meiotic metaphase chromosomes.

The contour length of the circular DNA molecule of *E. coli* is about 1100 μ. The *E. coli* cell has a diameter of only 1-2μ. Clearly, then, the chromosome must exist in a highly folded or coiled configuration within the cell. When the *E. coli* chromosome is isolated by very gentle procedures in the absence of ionic detergents (commonly used to lyse cells) and is kept in the presence of a high concentration of cations such as polyamines (small basic or positively charged proteins) or 1 M salt to neutralize the negatively charged phosphate grops of DNA, the chromosome remains in a highly condensed state comparable in size to the nucleoid *in vivo*. This structure, called the "*folded genome*," is apparently the functional state, the single DNA molecule of *E. coli* is arranged into about 50 loops or domains, each of which is highly twisted or "*supercoiled*" (much like a tightly coiled telephone cord). This structure is dependent on RNA and protein, both of which are components of the folded genome. The folded genome can be relaxed by treatment with either deoxyribonuclease (DNase) or ribonuclease (RNase).

Supercoiling of DNA is an important feature of all chromosomes, from those of the smallest viruses to those of eukaryotes. It occurs whenever the DNA is either underwound ("negative supercoils") or overwound ("positive supercoils"). If one takes a covalently closed, circular double helix of DNA, breaks one strand, and rotates one of the ends that is produced for 360° around the complementary strand, while holding the other free end fixed, one supercoil will be introduced into the molecule. If the free end is rotated in the same direction as the DNA double helix is wound (right-handed), a negative supercoil will result. While this is probably the simplest way to visualize the phenomenon of supercoiling in DNA, it is not the mechanism used by enzymes to introduced supercoil into DNA.

Many biological functions of chromosomes can be carried out only when the participating DNA molecules are ngatively supercoiled. For example, the phage ØX174 gene A protein will nick only the ØX174 replicative form (RF) and initiate replication when the RF is in its negatively supercoiled form. All bacterial chromosomes studied to date appear to be negatively supercoiled in their functional states. When the basic proteins are carefully dissociated from the DNA of the chromosomes of *Drosophila melanogaster*, the DNA is found to contain the same amount of negative supercoiling as is found in the folded genomes of *E. coli*.

It is very likely that negative supercoiling is universally involved in certain of the biological functions of DNA molecules. Considerable evidence suggests that supercoiling is involved in recombination, gene expression, and the regulation of gene expression. In addition, negative supercoiling is almost certainly required for the replication of most, if not all, DNA molecules. An enzyme called *DNA gyrase*, which catalyzes the formation of negative supercoils in DNA, has now been isolated from sever?¹ different organisms, both prokaryotes and eukaryotes. The DNA gyrase from *E. coli* has been the most extensively studied. Its activity is inhibited by the drugs novobiocin and nalidixic acid, two potent inhibitors of DNA synthesis in bacteria. This clearly inhibitors of DNA synthesis in bacteria. This clearly indicates that DNA gyrase activity is required for DNA replication.

Although the exact role (or roles) of DNA gyrase in DNA replication is not yet established, an obvious possibility is that the introduction of negative supercoils may aid in the unwinding of the strands of the double helix. Mechanistically, DNA gyrase is a most interesting enzyme. *In vitro*, it can tie knots in DNA molecules or join two circular molecules to produce interlocking rings. DNA gyrase is now known not to introduce negative supercoils into DNA molecules by cleaving one strand and rotating one of the ends as originally proposed. Rather, it produces negative supercoils two at a time by cleaving both strands of one segment of a DNA molecule, passing another segment of the molecule through the temporary gap, and then rejoining the ends. During each catalytic event, DNA gyrase "holds on" to the cut ends as the other DNA molecule or segment of the DNA molecule is passed through the transient gap, so that it can efficiently region the ends to complete the process. DNA gyrase "holds on" by means of covalent linkage of the transient ends of the cleaved DNA molecule to itself, in the same manner as the phage ØX174 gene A protein.

MORPHOLOGY

Size

The size of the chromosomes varies from species to species and relatively remains constant for a particular species. The length of the chromosomes may vary from 0.2 to 50μm. The diameter of the chromosomes may be from 0.2 to 20μm. For instance, the human chromosomes are upto 6μm in length. Moreover, the organisms with less number of chromosomes contain comparatively large-sized chromosomes than the chromosomes of the organisms having many chromosomes.

The monocotyledon plants contain large-sized chromosomes than the dicotyledon plants. The plants in general have large-sized chromosomes in comparison to the animals. Further, the chromosomes in a cell are never alike in size, some may be exceptionally large and other may be too small. The largest chromosomes are lampbrush chromosomes of certain vertebrate oocytes and polytene chromosomes of certain dipteran insects.

Shape

The shape of the chromosomes is changeable from phase to phase in the continuous process of the cell growth and cell division. In the resting phase or interphase stage of the cell, the chromosomes occur in the form of thin, coiled, elastic and contractile, thread-like stainable structures, the chromatin threads. In the metaphase and the anaphase, the chromosomes become thick and filamentous. Each chromosome contains a clear zone, known as *centromere* or *kinetochore*, along their length. The centromere divides the chromosomes into two parts, each part is called *chromosome arm*. The position of centromere vary from chromosome to chromosome and it provides different shapes to the latter which are follows:

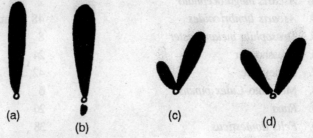

(a)   (b)   (c)   (d)

Fig. 2.1. Four morphologic types of chromosomes (a) Telocentric, (b)Acrocentric, (c) Submetacentric and (d) Metacentric.

1. *Telocentric*. The rod-like chromosomes which have the centromere on the proximal end are known as the *telocentric chromosomes*.

2. *Acrocentric*. The acrocentric chromosomes are also rod-like in shape but these have the centromere at one end and thus giving a very short arm and an exceptionally long arm. The locusts (Acridiadae) have the acrocentric chromosomes.

3. *Submetacentric*. The submetacentric chromosomes are J- or L-shaped. In these, the centromere occurs near the centre or at medium portion of the chromosome and thus forming two unequal arms.

4. *Metacentric*. The metacentric chromosomes are V-shaped and in these chromosomes the centromere occurs in the centre and forming two equal arms. The amphibians have metacentric chromosomes.

Number

The number of chromosomes in the somatic cells of higher animals and plants is known as *diploid* or *somatic* or *zygotic number*, while in the gametes (sperms and eggs) it is *haploid*, *gametic* or *reduced*. The number of chromosomes is constant in all the somatic cells of all the individuals of a species. Chromosome number is used in the identification of species and in tracing the relationship within the species. The chromosome number of some animals and plants is given in the following table:

Table 2.1. Number of chromosomes in some plants and animals.

S. No.	Name of organism	Number of chromosomes
A. Animals		
1.	*Paramecium aurellia*	30-40
2.	*Hydra vulgaris*	92
3.	*Ascaris megalocephala*	2
4.	*Ascaris lumbricoides*	48 in male
5.	*Drosophila melanogaster*	8
6.	Grasshopper	24
7.	Honey bee	42, 16
8.	Mosquito-*Culex pipens*	6
9.	*Rana*	26
10.	*Felis domesticus*	38
11.	Mouse, *Mus musculus*	40
12.	*Gallus domesticus* (fowl)	78 in male
13.	*Rattus rattus* (common rat)	42
14.	*Canis familiaris*	78
15.	Chimpanzee	48
16.	Monkey-*Macaca*	42
17.	*Homo sapiens*	46
B. Plants		
1.	*Alium cepa* (onion)	16
2.	*Brassica oleracea* (Cabbage)	18
3.	*Raphanus sativus* (Raddish)	18
4.	*Gossypium hirsutum* (upland cotton)	52
5.	*Zea mays* (Indian corn)	20
6.	*Triticum vulgare* (bread wheat)	42
7.	*Pisum sativum* (pea)	14
8.	*Oryza sativa* (rice)	24
9.	*Neurospora crassa* (red bread mold)	7

Chromosome Cycle and Cell Cycle

Chromosomes exhibit cyclic changes in shape and size during cell cycle. In the nondividing interphase nucleus, the chromosomes form interwoven network of fine twisted but uncoiled threads of chromatin, and are invisible. During cell division the chromatin threads condense into compact structures by helical coiling. In *prophase* of cell division the chromosomes appear as distinct threads and by *metaphase* and also in *anaphase* these become short, compact bodies having definite shapes and sizes. In anaphase these appear as rod-shaped, V-shaped, L-shaped or J-shaped. The chromosomes are studied and described at this state or at anaphase stage. In *telophase* these again uncoil to form the chromatin net.

STRUCTURE OF THE CHROMOSOME

In earlier light microscopic descriptions the chromosome, or chromatid, was though to consist of a coiled thread called the chromonema lying in a matrix. The chromosome was supposed to be convered by a membranous pellicle. Electron microscopic studies later showed that there is no definite membranous pellicle surrounding the chromosome. Other structure present in the chromosome include the chromatids, centromere, secondary constrictions, nucleolar organizers, telomeres and satellites are given under the following heads:

Chromatids

During metaphase a chromosome appears to possess two threads called *chromatids*, which become interwined in the matrix of chromosome. These two chromatids are held together at a point along their length in the region of constriction of the chromosome. These chromatids are really spirally coiled *chromonemata* (sing., chromonema) at metaphase. The coiled filament was first of all observed by *Baranetzky*, in 1880, in the pollen mother cells of *tradescantia* and was called chromonema by *Vejdovsky* in 1912. The chromonema may be composed of 2, 4 or more fibrils depending upon the species. This number of fibrils in the chromonema may depend on the different phases since at one phase it may contain one fibril and at other phase it may contain two or four fibrils. These fibrils of the chromonema are coiled with each other. The coils are of two types:

1. *Paranemic coils.* When the chromonemal fibrils are easily separable from each other, such coils are called paranemic coils.
2. *Plectonemic coils.* Here the chromonemal fibrils are closely interwined and they cannot be separated easily. Such coils are called plectonemic coils.

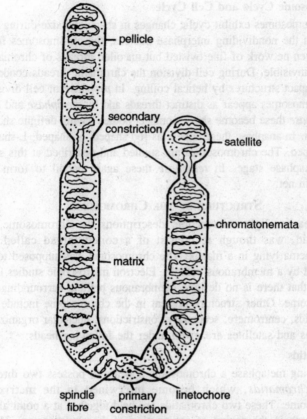

Fig. 2.2. Structure of a typical somatic chromosome at anaphase.

The degree of coiling of the chromonemal fibrils during cell divisions depend on the length of the chromosome. There are three types of coils: (i) *Major coils* of the chromonema posses 10-30 gyres, (ii) *Minor coils* of the chromonema are perpendicular to the major coils and have numerous gyres as observed in meiotic chromosomes. If splitting has not yet occurred at this stage, there will be a single chromonema, if it has already taken place there would be two chromonemata. (iii) *Standard* or *somatic coils* are found in the chromonema of mitosis where chromonemata possess helical structure, resembling the major coils of the meiotic chromosome.

Chromomeres

The chromonema of the chromosomes of mitotic and meiotic prophases have been found to contain alternating thick and thin regions and thus giving the appearance of a necklace in which several beads occur on a string. The thick or beak-like structures of the chromonema are known as the *chromomeres* and the thin region in between the chromomeres is termed as the *inter-chromomeres*. The position of the chromomeres in the chromonema is found to be constant for a given chromosome.

The cytologists have given various interpretations about the chromomers. Some consider chromomeres as condensed nucleoprotein material, while other postulated that the chromomeres are regions of the super-imposed coils. The later view has been confirmed by the electron microscopic observations. For long time most geneticists considered these chromomeres as *genes*, i.e. the units of heredity.

Centromere

The centromere is a specific region of the eukaryotic chromosome that becomes visible as a distinct morphological entity along the chromosome during condensation. It is responsible for chromosome movement in both mitosis and meiosis, functioning, at least in part, by serving as an attachment site for one or more spindle fibers. It is also the site at which the spindle fibers shorten, causing the chromosomes to move toward the poles. Electron microscopic analysis has shown that in some organisms—for example, the yeast *Saccharomyces cerevisiae*—a single spindle-protein fiber is attached to centromeric chromatin. Most other organisms have multiple spindle fibers attached to each centromeric region.

The chromatin segment of the centromeres of *Saccharomyces cerevisiae* has a unique structure in that it is exceeding resistant to the action of various DNases and has been isolated as a protein-DNA containing from 220 to 250 base pairs. The nucleosomal constitution and DNA base sequences of many of the yeast chromosomes have been determined. There are four regions, labeled I through IV. All yeast centromeres have the sequence characteristics indicated for regions I, II, and III, but the sequence of region IV varies from one centromere to another. Region II is noteworthy in that more than 90 percent of the base pairs are AT pairs. The centromeric DNA is contained in a structure (the centromeric core particle) that contains more DNA than a typical yeast nucleosome core particle (160 base pairs) and is larger. This structure is responsible for the resistance of centromeric DNA to DNase. The spindle fiber is believed to be attached directly to this particle.

The base-sequence arrangement of the yeast centromeres is not typical of other eukaryotic centromeres. In higher eukaryotes, the chromosomes are about one hundred times as large as yeast chromosomes, and several spindle fibers are usually attached to each chromosome. Furthermore, the centromeric regions of the chromosomes of many eukaryotes contain large amounts of heterochromatin, consisting of repetitive satellite DNA. For example, the centromeric regions of human chromosomes contain a tandemly repeated DNA sequence of about 170 base pairs called the alpha satellite. The number of copies in the centromeric region ranges from 5000 to 15,000, depending on the chromosome. The DNA sequences needed for spindle-fiber attachment may be interspersed among the alpha-satellite sequences. Whether the alpha-satellite sequences themselves contribute to centromere activity is unknown.

Telomeres

The sequences at the ends of eukaryotic chromosomes, called *telomeres*, play critical roles in chromosome replication and maintenance. Telomeres were initially recognized as distinct structures because broken chromosomes were highly unstable in eukaryotic cells, implying that specific sequences are required at normal chromosomal termini. This was subsequently demonstrated by experiments in which telomeres from the protozoan *Tetrahymena* were added to the ends of linear molecules of yeast plasmid DNA. The addition of these telomeric DNA sequences allowed these plasmids to replicate as linear chromosome-like molecules in yeasts, demonstrating directly that telomeres are required for the replication of linear DNA molecules.

The telomere DNA sequences of a variety of eukaryotes are similar, consisting of repeats of a simple-sequence DNA containing clusters of G residues on one strand. For example, the sequence of telomere repeats in humans and other mammals is AGGGTT, and the telomere repeat in *Tetrahymena* is GGGGTT. These sequences are repeated hundreds or thousands of times, thus spanning up to several kilobases.

Telomeres play a critical role in replication of the ends of linear DNA molecules. DNA polymerase is able to extend a growing DNA chain but cannot initiate synthesis of a new chain at the terminus of a linear chromosomes cannot be replicated by the normal action of DNA polymerase. This problem has been solved by the evolution of a special mechanism, involving reverse transcriptase activity, to replicate telomeric DNA sequences.

Euchromatin and Heterochromatin

When interphase chromosomes of metabolically active cells are chemically stained and examined under the microscope, it becomes apparent that there are two distinct types of organization of the chromatin material. One type is lightly staining and is called *euchromatin*, and the other type is darkly staining and is called *constitutive heterochromatin*. The former involves chromatin that is in a relatively uncoiled state, whereas the latter exhibits higher-order folding of the chromatin.

The distribution of constitutive heterochromatin varies from organism to organism, and examples are known where parts of chromosomes or whole chromosomes are heterochromatinized. In general, constitutive heterochromatin is found interspersed in short

Fig. 2.3. Model of constitutive heterochromatin in a mammalian metaphase chromosome. A—Constitutive heterochromatin; B—Secondary constriction I or nucleolar organizer; C—Primary constriction or centromere; D—Euchromatin; E—Secondary constriction II possible site of 5S rRNA cistrons; F—Telomere.

segments among euchromatin and is also located around the centromeres. Functionally, euchromatin contains DNA in an active or potentially active state (that is, capable, of being transcribed), whereas heterochromatin contains DNA in a transcriptionally inactive configuration. Characteristically, heterochromatin replicates later than euchromatin in the cell cycle.

CHROMOSOME BANDING

In 1969, *T.C. Hsu* and others introduced new methods for staining chromosomes by which distinct patterns of stained bands and lightly stained interbands became evident. These staining methods were enormously important since they permitted each chromosome to be identified uniquely, even if the overall morphology was identical. Distinctions can now be made among the relatively similar C group chromosomes, for example, so that we may reer to chromosome 9 or chromosome 12 instead of merely a C-group chromosome. Using the group reference is still convenient in many instances, but we now more often refer to a specific chromosome by its number as set by the karyotype conventional ordering.

The most useful chromosome banding method is *G-banding*. The earlier methods including some special steps in the staining procedure, but these were found to be unnecessary and no special conditions are really needed to visualize G-bands by staining with the Giemsa reagent. Giemsa staining had been used for many years to bring out contrast in nuclear material, and it was one of the first stains to delinete the bacterial nucleoid by microscopy.

Two main categories of chromosome banding patterns are recognized:

1. *G-bands* from Giemsa staining and *Q-bands*, which develop after staining with quinacrine and other fluorescent dyes, give relatively similar, but not identical, patterns. Fluorescent stains fade after a short time, and special microscope optics plus ultraviolet illumination are needed to see fluorescent bands. Giemsa-stained preparations are more permanent and require ordinary microscope optics and illumination. For these reasons, G-staining is used routinely.

2. *C-bands* are visualized by Giemsa staining after pretreatments using HCl and NaOH to partially denature the chromosomes in a preparation. C-bands are especially evident around the centromere and in other chromosome regions that contain substantial amounts of highly repetitive constitutive heterochromatin. The Giemsa stain

is not specific, but it binds to regions of DNA that have responded differently from non-banded regions to HCl and NaOH pretreatments.

Despite many attempts to interpret banding reactions on a molecular basis, we still know relatively little about specific interactions between DNA and any staining reagents in use Q-bands apparently result from binding between quinacrine dye and DNA regions that are rich in adenine and thymine. Since guanine and cytosine quench fluorescence GC-rich regions of DNA generally appear as unstained interbands. Since Q-bands and G-bands are relatively similar, it seems likely that a common mechanism of interaction exists between DNA and the dye. So far, this has not been shown to be true, and G-banding mechanisms remain unclear.

C-bands are very distinctively located and arise as the result of binding between Giemsa stain and residual chromatin remaining after pretreatments that extract nucleoproteins. More chromatin remains in areas of constitutive heterochromatin than in other parts of the chromosomes after denaturing steps, so more material is present to bind more of the stain and yield a band that is contrasted with lightly stained or unstained regions in between. (There is little or no nucleoprotein extraction in G- or Q-banding methods.) Locations of C-bands correlate very well with localizations of constitutive heterochromatin, according to several independent lines of evidence.

With new methods for G-banding chromosomes, investigators can unequivocally identify various structural and numerical changes in a normal complement. The greater certainty of identifying whole chromosomes or parts of chromosomes by G-bands often allows the investigator to know exactly which chromosomes are present and which chromosome parts have undergone structural rearrangements. Binding also provides a means to compare karyotypes of related species and to describe differences that apparently have an evolutionary basis.

ULTRASTRUCTURE OF CHROMOSOMES

Two views have been proposed for ultra-structure of chromosomes:

(a) Multistranded View

This was proposed by *Ris* (1906). By electron microscope the smallest visible unit of the chromosome is the fibril which is 100Å in thickness. This fibril contains two DNA double helix molecules separated by a space of 25Å across and associated protein. Next largest unit is the half chromatid. The half chromatid consists of four 100Å

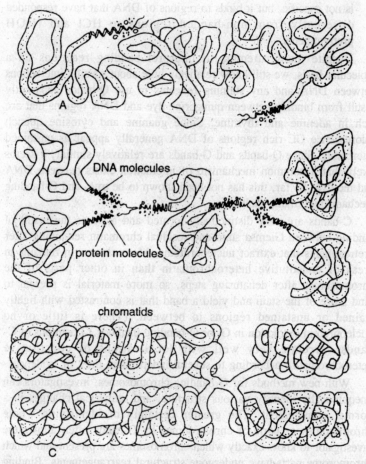

Fig. 2.4. Dupraw's fold fibre model of chromatin in interphase (A and B) and in metaphase.

fibrils so that it is 400Å in thickness and contains eight double helices of DNA and the associated protein. Two half-chromatids from a complete chromatid consisting of 16 double DNA helix molecules. As the chromosome consists of two chromatids, thus total number of helices will be 32 and diameter 1600Å thick before duplication or synthesis. After duplication chromosome has 64 double helices of DNA with corresponding diameter of 3200Å. The number of DNA helices in each unit above fibril level varies according to species. In summary, the chromosome is composed of numerous microfibrils, the smallest of which is a single nucleoprotein molecule.

(b) Folded-Fibril Model

DuPraw (1965) presented this model for the fine structure of chromosome. According to this model, a chromosome consists of single long chain of DNA and protein forming what is called as fibril. This fibril is folded many times and irregularly enterwined to form chromatid. This measure 250-300Å in thickness.

NUCLEOSOMES

Chromosomes are tight complexes between DNA and protein. It has long been known that the DNA in chromosomes is much longer than the chromosome length, and thus some means of compacting the genetic material must be available. Indeed, in chromatin the DNA is in a tightly packed state representing at least a 100-fold contraction. This is achieved by several levels of folding. The simplest level of

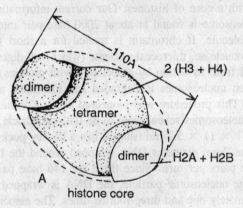

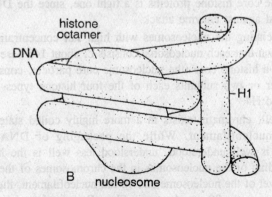

Fig. 2.5. A—Histone core; B—Nucleosome.

packing involves the coiling of DNA around a core of histones to form a structure called the *nucleosome*, and the most complex level of packing involves higher-order coiling of he DNA-histone complexes to produce chromosome morphologies exemplified by chromosomes in the division cycle.

When viewed under the microscope, the DNA—protein complex in chromosomes is seen as fibers, or nucleofilaments about 10 nm in diameter. If a nucleofilament is completely unraveled, the chromatin fiber looks like "beads on a string," where the beads are the nucleosome and the thinner thread connecting the beads is naked DNA, called linker DNA.

The nucleosome was first described in the 1970s by *A. Olins* and *D. Olins,* and by *C.L.F. Woodcock.* They described the nucleosome as 10-nm diameter, flattened spheres in which the DNA was somehow associated with a core of histones. Our current information indicates that the nucleosome is found at about 2000 base-pair intervals along the DNA molecule. If chromatin is treated for a short time with a bacterial endonuclease, microccal nuclease (which will digest any DNA not protected from its action by association with proteins), the linker DNA between nucleosomes is degraded and individual nucleosomes are related. (This procedure was pioneered by *R. Kornberg.*) Studies of isolated nucleosomes reveal them to be flat, cylindrical particles of dimensions 11 × 11 × 5.7 nm (shaped like a hockey puck or a can of tuna) with the 2-nm diameter DNA wrapped around the histone core with 80 base pairs per turn. Since there are 146 base pairs of DNA in the average nucleosome particle, the DNA is wrapped around the core approximately one and three-fourths times. The association of the DNA with the core histone proteins is a tight one, since the DNA is well protected against enzyme attack.

By dissociating the nucleosomes with high salt concentration, it has been shown that each nucleosome consists of about 146 base pairs of DNA and a histone core (the nucleosome core particle, consisting of an octamer or two subunits each of the four histone types H2A, H2B, H3, and H4.

In the cell, chromatin exists in a more highly coiled state than the 10 nm nucleofilament. While the packaging of DNA into nucleosomes is well understood, understood less well is the higher orders of folding of the nucleosomes in the chromosomes of the cell. Above the level of the nucleosome and 10 nm nucleofilament, the next level of packing is the 30 nm chromatin fiber. Examination of isolated

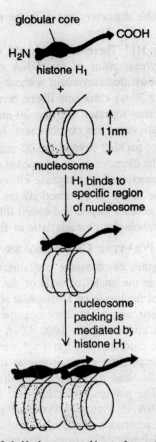

Fig. 2.6. Nucleosome packing to form solenoid.

30-nm chromatin fiber reveals the compact nature of this level of chromosome structure, making it difficult to distinguish individual nucleosomes. As a consequence, the arrangement of nucleosomes in the fiber is difficult to define. Based on biochemical and biophysical data, a recent model for the 30-nm fiber involves a zigzag ribbon of nucleosomes that is twisted to generate the 30-nm diameter chromatin fiber. In the figure, the least compact form is the relaxed zigzag ribbon, which can make the transition to the compact zigzag ribbon through no major changes in basic structure, especially the loss or addition of nucleosome-nucleosome contact. Then the 30-nm chromatin fiber is constructed by folding the compact zigzag ribbon in such a way as to minimize changes in nucleosome-nucleosome contacts. This coiling of the compact zigzag ribbon creates a double-helical ribbon with a range of possible diameters and with the nucleosomes in face-to-face contact.

What of histone H1? There is very good evidence that H1 is located at the entry/exit point of the DNA on the nucleosome. Experiments have shown that chromatin without H1 can form 10-nm nucleofilaments but not 30-nm chromatin fibers; hence, H1 must function to pack the nucleosomes together into the 30-nm fibers. Nothing is known about the regulation of this phenomenon, however.

The next levels of packing beyond the 30-nm chromatin fiber are poorly understood. The diameter of an interphase chromosome may be 300 nm while the diameter of a metaphase chromosome may be 700 nm. To achieve these levels of compaction, the simplest concept is that the 30-nm fiber becomes looped and coiled (like a rope) in various ways to give the morphologies characteristic of these chromosomes.

POLYTENE CHROMOSOMES

A typical eukaryotic chromosome contains only a single DNA molecule. However, in the nuclei of cells of the salivary glands and certain other tissues of the larvae of *Drosophila* and other two-winged (dipteran) flies, there are giant chromosomes, called *polytene chromosomes*, which contain about 1000 DNA molecules laterally aligned. Each of these chromosomes has a volume many times greater than that of the corresponding chromosome at mitotic metaphase in ordinary somatic cells, and a constant and distinctive pattern of transverse banding. The polytene structures are formed by repeated replication of the DNA in a closely synapsed pair of homologous chromosomes without separation of the replicated chromatin strands or of the two chromosomes. Polytene chromosomes are typical chromosomes and are formed in "terminal" cells; that is, the larval

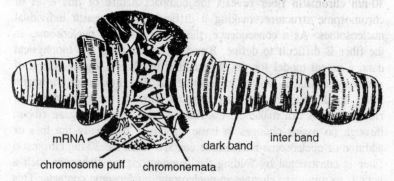

Fig. 2.7. Polytene chromosome of an insect.

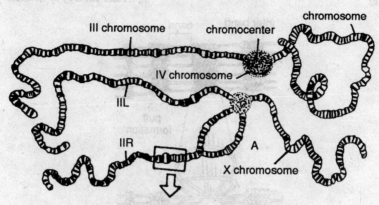

Fig. 2.8. Polytene chromosome of Drosophila.

cells containing them do not divide further during development of the fly and later eliminated in the formation of the pupa. However, they have been especially valuable in the genetics of *Drosophila*.

In polytene nuclei of *D. melanogaster* and other species, large blocks of heterochromatin (a particular type of chromatin described in the following section) adjacent of the centromeres are aggregated into a single compact mass called the *chromocenter*. Because the two largest chromosomes (numbers 2 and 3) have centrally located centromeres, the chromosomes appear in the configuration, the paired X chromosomes (in female), the left and right arms of chromosomes 2 and 3, and a short chromosome (chromosome 4) project from the chromocenter. In a male, the Y chromosome, which consists almost entirely of heterochromatin, is incorporated in the chromocenter.

The darkly staining transverse bands in polytene chromosomes have about a tenfold range in width. These bands result from side-by-side alignment of tightly folded regions of the individual chromatin strands that are often visible in mitotic and meiotic prophage chromosomes as chromomeres. More DNA is present within the bands than in the interband (lightly stained) regions. About 5000 bands have been identified in the *D. melanogaster* polytene chromosomes. This linear array of bands, which has a pattern that is constant and characteristic for each species, provides a finely detailed *cytological map* of the chromosomes. The banding pattern is such that short regions in any of the chromosomes can be identified.

Because of their large size and finely detailed morphology, polytene chromosomes are exceedingly useful for *in situ* nucleic acid hybridization. In the *in situ hybridization* procedure, labeled probe DNA or RNA is

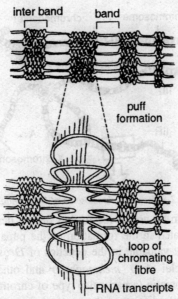

Fig. 2.9. A part of a giant polytene chromosome of Drosophila showing: A—Bands and interbands; B—Puff formation.

added to squashed polytene nuclei after denaturation of the chromosomal DNA, under conditions that favour renaturation. After washing, the only probe that remains in the chromosomes has formed hybrid duplexes with chromosomal DNA and its position can be identified cytologically.

THE ORGANIZATION OF NUCLEOTIDE

Sequences in Eukaryotic Genomes

In bacteria, the variation of average base composition from one part of the genome to another is quite small. However, in eukaryotes, some components of the genome can be detected their base composition is quite different from the average of the rest of the genome (for example, one component of crab DNA is only 3 percent GC). These components are called *satellite DNA*. In the mouse, satellite DNA accounts for 10 percent of the genome. A striking feature of satellite DNA is that it consists of fairly short nucleotide sequences that may be repeated *as many as a million times in a haploid genome*. Other *repetitive sequences* also are present in eukaryotic DNA.

Nucleotide Sequence Composition

Eukaryotic organisms differ widely in the proportion of the genome consisting of repetitive DNA sequences and in the types of these sequences that are present. A eukaryotic genome typically consists of three components.

1. *Unique,* or *single-copy, sequences.* This is usually the major component and is typically from 30 to 75 percent of the chromosomal DNA in most organisms.

2. *Highly repetitive sequences.* This component constitutes from 5 to 45 percent of the genome. Some of these sequences are satellite DNA referred to earlier. The sequences in this class are typically from 5 to 300 base pairs per repeat and are duplicated as many as 10^5 times per genome.

3. *Middle-repetitive sequences.* This component is from 1 to 30 percent of a eukaryotic genome and includes sequences that are repeated from a few times to 10^5 times per genome.

LAMPBRUSH CHROMOSOMES

In the oocytic nuclei of those animals which have large yolky eggs, the prophase of first meiotic division is extremely extended. During this phase the oocyte grows and synthesizes nutrients for the future embryo. In them, the chromosomes become greatly enlarged and assume unusual configuration. A large number of loops project out from the chromatid axis, giving a lampbrush appearance. Hence, these chromosomes are called *lampbrush chromosomes.*

The lampbrush chromosomes are bivalents each consisting of two chromatids. These persists during the prolonged diplotene phase of first meiotic prophase.

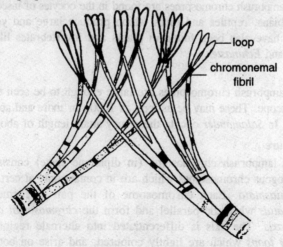

Fig. 2.10. A chromosomal loop of chromosome puff.

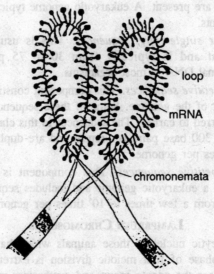

Fig. 2.11. Suggested form of the individual loops in chromosome puffs. Note the tiny fibrils with dense RNA granules attached to the loop.

History

Lampbrush chromosomes were first observed by *Flemming* (1882) in amphibian oocyte. A detailed study was made by *J. Ruckert* (1892) in the oocytes of sharks.

Occurrence

Lampbrush chromosomes are found in the oocytes of insects, sharks, amphibians, reptiles and birds which produce large and yolky eggs. These have also been found in plants and invertebrates like *Sagitta*, *Sepia* and *Echinaster*.

Size

Lampbrush chromosomes are large enough to be seen under light microscope. These may be as long as 1000μ or more and about 20μ in width. In *Salamander* oocyte these may attain length of about 5,900μ.

Structure

A lampbrush chromosome (in diplotene stage) consists of two homologous chromosomes which are in contact only at certain points, the *chiasmata*. Each chromosome of the pair is formed of two *chromatids* which lie parallel and form the *chromosomal axis* or the *main axis*. The axis is differentiated into alternate regions of high density *loops* which are lightly coloured, and arise on both sides of the chromosomal axis.

The *chromosomal axis*, the *chromomeres* and the *loop axis* and are formed of *DNA*.

The *chromomeres* are found in pairs, one chromomere on each chromatid. These are about .25 to 2.0μm in diameter and are spaced about 2μm from centre to centre along chromatid axis. These probably represent heterochromatic regions where axial filament remains tightly coiled.

The *lateral loops* arise from the chromomeres either 2 or in multiple of two. These extend on either side of the chromosomal axis about 550μm and are about 30-50 (3.-5 nm) in diameter. Each loop consists of an *axial fibre* formed of DNA. It is surrounded with the matrix composed of *RNA* and *Proteins*. This gives fuzzy appearance of lateral loops.

ELECTRON MICROSCOPIC STRUCTURE

Electron microscopic studies by *Miller* and *Beaty* (1969) on Lampbrush chromosomes of salamander oocyte have shown the presence of dense granules on the loop axis of DNA. These dense granules represent large molecules of enzyme *RNA polymerase*. On getting attachment of DNA, these initiate RNA synthesis. Arising from these RNA polymerase molecules are seen fine fibrils of RNA which increase in length.

Each loop is considered to be one operon consisting of a series of identical copies of the same structural genes (*cistrons*) separated by spacer DNA. Each gene locus probably produces a very long RNA molecule. This interacts with protein to form *ribonucleoprotein*.

(i) According to *Callan* and *Llyod* (1960) a chromosome is the *master gene* with solenoid super coiling which produces several identical copies of its own. These extend out as a lateral loop formed of linear strand of *nucleosomes*, representing the transcriptionally active stage. These are called *salve gene copies*.

(ii) According to *spinning out* and *retraction hypothesis*, a chromosome is fully transcribed from end to end by spinning out a transient loop. The new loop material spins out on one side of a chromomere at the thin end of loop and returns to a condensed stage on the other side after completing the synthesis of RNA. These are associated with the rapid synthesis of yolk and protein in the maturing ovum. These disappear by the end of first prophase when chromosomes become thick and more condensed.

3

GENETIC MUTUALISM

A study of inheritance of characters whether a particular gene is completely dominant or completely recessive. F_2 ration of 3 :1 in a monohybrid cross suggests that one gene is completely dominant and its allele is completely recessive. F_2 ration of 1 : 2 in a monohybrid cross indicates that none of the two alleles is completely dominant, but their dominance is incomplete. Sometimes the Interaction between alleles is more complex and we get a genotypic ration which is completely different from 3:1 or 1:2:1. Sometimes in dihybrid and polyhybrid crosses too, the expression of genes is not independent of each other and depends on the presence or absence of other gene or genes. The fact that genes are not merely separate entities producing distinct individual effects, but that they could interact with each other to give completely novel phenotypes, was discovered by Mendelism. The occurrence of such interactions suggests that the phenotype we observe is not due to individual genes but arises from complex developmental processes, although the genes themselves follow the regular laws of inheritance. The overall phenotype of organism, therefore, is the result of epigenetic interactions of a network of gene controlled reactions. A few simple genetic interactions are discussed in the following paragraphs:

LETHAL GENES

There are genes which control certain phenotypic traits, and at the same time also influence the viability of the individuals. For instance, white eyes and vestigial winged flies have lower viabilities than the wild types. There are still other genes which have no effect on the phenotype but influence the viability. This influence on viability may be of such an order that the individual may fail to survive. Such genes which cause the death of the individual carrying it are known as lethal genes.

In the lethal effect is dominant over its normal allele, all individuals carrying it will die and the gene cannot be transmitted to next generation. Such dominant lethal genes will therefore be lost in the same generation.

On the other hand, recessive lethals are carried in heterozygous condition, and will express themselves only the homozygous condition.

Lethality in Mice

Cuenot (1905), a french geneticist, studied the inheritance of mouse body colour and discovered lethality in mice. He noted that the yellow body colour is controlled by a dominant gene but the yellow mice are never true breeding. When a cross is made between two yellow mice, yellow and black offspring are produced in a ration 2 : 1. A back cross of yellow to black revealed that yellow mice are always heterozygous for the yellow gene and that individuals homozygous for the yellow gene cannot be found. This is because yellow has a dominant

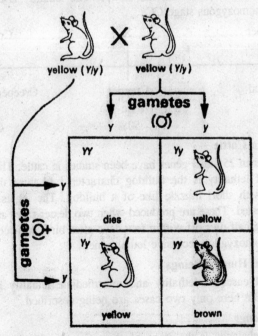

Fig. 3.1. Segregation for yellow body colour when yellow mice are intercrossed.

phenotypic effect and in homozygous condition the gene is lethal and the mice bearing such genes die in vitro.

Lethality in Drosophila

In Drosophila genes like curly wings (Cy), plum eyes (Pm) and stubble bristles (Sb) influence the viability of the flies when present in homozygous condition. For instance, an individual Cycy (heterozygous) will have curly wings and will survive. However, homozygous dominant i.e. Cycy will not survive. Homozygous recessive cycy will have normal phenotype and will survive. These genes, therefor, have dual effect. They are dominant with respect to the phenotype (e.g. curly wings, plum eyes and stubble bristles) but are recessive with respect to the lethal effect.

Lethality in Chicken

Some chicken develop abnormal short and crooked legs. This stage is called Creeper. This is due to a dominant gene C. The normal development is due to a recessive gene C. When a cross is made between two heterozygous creepers, the creepers and normal are produced in ratio of 2:1 instead of 3:1. The lethality is deserved in dominant homozygous stage CC.

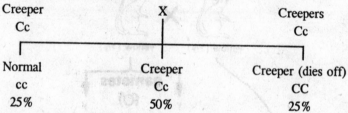

Lethality in Cattle

More than 25 lethal genes have been studies in cattle. The excellent example of lethality is the bulldog character. In this the head is abnormal with short muzzle like of a bulldog. The leg is short and palate is cleated. These are produced when two dexter races are crossed. The bulldog calf dies off within few days after birth on account of the effect of homozygous recessive lethal gene.

Lethality in Human Beings

Several cases of lethality and intermediate lethality have been observed. But here only two cases are being described.

Brachyphalangy

Brachyphalangy is the stage of short fingers with two joints, the middle bone being extremely shortened and often fused with one of the other two bones of the finger. Molir descried one case where one child was born without any fingers or toes and did not survive.

Sickle celled anemia

This abnormality is due to a recessive gene and in this the shape of erythrocyte is changed from circular to shaped and the amount of hemoglobin is also reduced. Such cases produced when a cross is made between two heterozygous individuals. It results carrier and normal offspring in a ration of 2:! instead of 3:1. The lethality is developed in a homozygous recessive case i.e. ss.

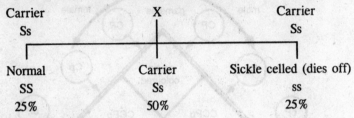

| Carrier | X | Carrier |
| Ss | | Ss |

Normal	Carrier	Sickle celled (dies off)
SS	Ss	ss
25%	50%	25%

Lethality in Plants

The first case of lethal genes in plants was discovered by *Baur* (1907) in *Arittirrhinum majus*. In this plant, a yellow leaved dominant genotype, aurea, when crossed *aurea* X *acurea*, produced normal green plants as well as aurea heterozygotes in a ratio of 1:2 Aurea homozygotes lack the availability to make chlorophyll and die as seedlings or sometimes even before germination.

COMPLEMENTARY GENES

A classical example of interaction of genes is the complementation between two genes meaning that both genes are necessary for the production of particular phenotype. *W. Bateson* and *R.C. Punnett* observed that, when two while flowered varieties of sweet pea, Lathyrus odoratus were crossed, F_1 progeny had coloured flowers. When F_2 progeny obtained from F_1 was classified plants with coloured flowers and those with white flowers were obtained in 9:7 ratio. This is again a modification 9:3:3:1 ratio, where only one character i.e., flower colour is involved and only two classes recognized (coloured and withe flowers).

It obvious in the above example that both the dominant alleles, C and P are necessary for the production of pigment in flowers. Each of the two parents lacks one of the two dominant alleles and, therefore, both bear only while flowers. The two dominants are brought together in F_1 generation and therefore coloured flowers are produced.

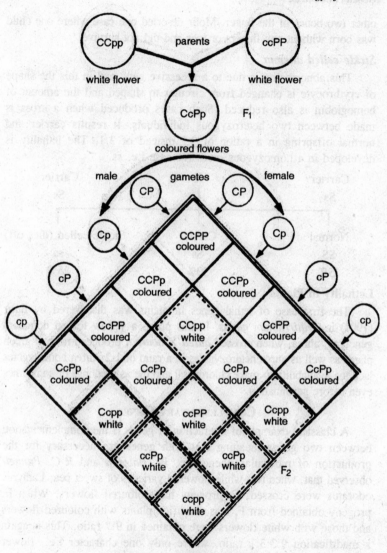

Fig. 3.2. Complementary factors.

SUPPLEMENTARY GENES

There are two independent pairs of genes interacting in such a manner that one dominant produces its effect whether the other is present or not while the second one produces it effect only in the presence of the first. This has been demonstrated in the inheritance of cot colour of rabbits and other rodents by *Castle*. In *guinea pigs* and other rodents the coat colour varies considerably and is inherited as a Mendelian trait. It has been found that the black colour of the coat (C) is dominant over albino (c). Apart from this there is a wild variety the *agouti* in which the colour of the coat is more or less grayish. Here the hairs are black at the base and tip with an yellow band in

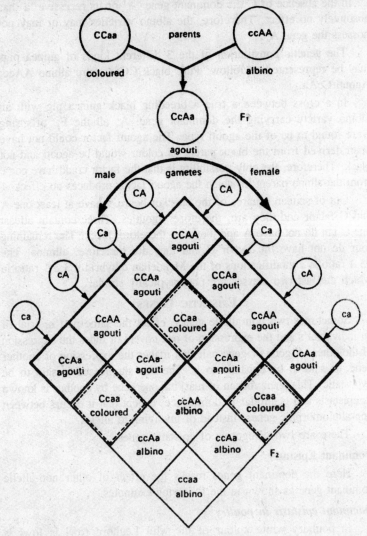

Fig. 3.3. Supplementary factors.

between. This produces a kind of neutral gray colour, a protective colour pattern characteristic of the wild variety, and it is due to the presence of a dominant gene A. This gene when present either in a single or double does turns black fur into agouti. It naturally follows that a black guinea pig is therefore, always homozygous for the recessive allele in a addition to possessing at least one dominant gene C. In the absence of C the dominant gene 'A' or its recessive 'a' has absolutely no effect. Therefore, the albino varieties may or may not possess the gene A.

The genetic constitution of the 3 different kinds of guinea pigs may be represented as follow: Pure black CCaa; pure albino AAcc; Agouti CcAa.

In a cross between a true a breeding black guinea pig with an albino variety carrying the dominant gene. A, all the F_1 offspring were found to be of the agouti type. The agouti factor could not have been derived from the black parent its colour would be agouti and not black. Therefore, the only possibility is that the factor could have come from the albino parent in which the agouti factor produces no effect.

Out of sixteen squares of the checker board 9 have at least one A and C factor and they are, therefore, agouties. Three contain atleast one C but do not have A and they are, therefore, black. The remaining four do not have the factor C and they are therefore, albinos. The 93.4 ratio is a modifications of the Mendelian dihybrid 9:3:3:1 ratio in which the last two classes are phenotypically similar.

EPISTATIC GENES

Sometimes two non-allelic genes, effect the same part or trial of an individual's and the expression of one covers or hides the expression of the other. A gene or gene pair that makes the expression of another gene, is said to be epistatic to it. The one suppressed is said to be hypostatic. This phenomenan of masking one gene by another is known as epistasis and is similar to dominance. except that it occurs between non-allelomorphic genes, instead of involving to alleles.

There are two categories of epistatic genes :

Dominant Epistasis

Here the dominant genes masks the effect of other non-allelic dominant gene as shown in the following examples.

Dominant epistasis in poultry

In poultary white colour of the whit Leghorn fowl is fowl is dominant over the coloured variety. But is the white plumage of the

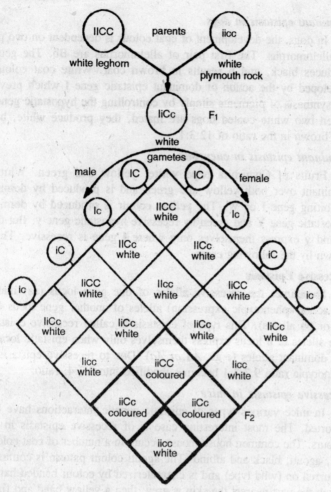

Fig. 3.4. Inhibiting factors.

white Wyandottes is recessive to the coloured plumage. The white Leghorns posses a colour factor C which is prevented from being expressed by an inhibiting gene I. Thus they are unable to develop their colour. The Wyandotte fowls are white because of the absence of the colour gene, as well as the inhibiting gene. When white leghorns (CCII) and white Wyandotte (ccii) are mated, the F_1 hybrids are all white (CcIi) with small black markings. But when the white fowls of the F_1 are crossed among themselves, the offspring are in the peculiar ration of 13/16 white and 3/16 coloured.

Dominant epistasis in dogs

In dogs, the development of coat colour is dependent on two pairs of allelomorphs. The first pair of allelomorphs are Bb. The gene B produces black, and b results in brown coat. White coat colour is developed by the action of dominant epistatic gene I which prevents the synthesis of pigments simply by controlling the hypostatic gene B. When two white coated dogs are mated, they produce white, black and brown in the ratio of 12:3:1:.

Dominant epistasis in cucurbita

Fruits of Cucurbita pepo white, yellow and green. White is dominant over both yellow and green and is produced by dominant inhibiting gene I or W. The yellow colour is produced by dominant hypostatic gene Y and green by recessive hypostatic gene y. But these Y and y express themselves only where I gene is recessive. This is shown by the following cross.

Recessive Epistasis

Sometimes the recessive alleles of one gene locus (aa) masked the action (phenotypic expression) alleles of another gene locus (BB, Bb or bb alleles). This type of epistasis is called recessive epistasis. The alleles of b locus express themselves only when epistatic locus–A has dominant alleles (e.g., *AA or Aa*). Due to recessive epistasis the phenotypic ratio 9:3:3:1 becomes modified into 9:3:4: ratio.

Recessive epistasis in mice

In mice various types of epistatic genetic interactions have been reported. The most interesting case is of recessive epistasis in coat colours. The common house mouse occurs in a number of coat colours, i.e., agouti, black and albino. The agouti colour pattern is commonly occurred on (wild type) and is characterized by colour banded hairs in which the part nearest the skin is grey, then a yellow band and finally the distal part is either black or brown. The albino mouse lacks totally in pigments and has white hairs and pink eyes.

When a homozygous agouti or grey (BB AA) is crossed with a homozygous albino (*bb aa*) in F_1 all agouti offsprings appear. When, the F_1 agouti are crossed among themselves in F_2 agouti, black and albino offspring appear in the ratio of 9:3:4.

Recessive epistasis in man

This is seen in the inheritance of albunism in man. Sometimes an albino child is born to parents who are normal or have dark skin. Each of these parents carries a recessive gene for albunism. The child who is homozygous for the genes for albinism, is unable to develop any pigment in the skin although the might inherit genes for pigmentation also. This is because the gene for albinism is epistatic to genes for pigmentation of the skin, hair and eyes.

Deaf-mutism man

Sometimes a child who is deaf and mute is born to normal parents. The normal hearing trait is due to the presence of two dominant genes (*AA BB*). The abnormal condition of deaf mutism is due to the presence of either of the two recessive genes (*a or b*) in homozygous condition. Thus, a person with the genotype *aa BB* would be a deaf-mute because the gene 'a' is epistatic to B for normal hearing. Similarly, a person with the genotype AA bb is also a deaf mute, because the gene b is epistatic to the gene A for normal hearing. This is called *duplicate recessive epistasis*. Thus, deaf and mute children are born to parents who are normal but heterozygous for the genes for normal hearing as shown in the Figure. When two-deaf-mutes, all of the children may have normal hearing and speech as both the genes for deafness are recessive.

DUPLICATE GENES

Sometimes two different genes determine the same phenotype. Such genes are called duplicate genes. For example, endosperm colour in maize is determined by two genes such as Y_1 and Y_2. When both or either of the genes are dominant endosperm is yellow. When both the genes are recessive, endosperm is colourless is white. Yellow colour is dominant and white recessive. A cross between plants with yellow ($Y_1\ Y_1\ Y_1\ Y_2$) and ($y_1\ y_1\ y_2 y_2$) endosperms yield progeny which are heterozygous for both the genes ($Y_1\ y_2\ Y_2\ y_2$) and therefore, have yellow endosperm. Plants of F_2 generation have either yellow or colourless endosperm and segregation yellow; white is in the ratio of 15:1. Seven out of sixteen progeny are homozygous dominant for both or either of the genes and are true breeding, producing only yellow seeded progeny on selfing. Four out of sixteen are dominant and heterozygous for only one and, therefore, on selfing segregate into three yellow-seeded: one white seeded progeny. Another four out of sixteen F_2 progeny are heterozygous for both the genes and produce 15 yellow seeded: one white seeded progeny on selfing. One of sixteen is homozygous recessive for the both genes and remains true-breeding, producing only white-seeded plants. Inheritance of fruit shape in Capsella bursa pastor is follows the same pattern. Fruits are triangular in the presence of two ($T_1\ T_2$) or one ($T_1\ or\ T_2$) dominant gene.

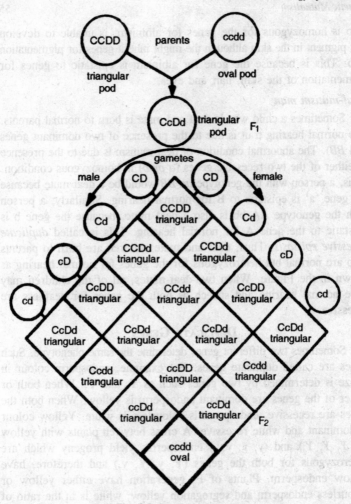

Fig. 3.5. Duplicate factors.

Recessive homozygosity for both the genes $(t_1t_1t_2t_2)$ results into oblong fruits.

CUMULATIVE OR QUANTITATIVE GENES

These genes are quantitative in nature and bring out different degrees of phenotypic expression according to the number of doses of determiners. The greater the genes will be, larger will be its effect. The traits influenced by duplicate factors are also of this type. A case of this type came to the notice of the famous plant breeder Kolreuter.

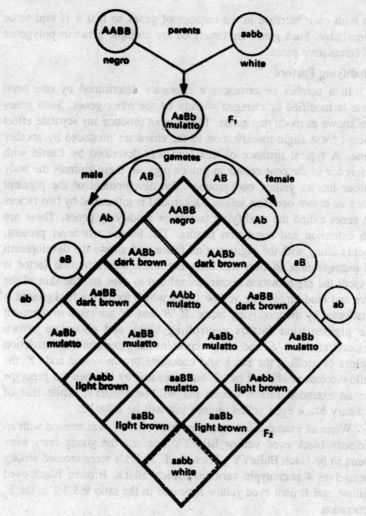

Fig. 3.6. Cumulative factors.

He crossed a tall variety of tobacco with a dwarf variety. The F_1 were intermediate between the two parents. The melanin pigment in the human skin experimented by Davenport by crossing Negro white crosses in an another classical example of cumulative genes. The inheritance of quantitative characters was also explained by the Swedish plant breeder, Nilson-Ehle. According to his explanation one gene will have a positive effect, two genes will have a greater effect and total effect of three genes will be still greater and so on. The effect adds up with each increase in the number of genes so that it is said to be cumulative. Such genes are described are multiple genes or polygenes or cumulative genes.

Modifying Factors

In a number of instances a character determined by one main gene is modified or changed slightly by the other genes. Such genes are known as modifying genes. They cannot produce any separate effect except for a slight modification in the character produced by another gene. A typical instance of this kind was described by Castle with reference to the coat colour in guinea pigs. In these animals the body colour has an yellow background. The development of the pigment black or brown over this yellow background is influenced by two factors or genes called the modifying factors or modifying genes. These are the extension and restriction factors. The former whenever present, occurs along with the pigmentation factor and allows the development of pigmentation all over the body but when the restriction factor is present the pigmentation becomes confined to eyes and the skin of the fore and hind limbs. The yellow factor which forms the background is unaffected by the modifying factor. If 'B' and 'b' are taken to represent the pigmentation factors controlling black and chocolate brown respectively, and 'E' and 'e' to represent the extension and restriction factors controlling the black and chocolate brown colour and 'Y' the yellow colour unaffected by 'E' but concealed by 'B' then the genotype for an extended brown guinea pig will be *bbEEYY*; while that of ordinary black eyed yellow guinea pig will be *BBeeYY*.

When an extended brown guinea pig bbEEYY was crossed with an ordinary black eyed yellow BBeeYY one; all the young ones were found to be black BbEeYY. When the F_1 hybrids were crossed among themselves 4 phenotypic varieties namely Black, Brown, Black eyed yellow, and Brown eyed yellow appeared in the ratio 9:3:3:1 in the F_2 generation.

Pleiotropy

The term pleiotropy refers to the situation in which a gene influences more than one trait. Many such instances have been discovered. In fact all genes (whether mutant or wild-type allelic forms) may be pleiotropic, with their various effects simply not yet recognized. Even though a structural gene may have many end effects, if has only one primary function, that of producing one polypeptide (in some cases, one RNA molecule). This polypeptide may give rise to different expressions at the phenotypic level.

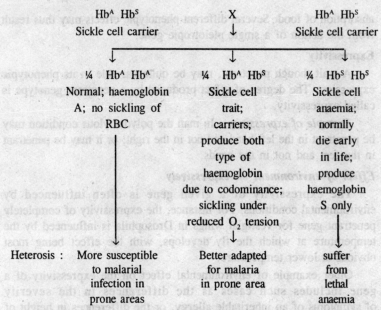

Hb^A Hb^S   X   Hb^A Hb^S
Sickle cell carrier   Sickle cell carrier

¼ Hb^A Hb^A
Normal; haemoglobin
A; no sickling of
RBC

¼ Hb^A Hb^S
Sickle cell
trait;
carriers;
produce both
type of
haemoglobin
due to codominance;
sickling under
reduced O₂ tension

¼ Hb^S Hb^S
Sickle cell
anaemia;
normlly
die early
in life;
produce
haemoglobin
S only

Heterosis : More susceptible   Better adapted   suffer
to malarial   for malaria   from
infection in   in prone area   lethal
prone areas   anaemia

The *Hb* allele provides a classic example of pleiotropy. It not only causes hemolytic anemia (in the homozygous status) but also results in increased resistance to one type of malaria, that caused by the parasite Plasmodium falciparum. Because the increased resistance of falciparum malaria occurs in Hb^AB Hb^bB heterozygotes, such heterozygous individuals have a selective advantage in geographical region where this type of malaria is prevalent. The sickle-cell-allele also has pleiotropic effects on the development of many tissues and organs such as bones, the lungs, the kidneys, the spleen and the heart.

Cystic fibrosis is a hereditary, metabolic disorder in children that is controlled by a single autosomal recessive gene. The gene apparently specifies an enzyme that produces a unique glycoprotein. This glycoprotein results in the production of mucus with abnormally high viscosity. Overly viscous mucus interferes with the normal functioning of several exocrine glands, including those in the skin (sweat), lungs (mucus), liver and pancreas. The syndrome (group of symptoms that characterizes the disease) is related directly or indirectly to the abnormal mucus. Abnormally high levels of sodium chloride occur in the sweat. Mucus stagnates in tabules of the lungs, which frequently become infected, giving rise to bronchitis. Secreting cells in the liver and the pancreas are impaired, curtailing production of fat-emulsifying agents and digesting enzymes and thus interfering with digestion and absorption of food. Several different phenotypic effects may thus result from the action of a single pleiotropic gene.

Expressivity

A trait though penetrant, may be quite variable in its phenotypic expression. The degree of effect produced by a penetrant genotype is called expressivity.

Example of expressivity : In man the polydactylous condition may be penetrant in the left hand and not in the right; or it may be penetrant in the feet and not in the hands.

Effect of environment on expressively

The expressivity or a given gene is often influenced by environmental conditions. For instance, the expressivity of completely penetrant gene for vestigial wings in Drosophila is influenced by the temperature at which the fly develops, with the effect being most obvious at lower temperature.

Other example of environmental effect on the expressivity of a gene includes such cases as the differences in the severity of symptoms of an inheritable allergy, or the differences in height of identical twins who have been raised in different home (with different diets), or who have had different medical histories (one with a serious childhood disease, the other escaping this disease).

Atavism

Characters may and often remain hidden generation after generation through the effect of inhibiting or epistatic factor or some other gene interaction. Occasionally, some wild character which was present in the ancestral forms reappears in the offsprings. This was first discussed by Charles Darwin and was called *atavism*.

Atavism results on account of chance combination of genes that allows a long suppressed character to reappear. For example, homozygous gene c is albino rats does not permit the appearance of agouti pattern. But in an outcross, when gene c is replaced by its allele C, agouti colour appears in the offsprings.

```
        Black        ×        Albino
        CCaa                   ccAA
         Ca          ↓          cA
                   Agouti
                    CcAa
```

The appearance of agouti colour pattern is rodents is an example of atavism.

4

HAPLOID GENES

A genome sequence is not an end in itself. A major challenge still has to be met in understanding what the genome contains and how the genome functions. The former is addressed by a combination of computer analysis and experimentation with the primary aim of locating the genes and their control regions and assigning a role to each gene. The bulk of this chapter will be devoted to these methods. The second question, understanding how the genome functions is, to a certain extent, merely a different way of stating the objectives of molecular biology over the last 30 years. The difference is that in the past attention has been directed at the expression pathways for individual genes, with groups of genes being considered only when the expression of one gene is linked to that of another. Now the issues have become more general and relate to the expression of the genome as a whole. We will familiarize ourselves with the relevant points at the end of this chapter.

LOCATING GENES IN DNA SEQUENCES

Once a DNA sequence has been obtained, whether it is the sequence of a single cloned fragment or of an entire chromosome, then various methods can be employed to locate the genes that are present. These methods can be divided into those that involve simply inspecting the sequence, by eye or more frequently by computer, to look for the special sequence features associated with genes, and those methods that locate genes by experimental analysis of the DNA sequence.

Gene Location by Sequence Inspection

Sequence inspection can be used to locate genes because genes are not random series of nucleotides but instead have distinctive features.

These features determine whether a sequence is a gene or not, and so by definition are not possessed by noncoding DNA. If in the future we can fully understand the exact nature of the specific sequence features that define a gene then sequence inspection will become a foolproof way of locating genes. We are not yet at this stage but sequence inspection is still a powerful tool in genome analysis.

Open Reading Frame of Genes

Genes that code for proteins comprise *open reading frames* (*ORFs*) consisting of a series of *codons* that specify the amino acid sequence of the protein that the gene codes for. The ORF begins with an *initiation codon*, usually but not always ATG, and ends with a *termination codon*, either TAA, TAG or TGA: Searching a DNA sequence for ORFs that begin with an ATG and end with a termination triplet is therefore one way of looking for genes. The analysis is complicated by the fact that each DNA sequence has six *reading frames*, three in one direction and three in the reverse direction on the complementary strand, but computers are quite capable of scanning all six reading frames for ORFs. How effective is this as a means of gene location?

The key to the success of ORF scanning is the frequency with which termination triplets appear in the DNA sequence. If the DNA has random sequence and a GC content of 50% then each of the three termination triplets - TAA, TAG and TGA - will appear, on average, once every $4^3 = 64$ bp. If the GC content is >50% then the termination triplets, being AT-rich, will occur less frequently but one would still be expected every 100-200bp. As there are three termination triplets and three reading frames in either direction, random DNA should not show many ORFs longer than 50 triplets in length, especially if the presence of a starting ATG is used as part of the definition of an 'ORF'. Most genes, on the other hand, are longer than 50 codons (the average lengths are 317 codons for *Escherichia coli* and 483 codons for *Saccharomyces cerevisiae*). ORF scanning, in its simplest form, therefore takes a figure of, say, 100 codons as the shortest length of a putative gene and records positive hits for all ORFs longer than this.

How well does this strategy work in practice? With bacterial genomes, simple ORF scanning is an effective way of locating most of the genes in a DNA sequence. The real genes in the sequence cannot be mistaken because they are much longer than 50 codons in length. With bacteria the analysis is further simplified by the fact that there is relatively little noncoding DNA in the genome (only 11% for *E. coli*). If we assume that the real genes do not overlap, and there

$$GAS \rightarrow$$

$$TGA \rightarrow$$

$$ATG \rightarrow$$

5'-ATGACGAGAGAGCAGCCA TTTT AG-3'

3'- T ACTGCTCTCTCGTCGGT AAAA TC-5'

$$\leftarrow ATC$$

$$\leftarrow AAT$$

$$\leftarrow AAA$$

Fig. 4.1. A double-stranded DNA molecule has six reading frames. Both strands are read in the 5´ -+3´ direction.

are no genes-within-genes, which are valid assumptions for bacterial DNA, then it is only in the noncoding regions that there is a possibility of mistaking a short, spurious ORF for a real gene. So if the noncoding component of a genome is small then there is a reduced chance of making mistakes in interpreting the results of a simple ORF scan.

Simple ORF Scans

Although ORF scans work well for simple bacterial genomes, they are less effective for locating genes in DNA sequences from higher eukaryotes. This is partly because there is substantially more space between real genes (70% of the human genome is intergenic), increasing the chances of finding spurious ORFs. But the main problem with the human genome and those of higher eukaryotes in general is that their genes are often split by introns and so do not appear as continuous ORFs in the DNA sequence. Many exons are shorter than 100 codons, some less than 50 codons, and continuing the reading frame into an intron usually leads to a termination sequence that appears to close the ORF. In other words, the genes of higher eukaryotes do not appear in their DNA sequences as long ORFs and simple ORF scanning cannot locate them.

Solving the problem posed by introns is the main challenge for bioinformaticists writing new software programs for ORF location. Three modifications to the basic procedure for ORF scanning have been adopted:

(i) *Codon bias* is taken into account. 'Codon bias' refers to the fact that not all codons are used equally frequently in the genes of a particular organism. For example, in human genes the amino acid alanine is only infrequently specified by the codon GCG, usually one of the other three codons for alanine (GCA, GCC or GCT) is used. Similarly, threonine is most frequently coded by ACA, ACC or ACT and less often by ACG. The biological reason for codon bias is not understood, but all organisms have a bias, different in different species. Real exons are expected to display the codon bias but chance series of triplets do not. The codon bias of the organism being studied is therefore written into the ORF scanning software.

(ii) *Exon-intron boundaries* can be searched for as these have distinctive sequence features, though unfortunately the distinctiveness of these sequences is not so great as to make their location a trivial task. The sequence of the upstream, exon-intron boundary is usually described as

$$5'-AG\downarrow GTAAGT-3'$$

the arrow indicating the precise boundary point. However, only the 'GT' immediately after the arrow is invariable, at the preceding positions nucleotides other than the ones shown are quite often found. In other words, the sequence shown is a consensus, the average of a range of variabilities. The downstream, intron-exon boundary is even less well defined:

$$5'-PyPyPyPyPyPyNCAG^{-}-3'$$

where 'Py' means one of the pyrimidine nucleotides, T or C, and 'N' is any nucleotide. Simply searching for the consensus sequences will not locate more than a few exon-intron boundaries because most have sequences other than the ones shown. Writing software to take account of the known variabilities has proven difficult, and at present locating exon-intron boundaries by sequence analysis is a hit and miss affair.

(iii) *Upstream control sequences* can be used to locate the regions where genes begin. This is because these control sequences, like exon-

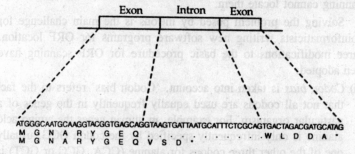

Fig. 4.2. ORF scans are complicated by introns. The nucleotide sequence of a short gene containing a single intron is shown.

intron boundaries, have distinctive sequence features that they possess in order to carry out their role as recognition signals for the DNA-binding proteins involved in gene expression. Unfortunately, as with exon-intron boundaries, the control sequences are variable, more so in eukaryotes than prokaryotes, and in eukaryotes not all genes have the same collection of control sequences. Using these to locate genes is therefore, problematical.

These three extensions of simple ORF scanning are generally applicable to all higher eukaryotic genomes. Additional strategies are also possible with individual organisms, based on the special features of their genomes. For example, vertebrate genomes contain *CpG islands* upstream of many genes, these being sequences of approximately 1 kb in which the GC content is greater than the average for the genome as a whole. For example, some 56% of human genes are associated with an upstream CpG island. These sequences are distinctive and when one is located in vertebrate DNA a strong assumption can be made that a gene begins in the region immediately downstream.

Homology Searches to Sequence Inspection

The limitations of ORF scanning with higher eukaryotic genomes are offset to a certain extent by the use of a *homology search* to test whether a series of triplets is a real exon or a chance sequence. In this analysis the DNA databases are searched to determine if the test sequence is identical or similar to any genes that have already been sequenced. Obviously, if the test sequence is part of a gene that has already been sequenced by someone else then an identical match will be found, but this is not the point of a homology search. Instead the intention is to determine if an entirely new sequence is similar to any known genes, because if it is then there is a chance that the test and match sequences are *homologous*, meaning that they represent genes that are evolutionarily related. The main use of homology searching is to assign functions to newly discovered genes, and we will therefore return to it when we deal with this aspect of genome analysis later in the chapter. At this point, we will note simply that the technique is also central to *gene location*, as it enables tentative exon sequences located by ORF scanning to be tested for functionality. If the tentative exon sequence gives one or more positive matches after a homology search then it probably is a real exon, if it gives no match then its authenticity must remain in doubt until it is assessed by one or other of the experiment-based gene location techniques. The value of this approach is increasing rapidly as the numbers of authentic gene sequences in databases multiply.

Experimental Techniques for Gene Location

It is to the experiment-based gene location techniques that we now turn our attention. These procedures locate genes by examining the RNA molecules that are transcribed from a DNA fragment. All genes are transcribed into RNA, and if the gene is discontinuous then the primary transcript is subsequently processed to remove the introns and link up the exons. Techniques which map the positions of transcribed (or 'expressed') sequences in a DNA fragment can therefore be used to locate exons and entire genes. The only problem to be kept in mind is that the transcript is usually longer than the coding part of the gene because it begins several tens of nucleotides upstream of the initiation codon and continues several tens or hundreds of nucleotides downstream of the termination codon. Transcript analysis does not therefore give a precise definition of the start and end of the coding region of a gene, but it does tell you that a gene is present in a particular region and it can locate the exon-intron boundaries. Often this is sufficient information to enable the coding region to be delineated.

Hybridization Tests

The simplest procedures for studying expressed sequences are based on hybridization analysis. RNA molecules can be separated by specialized forms of agarose gel electrophoresis and transferred to a nitrocellulose or nylon membrane by the process called *northern blotting*. This differs from Southern blotting only in the precise conditions under which the transfer is carried out and the fact that it was not invented by a Dr Northern and so does not have a capital 'N'. If a northern blot is probed with a labeled DNA fragment, then RNAs expressed from the fragment will be detected. Northern hybridization is therefore, theoretically, a means of determining the number of genes present in a DNA fragment and the size of each coding region. There are two weaknesses with this approach

- Some individual genes give rise to two or more transcripts, of different lengths, because some of their exons are optional and may or may not be retained in the mature RNA. If this is the case, then a fragment that contains just one gene could detect two or more hybridizing bands in the northern blot. A similar problem can occur if the gene is a member of a multigene family.

- With many species, it is not practical to make a preparation from an entire organism so the RNA extract is obtained from a single organ or tissue. Consequently any genes not expressed in that organ or tissue will not be represented in the RNA population, and so will not be detected when the RNA is probed with the DNA fragment being studied. Even if the whole organism is used, not all genes will give hybridization signals because many are expressed only at a particular developmental stage, and others are weakly expressed, meaning that their RNA products are present in amounts too low to be detected by hybridization analysis.

A second type of hybridization analysis avoids the problems with poorly expressed and tissue-specific genes by searching not for RNAs but for related sequences in the DNAs of other organisms. This approach, like homology searching, is based on the fact that homologous genes in related organisms have similar sequences, whereas the noncoding DNA is quite different. If a DNA fragment from one species is used to probe a Southern blot of DNAs from related species, and one or more hybridization signals are obtained, then it is likely that the probe contains one or more genes. This is called *zoo-blotting*.

cDNA Sequencing

Northern hybridization and zoo-blotting enable the presence or absence of genes in a DNA fragment to be determined, but give no positional information relating to the location of those genes in the DNA sequence. The easiest way to obtain this information is to sequence the relevant cDNAs. A cDNA is a copy of an mRNA and so corresponds to the coding region of a gene, plus any leader or trailer sequences' that are also transcribed. Comparing a cDNA sequence with a genomic DNA sequence therefore delineates the position of the relevant gene and reveals the exon-intron boundaries.

The degree of success of cDNA sequencing as a means of gene location depends on two factors. The first is the frequency of the appropriate cDNAs in the cDNA clone library that has been prepared. As with northern hybridization, the problem relates to the different expression levels of different genes. If the DNA fragment being studied contains one or more poorly expressed genes, then the relevant cDNAs will be rare in the library and it might be necessary to screen many clones before the desired one is identified. To get around this problem various methods of *cDNA capture* or *cDNA selection* have been devised, based around repeated hybridization between the DNA fragment being studied and the pool of cDNAs. Because the cDNA pool contains so many different sequences it is generally not possible to discard all irrelevant clones by these repeated hybridizations, but it is possible to enrich the pool for those clones that specifically hybridize to the DNA

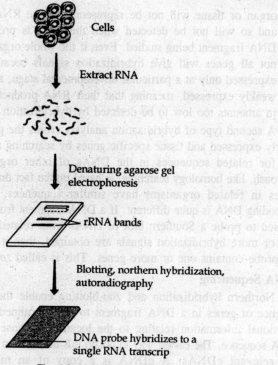

Cells

Extract RNA

Denaturing agarose gel electrophoresis

rRNA bands

Blotting, northern hybridization, autoradiography

DNA probe hybridizes to a single RNA transcrip

Fig. 4.3. Northern hybridization.

fragment. This reduces the size of the library that must subsequently be screened under stringent conditions to identify the desired clones.

A second factor determining success or failure is the completeness of the individual cDNA molecules. Traditionally, cDNAs are made by copying RNA molecules into single-stranded DNA with *reverse transcriptase* and then converting the single-stranded DNA into double stranded DNA with a DNA polymerase. There is always a chance that one or other of the strand synthesis reactions will not proceed to completion, resulting in a truncated cDNA. The presence of intramolecular base pairs in the RNA can also lead to incomplete copying. Truncated cDNAs may lack some of the information needed to locate the start and end points of a gene and all its exon-intron boundaries.

Methods for Mapping of the Ends

The problems with incomplete cDNAs means that more robust methods are needed for locating the precise start and end points of gene transcripts. One possibility is a special type of PCR which uses RNA rather than DNA as the starting material. The first step in this

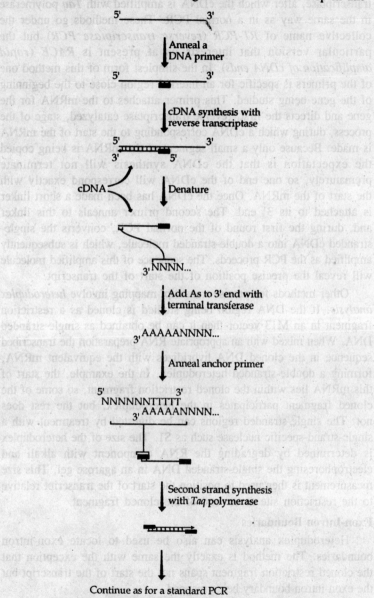

Fig. 4.4. RACE—rapid amplification of cDNA ends.

type of PCR is to convert the RNA into cDNA with reverse transcriptase, after which the cDNA is amplified with *Taq* polymerase in the same way as in a normal PCR. These methods go under the collective name of *RT-PCR* (*reverse transcriptase PCR*) but the particular version that interests us at present is *RACE* (*rapid amplification of cDNA ends*). In the simplest form of this method one of the primers is specific for an internal region close to the beginning of the gene being studied. This primer attaches to the mRNA for the gene and directs the first, reverse transcriptase catalyzed, stage of the process, during which a cDNA corresponding to the start of the mRNA is made. Because only a small segment of the mRNA is being copied the expectation is that the cDNA synthesis will not terminate prematurely, so one end of the cDNA will correspond exactly with the start of the mRNA. Once the cDNA has been made a short linker is attached to its 3' end. The second primer anneals to this linker and, during the first round of the normal PCR, converts the single-stranded cDNA into a double-stranded molecule, which is subsequently amplified as the PCR proceeds. The sequence of this amplified molecule will reveal the precise position of the start of the transcript.

Other methods for precise transcript mapping involve *heteroduplex analysis*. If the DNA region being studied is cloned as a restriction fragment in an M13 vector then it can be obtained as single-stranded DNA. When mixed with an appropriate RNA preparation the transcribed sequence in the cloned DNA hybridizes with the equivalent mRNA, forming a double-stranded heteroduplex. In the example, the start of this mRNA lies within the cloned restriction fragment, so some of the cloned fragment participates in the heteroduplex, but the rest does not. The single-stranded regions can be digested by treatment with a single-strand-specific nuclease such as S1. The size of the heteroduplex is determined by degrading the RNA component with alkali and electrophoresing the single-stranded DNA in an agarose gel. This size measurement is then used to position the start of the transcript relative to the restriction site at the end of the cloned fragment.

Exon-Intron Boundaries

Heteroduplex analysis can also be used to locate exon-intron boundaries. The method is exactly the same with the exception that the cloned restriction fragment spans not the start of the transcript but the exon-intron boundary being mapped.

A second method for finding exons in a genome sequence is called *exon trapping*. This requires a special type of vector that contains a

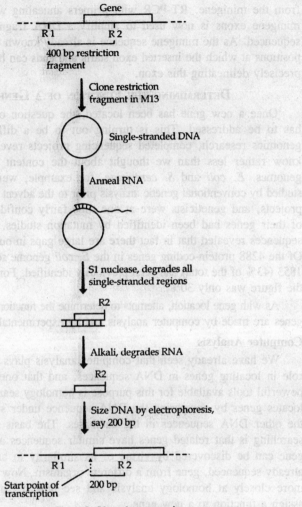

Fig. 4.5. S1 nuclease mapping

minigene consisting of two exons flanking an intron sequence, the first exon being preceded by the sequence signals needed to initiate transcription in a eukaryotic cell. To use the vector the piece of DNA to be studied is inserted into a restriction site located within the vector's intron region. The vector is then introduced into a suitable eukaryotic cell line, where it is transcribed and the RNA produced from it is spliced. The result is that any exon contained in the genomic fragment becomes attached between the upstream and downstream exons from the minigene. RT-PCR with primers annealing within the two minigene exons is now used to amplify a DNA fragment which is sequenced. As the minigene sequence is already known the nucleotide positions at which the inserted exon starts and ends can be determined, precisely delineating this exon.

DETERMINING THE FUNCTION OF A GENE

Once a new gene has been located, the question of its function has to be addressed. This is turning out to be a difficult area of genomics research, completed sequencing projects revealing that we know rather less than we thought about the content of individual genomes. *E. coli* and *S. cerevisiae*, for example, were intensively studied by conventional genetic analysis prior to the advent of sequencing projects, and geneticists were at one time fairly confident that most of their genes had been identified by mutation studies. The genome sequences revealed that in fact there are large gaps in our knowledge. Of the 4288 protein-coding genes in the *E. coli* genome sequence, only 1853 (43% of the total) had been previously identified. For *S. cerevisiae* the figure was only 30%.

As with gene location, attempts to determine the functions of unknown genes are made by computer analysis and by experimental studies.

Computer Analysis

We have already seen that computer analysis plays an important role in locating genes in DNA sequences, and that one of the most powerful tools available for this purpose is homology searching, which locates genes by comparing the DNA sequence under study with all the other DNA sequences in the databases. The basis of homology searching is that related genes have similar sequences and so a new gene can be discovered by virtue of its similarity to an equivalent, already sequenced, gene from a different organism. Now we will look more closely at homology analysis and see how it can be used to assign a function to a new gene.

Evolutionary Relationships

Homologous genes are ones that share a common evolutionary ancestor, revealed by sequence similarities between the genes. These similarities form the data on which molecular phylogenies are based. Homologous genes fall into two categories:

  • *Orthologous* genes are those homologs that are present in different organisms and whose common ancestor predates the split between the species.

- *Paralogous* genes are present in the same organism, often members of a recognized multigene family their common ancestor possibly or possibly not predating the species in which the genes are now found.

A pair of homologous genes do not usually have identical nucleotide sequences, because the two genes undergo different random changes by mutation, but they have similar sequences because these random changes have operated on the same starting sequence, the common ancestral gene. Homology searching makes use of these sequence similarities. The basis of the analysis is that if a newly sequenced gene turns out to be similar to a second, previously sequenced gene, then an evolutionary relation-ship can be inferred and the function of the new gene is likely to be the same, or at least similar, to the function of the second gene.

It is important not to confuse the words *homology* and *similarity*. It is incorrect to describe a pair of related genes as '80% homologous' if their sequences have 80% nucleotide identity. A pair of genes are either evolutionarily related or they are not, there are no in between situations and it is therefore meaningless to ascribe a percentage value to homology.

Homology Analysis

A homology search can be conducted with a DNA sequence but usually a tentative gene sequence is converted into an amino acid sequence before the search is carried out. One reason for this is because there are twenty different amino acids in proteins but only four nucleotides in DNA, so genes that are unrelated usually appear to be more different from one another when their amino acid sequences are compared. A homology search is therefore less likely to give spurious results if the amino sequence is used. The practicalities of homology searching are not at all daunting. Several software programs exist for carrying out this type of analysis, the most popular being BLAST. The search can be carried out simply by sending a correctly formatted email to the BLAST server at a DNA database. Several hours later the server sends you back an email giving the results of the search. There is currently approximately a 50% chance that a newly sequenced gene will-give a positive homology match with a gene already in the databases.

A positive match may give a clear indication of the function of the new gene or the implications of the match might be more subtle. In particular, genes that have no obvious evolutionary relatedness might

Sequence 1   GGTGAGGGTATCATCCCATCTGACTACACCTCATCGGGAGACGGAGCAGT
Sequence 2   GGTCAGGATATGATTCCATCACACTACACCTTATCCCGAGTCGGAGCAGT
Identities   *** *** *** ** ***** ********* *** *** *********

Fig. 4.6. Two DNA sequences with 80% sequence identity.

have short segments that are similar to one another. The explanation of this is often that, although the genes are unrelated, their proteins have similar functions and the shared sequence encodes a domain within each protein that is central to that shared function. Although the genes themselves have no common ancestor, the domains do, but with their common ancestor occurring at a very ancient time, the homologous domains having subsequently evolved not only by single nucleotide changes, but also by more complex rearrangements that have created new genes within which the domains are found. An interesting example is provided by the tudor domain, an approximately 120-amino-acid motif which was first identified in the sequence of the *Drosophila melanogaster* gene called *tudor*. The protein coded by the *tudor* gene, whose function is unknown, is made up often copies of the tudor domain, one after the other. A homology search using the tudor domain as the test revealed that several known proteins contain this domain. The sequences of these proteins are not highly similar to one another and there is no indication that they are true homo logs, but all possess the tudor domain. These proteins include one involved in RNA transport during *Drosophila* oogenesis, a human protein with a role in RNA metabolism, and others whose activity appears to involve RNA in one way or another. The homology analysis therefore suggests that the tudor sequence plays some part in RNA binding, RNA metabolism or some other function involving RNA. The information from the computer analysis is incomplete by itself, but it points the way to the types of experiment that should be done to obtain more clear-cut data on the function of the tudor domain.

Yeast Genome Project

The *S. cerevisiae* genome project has illustrated both the potential and limitations of homology analysis as a means of assigning functions to new genes. The yeast genome contains approximately 6000 genes, of which 30% had been identified by conventional genetic analysis before the sequencing project got underway. The remaining 70% were studied by homology analysis, giving the following results.

1. Almost another 30% of the genes in the genome could be assigned functions after homology searching of the sequence databases. About half of these were clear homologs of genes whose functions had previously been established, and about half had less striking

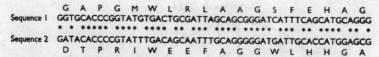

```
            G  A  P  G  M  W  L  R  L  A  A  G  S  F  E  H  A  G
Sequence 1  GGTGCACCCGGTATGTGACTGCGATTAGCAGCGGGATCATTTCAGCATGCAGGG
            *  *  *****  ****  ****  **  ***  ****  *****  ***  **  ****  **  *
Sequence 2  GATACACCCCGTATTTGACAGCAATTTGCAGGGGGATGATTGCACCATGGAGCG
            D  T  P  R  I  W  E  E  F  A  G  G  W  L  H  H  G  A
```

Fig. 4.7. Lack of homology between two sequences is often more apparent when comparisons are made at the amino acid level.

similarities, including many where the similarities were restricted to discrete domains. For all these genes the homology analysis could be described as successful, but with various degrees of usefulness. For some genes the identification of a homolog enabled the function of the yeast gene to be comprehensively determined: examples included identification of yeast genes for DNA polymerase subunits and aminoacyl-tRNA synthetases. For other genes the functional assignment could only be to a broad category, such as 'gene for a protein kinase', in other words the biochemical properties of the gene product could be inferred but not the exact role of the protein in the cell. Some identifications were initially puzzling, the best example being the discovery of a yeast homolog of a bacterial gene involved in nitrogen fixation. Yeasts do not fix nitrogen so this could not be the function of the yeast gene. In this case, the discovery of the yeast homolog refocused attention on the previously characterized bacterial gene, with the subsequent realization that, although being involved in nitrogen fixation, the primary role of the bacterial gene product was in the synthesis of metal-containing proteins, which have broad roles in all organisms, not just nitrogen-fixing ones.

(ii) About 10% of all the yeast genes had homologs in the databases, but the functions of these homologs were unknown. The homology analysis was therefore unable to help in assigning functions to these yeast genes. These yeast genes and their homologs are called *orphan families*.

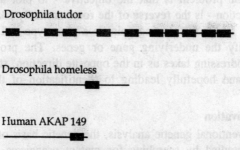

Drosophila tudor

Drosophila homeless

Human AKAP 149

Fig. 4.8. The tudor domain.

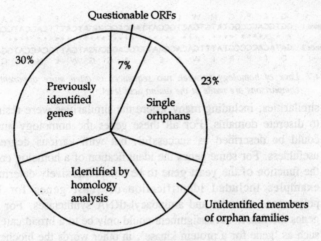

Fig. 4.9. Categories of gene in the yeast genome.

(iii) The remaining yeast genes, about 30% of the total, had no homologs in the databases. A small proportion of these (about 7% of the total) were questionable ORFs which might not be real genes, being rather short or having an unusual codon bias. The remainder look like genes but at present are unique. The latter group are called single orphans.

Assigning Gene Function

It is clear that homology analysis is not a panacea that can identify the functions of all new genes. Experimental methods are therefore needed to complement and extend the results of homology studies. This is proving to be one of the biggest problems in genomics research and most molecular biologists agree that the methodologies and strategies currently in use are not entirely adequate for assigning functions to the vast numbers of unknown genes being discovered by sequencing projects. The problem is that the objective - to plot a course from gene to function - is the reverse of the route normally taken by genetic analysis, in which the starting point is a phenotype and the objective is to identify the underlying gene or genes. The problem we are currently addressing takes us in the opposite direction, starting from a new gene and hopefully leading to identification of the associated phenotype.

Gene Inactivation

In conventional genetic analysis, the genetic basis of a phenotype is usually studied by searching for mutant organisms in which the phenotype has become altered. The mutants might be obtained experimentally, for example by treating a population of organisms (*e.g.* a culture of bacteria) with ultraviolet radiation or a mutagenic chemical or the mutants might be present in a natural population. The gene or genes that have been altered in the mutant organism are then studied by genetic crosses, which can locate the position of a gene in a genome and also determine if the gene is the same as one that has already been characterized. The gene can then be studied further by molecular biology techniques, for example by cloning and sequencing.

The general principle of this conventional analysis is that the genes responsible for a phenotype can be identified by determining which genes are inactivated in organisms that display a mutant version of the phenotype. If the starting point is the gene, rather than the phenotype, then the equivalent strategy would be to mutate the gene and identify the phenotypic change that results. This is the basis of most of the techniques used to assign functions to unknown genes.

Methods for inactivating specific genes

The easiest way to inactivate a specific gene is to disrupt it with an unrelated segment of DNA. This can be achieved by *homologous recombination* between the chromosomal copy of the gene and a second piece of DNA that shares some sequence identity with the target gene. Homologous, and other types of, recombination are complex events, for present purposes it is enough to know that if two DNA molecules have similar sequences, then recombination can result in segments of the molecules being exchanged.

How is gene inactivation carried out in practice? We will consider two examples, the first with *S. cerevisiae*. Since completing the genome sequence in 1996, yeast molecular biologists have embarked

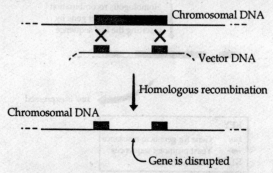

Fig. 4.10. Gene inactivation by homologous recombination.

on a coordinated, international effort to determine the functions of as many orphan genes as possible. The central component is the 'deletion cassette', which carries a gene for antibiotic resistance. This gene is not a normal component of the yeast genome but it will work if transferred into a yeast chromosome, giving rise to a transformed yeast cell that is resistant to the antibiotic geneticin. Before using the deletion cassette new segments of DNA are attached as tails to either end. These segments have sequences identical to parts of the yeast gene that is going to be inactivated. After the modified cassette is introduced into a yeast cell, homologous recombination occurs between the DNA tails and the chromosomal copy of the yeast gene, replacing the latter with the antibiotic resistant gene. Cells which have undergone the replacement are therefore selected by plating the culture on to agar medium containing geneticin. The resulting colonies lack the target

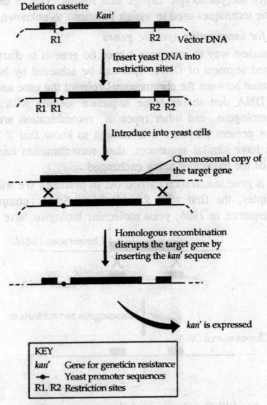

Fig. 4.11. The use of a yeast deletion cassette.

gene and their phenotypes can be examined to gain some insight into the function of the gene.

The second example of gene inactivation uses an analogous process but with mice rather than yeast. The mouse is frequently used as a *model organism* for humans, because the mouse genome is similar to the human genome, containing many of the same genes. Identifying the functions of unknown human genes is therefore being carried out largely by inactivating the equivalent genes in the mouse, these experiments being ethically unthinkable with humans. The homologous recombination part of the procedure is identical to that described for yeast and once again results in a cell in which the target gene has been inactivated. The problem is that we do not want just one mutated cell, we want a whole mutant mouse, as only with the complete organism can we make a complete assessment of the effect of the gene inactivation on the phenotype. To achieve this it is necessary to use a special type of mouse cell, an *embryonic stem* or *ES* cell. Unlike most mouse cells, ES cells are *totipotent*, meaning that they are not committed to a single developmental pathway and can therefore give rise to all types of differentiated cell. The engineered ES cell is therefore injected into a mouse embryo, which continues to develop and eventually give rise to a *chimera*, a mouse whose cells are a mixture of mutant ones, derived from the engineered ES cells, and nonmutant ones, derived from all the other cells in the embryo. This is still not quite what we want, so the chimeric mice are allowed to mate with one another. Some of the offspring result from fusion of two engineered gametes, and will therefore be nonchimeric, as every one of their cells will carry the inactivated gene. These are *knockout mice*, and it is hoped that examination of their phenotypes provides the desired information on the function of the gene being studied. This works well for many gene inactivations but some are lethal and so cannot be studied in a homozygous knockout mouse. Instead, a heterozygous mouse is obtained, the product of fusion between one normal and one engineered gamete, in the hope that the phenotypic effect of the gene inactivation will be apparent even though the mouse still has one correct copy of the gene being studied.

Phenotypic Effect

Once a gene-inactivated yeast strain, knockout mouse, or equivalent with any other organism has been obtained the next stage is to examine the phenotype of the mutant in order to assign a function to the unknown gene. This can be much more difficult than it sounds. With any organism the range of phenotypes that must be examined is immense. Even with yeast, the list is quite lengthy and with higher organisms some phenotypes (*e.g.* behavioural ones) are difficult if not impossible to assess in a comprehensive fashion. Furthermore, the effects of some gene inactivations are very subtle and may not be recognized when the phenotype is examined. A good example was provided by the longest gene on yeast chromosome III which, at 2167 codons and with typical yeast codon bias, simply had to be a functional gene rather than a spurious ORE. Inactivation of this gene had no apparent effect, the mutant yeast cells appearing to have an identical phenotype to normal yeast. For some time it was thought that perhaps this gene is dispensable, its protein product either involved in some completely nonessential function, or having a function that is duplicated by a second gene. Eventually it was shown that the mutants died when they were grown at low pH in the presence of glucose and acetic acid, which normal yeasts can tolerate, and it was concluded that the gene codes for a protein that pumps acetate out of the cell. This is definitely an essential function as the gene plays a vital role in protecting yeast from acetic acid induced damage, but this essentiality was difficult to track down from the phenotype tests.

These problems, together with the daunting prospect of having to perform a gene inactivation and full phenotype screen for everyone of the 2500 yeast orphans, has prompted yeast biologists to pioneer the search for more efficient methods of assigning functions to unknown genes.

Gene Overexpression

So far we have concentrated on techniques that result in inactivation of the gene being studied ('loss of function'). The complementary approach is to engineer an organism in which the test gene is much more active than normal ('gain of function') and to determine what changes, if any, this has on the phenotype. The results of these experiments must be treated with caution because of the need to distinguish between a phenotype change that is due to the specific function of an over expressed gene and a less specific phenotype change that reflects the abnormality of the situation where a single gene product is being synthesized in excessive amounts, possibly in tissues in which the gene is normally inactive. Despite this qualification, over expression has provided some important information on gene function.

To overexpress a gene a special type of cloning vector must be used, one designed to ensure that the cloned gene directs the synthesis

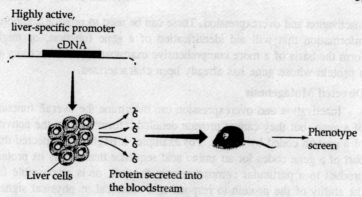

Fig. 4.12. *Functional analysis by gene overexpression.*

of as much protein as possible. The vector is therefore *multicopy*, meaning that inside the host organism it multiplies to 40-200 copies per cell, so there are many copies of the test gene. The vector must also contain a highly active promoter so that each copy of the test gene is converted into large quantities of mRNA, again ensuring that as much protein as possible is made. In this project the genes to be studied were identified from EST sequences and so each one was cloned as a cDNA. The genes were selected because their sequences suggested that they code for proteins that are secreted into the bloodstream. The cloning vector that was used contained a highly active promoter that is expressed only in the liver, so each *transgenic mouse* overexpressed the test gene in its liver and then secreted the resulting protein into the blood.

The phenotype of each transgenic mouse was examined in the search for clues regarding the functions of the cloned genes. An interesting discovery was made when it was realized that one transgenic mouse had bones that were significantly more dense than those of normal mice. This was important for two reasons: first, it enabled the relevant gene to be identified as one involved in bone synthesis; and second, the discovery of a protein that increases bone density has implications for the development of treatments for human osteoporosis, a fragile-bone disease.

Activity of a Protein Coded by an Unknown Gene

Gene inactivation and overexpression are the primary techniques used by genome researchers to determine the function of a new gene, but these are not the only procedures that can provide information on gene activity. Other methods can extend and elaborate the results of inactivation and overexpression. These can be used to provide additional information that will aid identification of a gene function, or might form the basis of a more comprehensive examination of the activity of a protein whose gene has already been characterized.

Directed Mutagenesis

Inactivation and overexpression can determine the overall function of a gene, but they cannot provide detailed information on the activity of a protein coded by a gene. For example, it might be suspected that part of a gene codes for an amino acid sequence that directs its protein product to a particular compartment in the cell, or is responsible for the ability of the protein to respond to a chemical or physical signal. To test these hypotheses it would be necessary to delete or alter the relevant part of the gene sequence, but to leave the bulk unmodified so that the protein is still synthesized and retains the major part of its activity. The various procedures of *sitedirected* or *in vitro mutagenesis* can be used to make these subtle changes. These are important techniques whose applications lie not only with the study of gene activity but also in the area of *protein engineering*, where the objective is to create novel proteins with properties that are better suited for use in industrial or clinical settings.

After mutagenesis the gene sequence must be introduced into the host cell so that homologous recombination can replace the existing copy of the gene with the modified version. This presents a problem because we must have a way of knowing which cells have undergone homologous recombination. Even with yeast this will only be a fraction of the total, and with mice the fraction will be very small. Normally we would solve this problem by placing a marker gene (*e.g.* one coding for antibiotic resistance) next to the mutated gene and looking for cells that take on the phenotype conferred by this marker. In most cases, cells that insert the marker gene into their genome also insert the closely attached, mutated gene and so are the ones we want. The problem is that in a site-directed mutagenesis experiment we must be sure that any change in the activity of the gene being studied is due to the specific mutation that was introduced into the gene rather than to the indirect result of changing its environment in the genome by inserting a marker gene next to it. The answer is to use a more complex, two-step gene replacement. In this procedure the target gene is first replaced with the marker gene, on its own, the cells in which this recombination takes place being identified by selecting for the marker gene phenotype. These cells are then used in the second stage

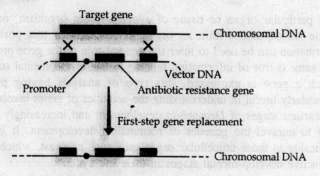

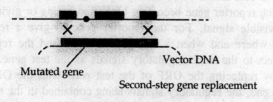

Fig. 4.13. Two-step gene replacement.

of the gene replacement, when the marker gene is replaced by the mutated gene, success now being monitored by looking for cells that have lost the marker gene phenotype. These cells contain the mutated gene and their phenotypes can be examined to determine the effect of the directed mutation on the activity of the protein product.

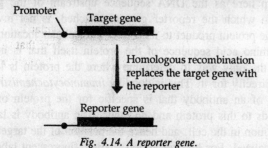

Fig. 4.14. A reporter gene.

Reporter Genes and Immunocytochemistry

Clues to the function of a gene can often be obtained by determining where and when the gene is expressed. If gene expression is restricted to a particular organ or tissue of a multicellular organism, or to a single set of cells within an organ or tissue, then this positional information can be used to infer the general role of the gene product. The same is true of information relating to the developmental stage at which a gene is expressed, this type of analysis having proved particularly useful in understanding the activities of genes involved in the earliest stages of *Drosophila* development and increasingly being used to unravel the genetics of mammalian development. It is also applicable to those unicellular organisms, such as yeast, which have distinctive develop-mental stages in their life cycle.

Determining the pattern of gene expression within an organism is possible with a *reporter gene*. This is a gene whose expression can be monitored in a convenient way, ideally by visual examination, cells that express the reporter gene becoming blue, fluorescing or giving off some other visible signal. For the reporter gene to give a reliable indication of where and when a test gene is expressed the reporter must be subject to the same regulatory signals as the test gene. This is achieved by replacing the ORF of the test gene with the ORF of the reporter gene, the regulatory signals being contained in the region of DNA upstream of an ORF. The reporter gene will now display the same expression pattern as the test gene, this expression pattern being determined by examining the organism for the reporter signal.

As well as knowing in which cells a gene is expressed, it is often useful to locate the position within the cell where the protein coded by the gene is found. For example, key data regarding gene function can be obtained by showing that the protein product is located in mitochondria, in the nucleus, or on the cell surface. Reporter genes cannot help here as the DNA sequence upstream of the gene, the sequence to which the reporter gene is attached, is not involved in targeting the protein product to its correct intracellular location. Instead it is the amino acid sequence of the protein itself that is important. Therefore the only way to determine where the protein is located is to search directly for it. This is done by *immunocytochemistry*, which makes use of an antibody that is specific for the protein of interest and so binds to this protein and no other. The antibody is labeled so that its position in the cell, and hence the position of the target protein, can be visualized. For low resolution studies, fluorescent labeling and light microscopy are used; alternatively, high resolution immunocytochemistry can be carried out by electron microscopy with an electron dense label such as colloidal gold.

Protein-protein Interactions

Important data pertaining to gene function can often be obtained by determining if the protein coded by the gene interacts with other, known proteins. If an interaction to a well characterized protein is identified, then it might be possible to infer the function of the unknown protein. For example, an interaction between an unknown protein and one known to be located on the cell surface might indicate that the unknown protein is involved in cell-cell signaling. There are several methods for studying protein-protein interactions, the two most useful being *phage display* and the *yeast two-hybrid system*.

In phage display a special type of cloning vector is used. This vector is based on λ bacteriophage or one of the filamentous bacteriophages such as M13. It is designed so that a new gene that is cloned into it is expressed in such a way that its protein product is synthesized as a fusion with one of the phage coat proteins. The phage protein therefore carries the foreign protein into the phage coat, where it is 'displayed' in a form that enables it to interact with other proteins that the phage encounters. There are several ways in which phage display can be used to study protein interactions. In one method, the test protein is displayed and interactions sought with a series of purified proteins or protein fragments of known function. This approach is limited as it takes time to carry out each test, so is feasible only if some prior information has been obtained about likely interactions. A more powerful strategy is to prepare a phage display library, a collection of clones displaying a range of proteins, and identifying which members of the library interact with the test protein.

The yeast two-hybrid system detects protein interactions in a more complex way. The proteins called *transcription factors* are responsible for controlling the expression of genes in eukaryotes. To carry out this function a transcription factor must bind to a DNA sequence upstream of a gene and activate the RNA polymerase enzyme that copies the gene into RNA. These two activities are specified by different parts of the transcription factor's protein structure, and some factors will work even after the protein has been cleaved into two segments, one segment containing the DNA-binding domain and one the activation domain. In the cell, the two segments interact to form the functional transcription factor.

The two-hybrid system makes use of an *S. cerevisiae* strain that lacks a transcription factor for a reporter gene. This gene is therefore switched off. The two segments of the transcription factor are coded by separate genes, both of which have been cloned. One of these genes, usually the one for the DNA-binding domain, is ligated to the gene for the protein whose interactions we wish to study. This protein can come from any organism, not just yeast: it is a human protein, which for convenience we will call 'Protein X'. After introduction into yeast, this engineered gene will specify synthesis of a fusion protein, made up of the DNA-binding domain of the transcription factor attached to Protein X. The second gene, the one for the activation domain of the transcription factor, is ligated with a mixture of DNA fragments so that many different constructs are made. The engineered genes are mixed together with yeast cells, some of which become cotransformed with an engineered DNA-binding gene and an engineered activation gene. If the fusion proteins coded by these two genes can cooperate then the reporter gene will be switched on. If this happens then the protein attached to the activation domain of the transcription factor must be one that can interact with Protein X.

COMPARATIVE GENOMICS

We have already seen how similarities between homologous genes from different organisms provide one way of assigning a function to an unknown gene. This is an example of how knowledge about the genome of one organism can help in understanding the genome of a second organism. The possibility that comparative genomics might be a valuable means of deciphering the human genome was recognized when the Human Genome Project was planned in the late 1980s, and the Project has actively stimulated the development of genome projects for model organisms such as the mouse and fruit fly. In this section we will explore the extent to which comparisons between different genomes are proving useful.

Gene Mapping

The basis of comparative genomics is that the genomes of related organisms are similar. The argument is the same one that we considered when looking at homologous genes. Two organisms with a relatively recent common ancestor will have genomes that display species-specific differences built onto the common plan possessed by the ancestral genome. The closer two organisms are on the evolutionary scale, the more related their genomes will be.

If the two organisms are sufficiently closely related then their genomes might display synteny, the partial or complete conservation of gene order. Then it is possible to use map information from one genome to locate genes in the second genome. At one time it was

(A) Production of a display phage

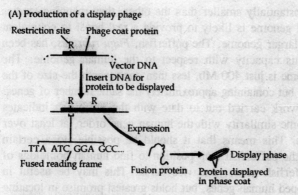

(B) Using a phage display library

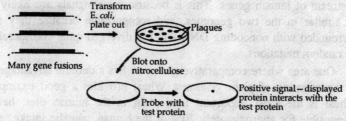

Fig. 4.15. Phage display. (A) The cloning vector used for phage display is a bacteriophage genome with a unique restriction site located within a gene for a coat protein. (B) A phage display library is produced by ligating many different DNA fragments into the cloning vector.

thought that mapping the genomes of mouse and other mammals, which are at least partially syntenic with the human genome, might provide valuable information that could be used in construction of the human genome map. The problem with this approach is that all the close relatives of humans have equally large genomes that are just as difficult to study, the only advantage being that a genetic map is easier to construct with an animal which, unlike humans, can be subjected to experimental breeding programs. Despite the limitations of human pedigree analysis, progress has been more rapid in mapping the human genome than those of any of our close relatives, so in this respect comparative genomics is proving more useful in mapping the animal genomes rather than our own. This is in itself a useful corollary to the Human Genome Project because it is revealing animal homologs of human genes involved in diseases, providing animal models in which these diseases can be studied.

Mapping is significantly easier with a small genome compared with a large one. This means that if one member of a pair of syntenic genomes is substantially smaller than the other, then mapping studies with this small genome is likely to provide a real boost to equivalent work with the larger genome. The pufferfish, *Fugu rubripes*, has been proposed in this capacity with respect to the human genome. The pufferfish genome is just 400 Mb, less than one-seventh the size of the human genome but containing approximately the same number of genes. The mapping work carried out to date with the pufferfish indicates that there is some similarity with the human gene order, at least over short distances. This means that it should be possible, to a certain extent, to use the pufferfish map position to find human homologs of sequenced pufferfish genes, and *vice versa*. This may be useful in locating unmapped human genes, but holds greatest promise in locating essential sequences such as promoters and other regulatory signals upstream of human genes. This is because these signals are likely to be similar in the two genomes, and recognizable because they are surrounded with noncoding DNA that has diverged quite considerably by random mutations.

One area where comparative genomics has a definite advantage is in the mapping of plant genomes. Wheat provides a good example. Wheat is the most important food plant in the human diet, being responsible for approximately 20% of the human calorific intake, and is therefore one of the crop plants that we most wish to study and possibly manipulate in the quest for improved crops. Unfortunately, the wheat genome is huge at 17000Mb, more than five times larger than even the human genome. A small model genome with a gene order similar to that of wheat would therefore be useful as a means of mapping desirable genes which might then be obtained from their equivalent positions in the wheat genome. Wheat, and other cereals such as rice, are members of the *Gramineae*, a large and diverse family of grasses. The rice genome is only 400Mb, substantially smaller than that of wheat, and there are probably other grasses with even smaller genomes. Comparative mapping of the rice and wheat genomes has revealed many similarities, and the possibility therefore exists that genes from the wheat genome might be isolated by first mapping the positions of the equivalent genes in a smaller *Gramineae* genome.

Study of Human Disease Genes

One of the main reasons for sequencing the human genome is to gain access to the sequences of genes involved in human disease. The hope is that the sequence of a disease gene will provide an insight into the biochemical basis of the disease and hence indicate a way of preventing or treating the disease. Comparative genomics has an important role to play in the study of disease genes because the discovery of a homolog of a human disease gene in a second organism is often the key to understanding the biochemical function of the human gene. If the homolog has already been characterized then the information needed to understand the biochemical role of the human gene may already be in place; if it is not then the necessary research can be directed at the homolog.

To be useful in the study of disease-causing genes, the second genome does not need to be syntenic with the human genome, nor even particularly closely related. *Drosophila* holds great promise in this respect, as the phenotypic effects of many *Drosophila* genes are already well known, so the data already exist for inferring the mode of action of human disease genes that have homologs in the *Drosophila* genome. But the greatest success has been with yeast. Several human disease genes have homologs in the *S. cerevisiae* genome. These disease genes include ones involved in cancer, cystic fibrosis and neurological syndromes, and in several cases the yeast homolog has a known function that provides a clear indication of the biochemical activity of the human gene. In some cases it has even been possible to demonstrate a physiological similarity between the gene activity in humans and yeast. For example, the yeast gene *SGSI* is a homolog of a human gene involved in the premature aging disease called Werner's syndrome. Yeasts with a mutant *SGSI* gene live for shorter periods than normal yeasts and display accelerated onset of aging indicators such as sterility. In yeast the underlying cause of the premature aging, and possibly the direct effect of the mutation, appears to be a change in the distribution of proteins in the nucleolus, a subcompartment of the nucleus. The link between *SGSI* and the Werner's syndrome gene, provided by comparative genomics, means that these findings are directly relevant to study of the human disease.

FROM GENOME TO CELL

Even if every gene in a genome can be identified and assigned a function, a challenge still remains. This is to understand how the genome as a whole operates within the cell, specifying and coordinating the various biochemical activities that take place. Describing and explaining this aspect of genome biology will be a mammoth task that will occupy researchers for many decades of the 21st century. Attempts are currently being made to chart the pattern of gene expression - which genes are switched on and which are switched off - in different tissues, during different developmental stages and, in the case of humans, in different disease states.

Patterns of Gene Expression

All organisms regulate expression of their genes, so that those genes whose protein products are not needed at a particular time are switched off. Understanding which genes are active in particular tissues at particular times, and assessing the relative degrees of activity of the genes that are switched on, is the first step in understanding how the genome as a whole functions within the cell.

Measuring Levels of RNA Transcripts

The first stage of gene expression involves copying the gene into an RNA transcript. Identifying if a transcript of a gene is present in a cell or tissue is therefore the most direct way of determining whether the gene is switched on. This can be done by immobilizing the DNA copy of the gene on a solid support and hybridizing it with a sample of RNA extracted from the cells being studied. In fact the RNA is usually converted into cDNA prior to being used as the hybridization probe, as cDNA synthesis is the most convenient way of obtaining labeled sequences representing RNA molecules. If transcripts of the gene are present in the RNA extract then a hybridization signal will be seen.

Determining if a gene is being expressed is therefore a routine task. The complications become apparent when one appreciates that, in order to assay the entire mRNA content of a cell (referred to as its *transcriptome*), this basic procedure has to be repeated for every proteincoding gene in the genome. The answer is to use a DNA chip or other kind of microarray. In an early experiment, all 6000 *S. cerevisiae* genes were immobilized as an 80 × 80 array in a 18 mm by 18 mm square on a glass slide, and changes in gene expression that accompany the transition from aerobic to anaerobic respiration assayed, using fluorescently labeled cDNA with hybridization of the cDNA to

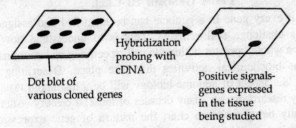

Hybridization
probing with
cDNA

Dot blot of
various cloned genes

Positivie signals-
genes expressed
in the tissue
being studied

Fig. 4.16. Assaying gene expression by dot blot hybridization analysis.

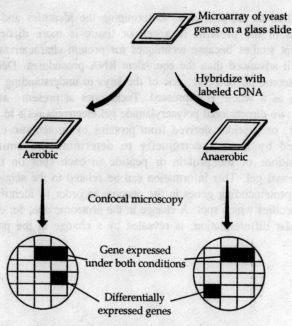

Fig. 4.17. *Assaying gene expression with a microarray.*

the microarray being visualized by scanning confocal microscopy. Twofold or greater changes in expression level, either up or down, were recorded for 1740 genes, over a quarter of the total, including many orphans whose functions are not known.

Not surprisingly, applying these and equivalent techniques to studies of human gene expression patterns has proved more difficult. Most effort has been directed at cancerous tissues because understanding the abnormal features of gene expression in these cells might lead to a means of diagnosing the disease state and monitoring progress during treatment, and might even point the way towards new therapies. One study discovered 289 genes whose expression patterns differed significantly when normal colon epithelial cells were compared with colon cancer cells, about half of these genes also showing abnormal expression levels in pancreatic cancer cells. The implication is that some genes are abnormally expressed in a range of cancers and some are specific for a particular type of cancerous tissue.

Proteome

In the second stage of gene expression, mRNA transcripts are translated into protein, the entire protein content of the cell being referred to as the *proteome*. Determining the identities and relative amounts of the proteins in a cell or tissue is more difficult than transcript studies because techniques for protein characterization are less well advanced than the equivalent RNA procedures. Delineating the proteome is, however, one of the keys to understanding how the genome as a whole is expressed. Techniques at present are based around two-dimensional polyacrylamide gel electrophoresis to separate proteins, or peptides derived from proteins by proteolytic cleavage, followed by mass spectrometry to determine the amino acid compositions of the protein or peptide in each spot on the two-dimensional gel. This information can be related to the sequences of all the proteincoding genes in the genome in order to identify which gene specifies which spot. A change in the proteome due, for example, to cellular differentiation, is revealed by a change in the pattern of spots.

5

GENETICS OF SEX

More than fifty sex-linked traits have been reported in man and most of these are due to recessive genes. Some of the sex-linked traits in man include red-green colour blindness, hemophilia, two forms of diabetes insipidus, nonfunctional sweat glands (anhidrotic ectodermal dysplasia), certain forms of deafness, absence of central incisors, spastic paraplegia, a form of cataract nystagmus, optic atropy, night blindness, juvenile muscular dystrophy, juvenile glaucoma, etc. (Burns, 1969). Most of these traits have been clearly found to be due to recessive genes. Defective tooth enamel, which results in early wearing of the teeth down to the gums, is a sex-linked trait in man and is due to a dominant sex-linked gene.

The criteria for identifying sex-linked recessive genes from pedigree studies may be summarized as follows (1) expressions occur much more frequently in males than in female; (2) traits are transmitted from an affected man through his daughters to half of their sons; (3) an X-linked gene is never transmitted directly from father to son; and (4) because the gene is transmitted through carrier females, affected males in a kindred may be related to one another through their mothers.

If the X-linked gene should be dominant, such as the Xg gene for a rare blood type, males expressing the trait would be expected to transmit it to all their daughters but none of their sons. Heterozygous females would transmit the trait to half of their children of either sex. If a female expressing the trait should be homozygous, all of her children would be expected to inherit the trait. Sex-linked dominant inheritance cannot be distinguished from autosomal inheritance in the progeny of females expressing the trait but only in the progeny of affected males.

Incompletely Sex-linked Genes in Man

Besides the nonhomologous part of the X chromosome that carries the usual sex-linked genes, the X chromosome of man has section that is homologous with a part of the Y chromosome. The situation is similar to the case described in Drosophila for the section carrying the gene (bb) for bobbed bristles. Several genes have gene postulated for this region on the basis of pedigree studies. These include the gene for total colour blindness; that for xeroderma pigmentosum, asking disease characterized by pigment patches and cancerous growths on the body; the gene for retinitis pigmentosa, a progressive degeneration of the retina, accompanied by deposition of pigment in the eye; and that for a type of nephritis, a kidney disease. These are presumably represented in the X and Y chromosomes as allelic pairs and segregate like ordinary autosomal pairs, although they do not segregate independently of sex as do autosomal genes. Even though these genes are located on the X chromosome, the usual crisscross pattern for sex linkage is not expected because of their paired (allelic) arrangement. Questions have been raised concerning the interpretation of genetic or pedigree data for incomplete sex linkage in man but the cytological evidence is good. Chiasmata have been observed between sex chromosomes. More extensive pedigree studies will undoubtedly provide evidence for this mode of inheritance.

Y Chromosome Linkage in Man

Certain published pedigrees have indicated that the Y chromosome may have a section with genes distinctive to that chromosome. Genes located in a nonhomologous part of the Y chromosome are expected to control "holandric" inheritance because they are transmitted exclusively through the male line. The pedigree evidence for transmission from father to son is the only criterion on which they have been predicted Published pedigrees interpreted to show this pattern, for the most part, have not been substantiated, and there is reason to suspect that at least some of the most spectacular cases are not accurately reported. One example, that of "hairy pianna" of the ear reported by Dronamraju in 1960, is well substantiated. Judgment on the extend of Y-linked genes in man must be withheld until more complete evidence is available.

Sex-Linked Lethals

One of the many well-known sex-linked lethals in Drosophila produces the notched-wing effect. Appropriate test crosses and cytological observation have demonstrated that females homozygous for a gene associated with the notch phenotype die before hatching. Numerous other sex-linked lethals have been induced by irradiation in experiments designed to identify mutagenic agents and determine mutations rates under different environmental conditions. Methods of detecting sex-linked lethal mutations are described in next chapter.

Induced sex-linked lethal mutations in man have been indicated by differences in the sex ratio following irradiation of parents. W. J. Schull and J. V. Neel have analyzed the sex ratios of children born to parents who were exposed to atomic bombing in Japan during World War II. The data were grouped according to whether the father, mother, or both parents were exposed to irradiation. A trend evicting from the sex ratio in the general population was detected among the children of mothers that are exposed. Male children occurred less frequently than expected. This trend was interpreted to indicate that sex-linked lethals had been induced in the mothers and were being expressed in their sons. Data on sex-linked lethals are thus utilized for determining mutations rates that occur spontaneously and under different environmental conditions.

Sex-Influenced Traits

The end product of some gene action is influenced by hormones. For example, autosomal genes responsible for horns in some breeds of sheep behave differently in the presence of the male and female sex hormones. More than a single pair of genes is involved in the production of horns, but assuming all other genes to be homozygous, the example can be treated as if only a single pair were involved. Among Dorset sheep, both sexes are horned, and the gene for the horned condition is homozygous (h^+h^+). In Suffolk sheep, neither sex is horned and the genotype is hh. Among the F_1 progeny from crosses between these two breeds, horned males and hornless females are produced. Because both sexes are genotypically alike (h^+h) the gene must behave as a dominant in males and as a recessive in females; that is, only one gene is required for an expression in the male, but the same gene must be homozygous for expression in the female.

When F_1 hybrids are mated together, a ratio of 3 horned to 1 hornless is produced among the F_2 males, whereas a ratio of 3 hornless to 1 horned is observed among the F_2 females. Genotypes and phenotypes of the two sexes are summarized. The only departure from the usual pattern is concerned with the heterozygous (h^+h) genotype. This genotype in the male results in the horned condition, but females with the same genotype are hornless. Dominance of the gene is apparently influenced by the sex hormone.

Table 5.1. Genotypes and corresponding phenotype in male and female hybrid sheep

Genotypes	Males	Females
h^+h^+	Horned	Horned
h^+h	Horned	Hornless
hh	Hornless	Hornless

Some human traits, such as certain type of white forelock, absence of the upper lateral incisor teeth, and a particular type of enlargement of the terminal joints of the fingers, have been reported to allow the sex-influenced mode of inheritance. Other abnormalities such as harelip, cleft palate, an stuttering have hereditary bases and occur more frequently and more severely among males than females. The inheritance mechanism is complex. Environmental as well as genetic factor are involved but autosomal and not sex-linked genes have been associated with the traits. The higher incidence of affected amelus presumably indicates some sort of sex influence on gene action.

Sex-Limited Traits

Some genes can not express themselves in the presence of certain hormones and therefore are considered to be sex-limited. In most breeds of domestic poultry, plumage of the two sexes is strikingly different, but in some Sebright bantams, for example, both sexes are hen-featherd. In the Hamburgh breed, both hen-feathered and cock-feathered males may be produced, but all females are hen-feathered. Results of appropriate crosses whom that hen feathering is due to a dominant gene h^+ and cock feather in to its recessive allele h. Cock feathering, however, not only requires a particular genotype, but also is limited to the male sex. Even though females carry the proper genotype (hh) for cock feathering, they are hen-featherd. Genotypes and corresponding phenotypes that might occur in mixed breeds of chickens are summarized as shown in Table 5.2.

The Hambrugh strain, in which males are cock-feathered and females are hen-feathered, carries the homozygous genotype hh. Sebright bantams, in which both sexes are hen-feathered, carry the homozygous genotype h^+h^+. In hybrids between the two breeds, the genotype and presence or absence of the male sex hormone determine the feathering pattern. Both alleles are apparently seggregating in populations that include hen-feathered and cock-feathered males. In such flocks, all females, regardless of genotype, are hen-feathered, and males carrying the gene h^+ are also hen-feathered; only hh males are cock-feathered. Experimental gonadectomies have elucidated the relation between genes and hormones. Removal of the ovary in a hen-feathered female (hh) results in cock feathering. This indicates that the female sex hormone normally in habits the hh genotype from producing cock-feathered. Furthermore, in castrated males, the h^+ gene is inhibited. Thus, the hormones of both sexes limit gene action.

Table 5.2. Genotypes and corresponding phenotypes in male and female hybrid chickens

Genotypes	Males	Females
h^+h^+	Hen-feathered	Hen-feathered
h^+h	Hen-feathered	Hen-feathered
hh	Cock-feathered	Hen-feathered

Premature (pattern) baldness in man has also been explained as a sex-limited trait. Other types of baldness are associated with abnormal ities in thyroid metabolism and infectious disease. About 26 percent of the men over 30 in the United States are baldheaded. Approximately half of these became bald prematurely, in their twenties or early thirties. Baldness is known to be more common in some families than in others. Several different modes of inheritance have been associated by different investigators with this trait. An explanation for a particular type of premature baldness based on sex-limed inheritance was set forth by J. B Hamilton and supported by statistical data accumulated by H. Harris. A single dominant gene that expresses itself only in the presence of an adequate level of androgenic hormone was postulated by these investigator to account for the observed facts. The level of hormone necessary for expression of the trait is seldom if ever reached in women, but is attained in all normal men.

A pedigree illustrating a hereditary pattern of baldness in one family group is presented in Fig. Affected males, symbolized by darkened squares, became bald before they reached the age of 35. Men symbolized by light squares had thick hair, some even in old age. No women in this family group were baldheaded.

Expressions of some genes are sex-limed for more basic reasons. For example, milk production among cattle and other mammals is limited to the sex that is equipped with developed mammary glands and appropriate hormones. It is true that milk production is affected by environmental factors, but inheritance plays a part, and it is well known that milk-yielded genes are carried in the chromosomes of bulls as well as cows. Certain bulls are in great demand along dairy breeders and artificial insemination associations because their mothers and daughters have good milk-production records.

The frequency of twins and other multiple births in human families is hereditary to some extent. Mothers are immediately involved, but evidence indicates that genes from their fathers may influence the tendency toward multiple births. Genes of both parents control directly or indirectly many anatomical and physiological characteristics that express themselves only in one sex. The width of the pelvis, age of onset of menstruation, and distribution of body hair in females depend on genes common to both sexes. Genes that directly or indirectly influence the fertility of one sex or sex linked what force in Drosophila.

SEX LINKED INHERITANCE IN DROSOPHILA

The first X-linked gene found in *Drosophila* was the recessive white eye mutation (*Morgan*, 1910). When a homozygous red-eyed female (dominant) is crossed with a white-eyed male (recessive), all individuals in the F_1 are red-eyed but when the cross is between a white-eyed female and red-eyed male, male offspring in the F_1 have white eyes. When heterozygous red eyed females are crossed with white-eyed males, both sexes segregate 1:1 rather than 3:1, for eye colour. These experiments demonstrate that the genes in this case are carried by the X chromosome, but not by the Y.

The inheritance of X-linked recessive gene can be understood more properly by considering the behaviour of X and Y chromosomes, such as follows:

In the cross between red-eyed female and white-eyed male *Drosophila*, the red eyed female contains the gene 'WW' for white colour of eye which remains located in X-chromosome. This one allelic condition of male is termed hemizygous in contrast to the homozygous or heterozygous possibilities in the female. The female being homogametic produces only one type of gametes or eggs each with the gene 'W' for red-coloured eyes. The male being heterogametic produces two types of gametes, 50% sperms with X chromosome containing 'w' gene and 50% sperms with 'Y' chromosome without any such gene. The gametes of both parents unite in fertilization to produce F_1 progeny. The F_1 hybrids which receive a X chromosome with 'W' gene from

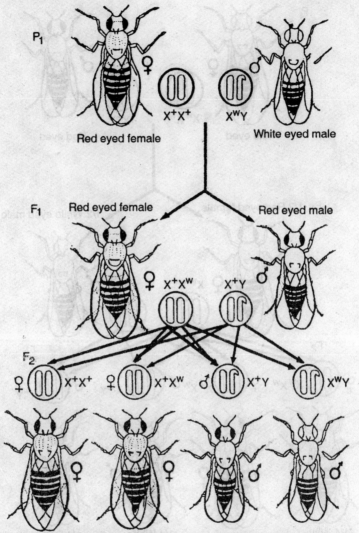

Fig. 5.1. A cross between red-eyed female and white-eyed male showing sex-linked inheritance in Drosophila.

the female and a X chromosome with 'w' gene from the male becomes red-eyed female because gene 'W' is dominant over gene 'w'. Further the hybrid which happens to receive a single gene 'W' from mother and Y chromosome from father produce red-eyed males.

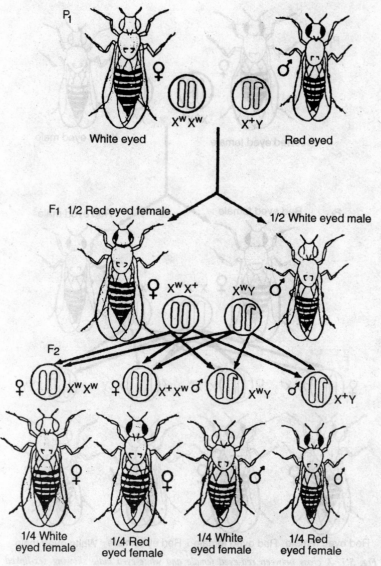

Fig. 5.2. A cross between white-eyed female and red-eyed male showing X-linked inheritance in Drosophila.

The F$_1$ red-eyed female with the gene 'Ww' when crossed with F$_1$ red-eyed male having the gene 'W'. The female hybrids produces two types of eggs, 50% eggs carry the gene 'W and the remaining 50% carry the gene 'w'. The males produce two types of sperms, half carry the gene 'W' and half carry no such gene on Y chromosomes. The union of sperm sand ova of F_1 offsprings may produce four possible types of F_2 individuals.

1. The eggs with 'W' genes if fertilized by sperms with 'W' genes produce homogametic red-eyed females.
2. The eggs with 'W' gene if fertilized by the sperms with 'Y' chromosome produce the red-eyed males.
3. The eggs with the gene 'w' when fertilized by the sperms having the gene 'W' produce heterogametic red-eyed females.
4. The eggs with the gene 'w' when fertilized by the sperms having the Y chromosome white-eyed males are produced.

Likewise in other experiment in which a white-eyed female is crossed with red eyed male. Similar X-linked inheritance of recessive gene for white eye colour is revealed. The white-eyed female contains the gene 'ww' located on both X chromosomes. The red-eyed male contains the gene 'W' located on single X-chromosome. The female being homogametic produces single type of eggs with single 'w' gene for whiteness, while the male beings heterogametic produces two types of sperms, 50% sperms carry the gene 'W' and remaining 50% sperms carry no such genes on the Y chromosomes. In the mating of both parents by the union of these eggs and sperms, two kinds of F_1 hybrids are produced. The eggs with 'w' genes by union with the sperms having 'W' genes produce heterogametic red-eyed female and the eggs with 'w' gene by union with the sperms having Y chromosome produce white-eyed male. When the F_1 brothers and sisters with the gene 'w' and 'Ww' bred together they produce four types of individuals in F_2 such as white-eyed female (ww), red-eyed female (Ww), white-eyed male (w) and red-eyed male (W).

The results of these experiments clearly indicate towards linkage of genes for red-eyes and genes for white-eyes on the X chromosomes. Further, from these experiments characteristic criss-cross pattern of inheritance of recessive X-linked from P_1 father to F_1 daughter, in which it remain phenotypically unexpressed (and such F_1 female is called carrier) and from F_1 daughter this trait is transmitted to F_2 son, in which it is expressed phenotypically.

INHERITANCE FOR Z-LINKED GENE FOR COLOURED (BLACK OR RED) FEATHERS IN CHICKEN

In case of birds, moths, butterflies, etc,, the females are heterogametic and males are homogametic quite unlike that of

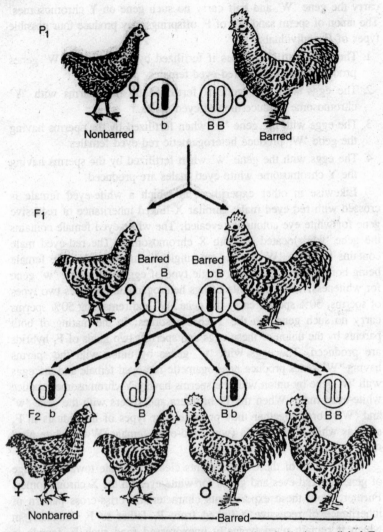

Fig. 5.3. A cross between a non-barred hen and a barred cock showing sex-linked (Z-linked) inheritance.

Drosophila and man. Here also sex-linked genes follows the "crisscross" pattern but from mother through heterozygous F_1 sons to grand-daughters of F_2. The common example of ZW-ZZ sex-linkage is Plymouth rock chicken.

In Plymouth rock chicken the gene fro barred feathers is dominant and the gene for black or red unbarred feathers is recessive. Both the genes are Z-linked. A barred male chicken contains two genes for barring because it has two sex chromosomes (ZZ). When this barred male with the gene BB is crossed with unbarred female containing single recessive gene 'b' in its Z chromosome (W chromosome contains no genes), produce in F_1 only barred males and females. These F_1 barred males and females when inbred produce in F_2, a hemizygous non-barred female, a hemizygous barred female, a heterozygous barred male and a homozygous barred male.

In another cross, when barred hens and non-barred cocks are crossed, the F_1 has half barred male and half non-barred female. These by inbreeding produce in F_2 half barred males and female and half non-barred males and females.

Besides fowl, many birds, e.g., pigeon, duck, canary, moths, butterflies, all reptiles, some fishes and amphibians which have XX male and XY or XO female type of sexes showing sex-linked inheritance of (ZW-ZZ) type.

MALES EXPRESS SEX-LINKED RECESSIVE GENES

Congenital hyperuricemia (Lesch-Nyhan syndrome), characterized by excess production of uric acid, is inherited through a *sex-linked recessive gene*. This means that the mother contributes the X chromosme with the defective gene to a male zy-gote. Half of the male children of carrier mothers may be expected to inherit the disease. These are deficient for the enzyme hypoxanthine-guanine phosphoribosyl-transferase (*HGPRT*). This enzyme is involved in nucleotide synthesis. Infants who receive the gene appear normal at birth and for several months, but may show symptoms of excessive uric acid in the urine, such as orange "sand" (uric acid crystals). By about 10 months of age, they may become abnormally irritable and lose motor control. Weak and flabby muscles prevent the child from sittings walking, or speaking normally. By the second year of life, the nervous condition has progressed to a degree that self-mutations occurs, manifested by lip-bitting, finger-chewing, teeth-grinding, and marked swinging of the arms. Death, which is usually secondary to severe renal and neurological damage, usually occurs within a few years, but some victims live into there 20s. Affected features as well as sex can be detected by amniocentesis.

Juvenile muscular dystrophy also depend son a *sex-linked recessive gene*. If the mother is known to be a carrier for this gene, either from her pedigree or through tests that are available, about half of her male children are expected to be affected. Male fetuses can be

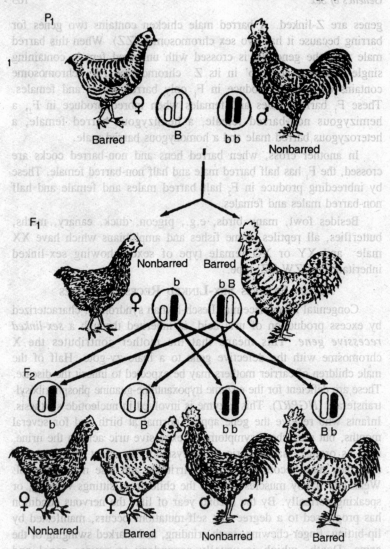

Fig. 5.4. A cross between a barred hen and non-barred cock showing sex linked (Z-linked) inheritance.

identified by a chromosme study. Juvenile muscular systrophy affects males, usually before they reach teen age, with muscular deterioraction that progresses rapidly during the early teen years. Muscles of the legs and shoulders become stiff, and the children usually become paralyzed and crippled during their middle or late teens. Virtually all die before age 21. All female children born to a carrier mother are expected to be normal, since the possibility for their being homozygous for a sex-linked recessive gene is virtually nonexistent.

Another severe disease following the pattern of *X-linked recessive* inheritance is the *Hunter syndrome*. It is characterized by mental retardation, coarse features, hirsutism (abnormal hairness), and a characteristic facial appearance that includes a broad bridge of the nose and a large protruding tongue. Symptoms appear in early childhood. A chemical means of diagnosing this condition is being developed. Certain constituents in the amniotic fluid indicate the presence of this disease, which is associated with an abnormal processing of mucopolysaccharides synthesized in early pregnancy. Mucopolysachharides also accumulate in skin cells of persons who are monozygous for the gene for Hunter syndrome. When amniotic or skin cells are grown in culture and stained with o-toludine blue, any mucopolysachharide cell inclusions will be stained pink. It is thus possible to identify a heterozygous carried of the gene as well as an affected fetus.

The pattern of mucopolysaccharide (containing an amino sugar as well as uronic acid units) metabolism by Hunter cells is so strikingly different from the normal that it can be used along with chromosome analysis for sex determination in prenatal diagnosis, a situation in which clinical observation is obviously impossible. Of the many cell types originally present in amniotic fluid, fetal fibroblasts are the only ones to multiply in culture. Like fibroblasts from skin biopsies, they show an excessive accumulation of mucopolysaccharide or stainable cell inclusions if the fetus is affected with the Hunter syndrome.

GLUCOSE 6-PHOSPHATE DEHYDROGENASE (G6PD) DEFICIENCY

One well-known gene on the X- chromosomes controls the production of an enzyme, *glucose 6-phosphate dehydrogenase* (G6PD), which is involved in carbohydrate metabolism and is important in maintaining the stability of red blood cells. Individuals who have abnormally low amounts of this enzymatic activity are prone to a severe anemia that occurs when many for their red blood cells cannot function normally and therefore break down and are destroyed. The anemia can be provoked by a number of environmental triggers such as inhaling pollen of the broad bean Vicia faba or eating the bean raw, in which the illness is known as *favism*. Such individuals are also sensitive to certain drugs such as naphthalene (used in mothballs), certain sulfa antibiotics (such as sulfanilamide), or the antimalarial drug primaquine. In the absence of the offending substances these individual are completely normal, and they recover from the anemia when the agents are eliminated. G6PD deficiency is found in high frequency in people of Mediterranean extractin (10 to 20 percent or more of males are affected) and among Asians (About 5 per cent of Chinese males are affected), and it occurs in about 10 percent of black American males. As noted, the locus of G6PD is X linked, and well over 50 alleles coding variant forms of the enzyme are known. However, only a few of these alleles lead to sufficiently defective form of G6PD to cause the drug sensitivity and anemia associated with G6PD deficiency.

COLOUR BLINDNESS

Almost everyone is familiar with the common form of colour blindness, called *red-green colour blindness*, which is inherited as an X-linked recessive condition. Several other kinds of defects in colour vision are known; a they differ according to which of the three pigments in the retina of the eye–red, green, or blue–is defective or present in an abnormally low amount. The most common types of colour blindness involve the red or green pigments; these are collectively known as red-green colour blindness, but they are not a single entity. Both

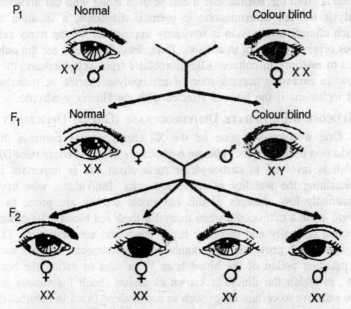

Fig. 5.5. Cross between a red-green colour blind female (XX) and a normal male (XY) showing X-linked inheritance in man.

conditions are X linked, however, and in different Caucasian populations the frequency of red-green colour-blind males is between 5 and 9 percent. Colour blindness in females is much rare, of course, but it does occur.

Two loci on the long arm of the X chromosoe seem to be involve in red-green colour blindness. Defects in green vision are due to mutations at one of the loci; defects in red vision are due to mutations at the other locus. Among Western European males, about 5 percent have defects in green perception and another 1 percent have defects in red perception. Two loci are known to be involved in red-green colour perception because the stations that cause the red defects and the green defects exhibit *complementation*. That is to say, women who carry a red-defect allele on one X chromosome and a green-defect allele on the other have normal colour vision. Such complementation is expected when two loci are involved because these women are actually heterozygous for a normal allele and a recessive mutation at each of two loci. Because of segregation, nearly half the sons of these women will have the green defect and the other half will have the red defect. Because of recombination, however, a proportion of their sons will have normal colour vision and an equal proportion will have defects

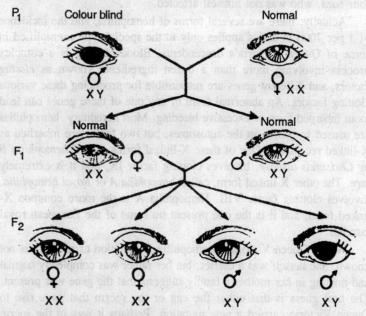

Fig. 5.6. A cross between a red-green colour blind male and normal female showing X-linked inheritance in man.

in both their red and green colour vision. The two loci are very close to each other on the X chromosome, so the actual proportion of sons who carry recombinant X chromosomes is very small.

HEMOPHILIA

Recall that hemophilia is a bleeding disorder due to an X-linked recessive that results from the excessively long time required for the blood to clot following an injury. Affecting about 1 in 7000 males, it is much rare than red-green colour blindness, yet is probably as well known. This is partly because it affects the blood; and even though we now know that blood has no magical or hereditary properties, we still carry a vestige of the old beliefs in such expressions as "cure blood" and "blood lines" and "blood relation." A second reason hemophilia is so well known is that it occurred in many members of the European royalty who descended from Queen Victoria of England (1819–1901).She was a carrier of the gene, and by the marriages of her carrier granddaughters, the gene was introduced into the royal houses of Russia and Spain. Ironically, the present royal family of Great Britain is free of the gene because it descends form King Edward VII, one of Victoria's four sons, who was not himself affected.

Actually, there are several forms of hemophilia, and the incidence of 1 per 7000 in males applies only to the special type exemplified in some of Queen Victoria's descendents. Blood clotting is a complex process involving more than a dozen ingredients known as *cloting factors*, and different genes are responsible for producing these various clotting factors. An abnormal form of any one of these genes can lead to an inherited form of excessive bleeding. Most hereditary hemophilias are caused by genes on the autosomes, but two forms are inherited as X-linked recessives. One of these X-linked forms, called *hemophilia B* or *Christmas disease*, involves clotting factor IX, and it is extremely rare. The other X-linked form, called *hemophilia A* or *Royal hemophilia*, involves clotting factor VIII. Hemophilia A is the more common X-linked form, and it is the one present tin some of the European royal families.

Where Queen Victoria's hemophilia-A mutation came from is not known. She herself was a carrier, but her father was completely normal and nothing in her mother's family suggests that the gene was present. The best guess is that either the egg or the sperm that gave rise to Queen Victoria carried a new mutation. Perhaps it was in the sperm of her father, Edward Duke of Kent, because it is thought that mutations are somewhat more likely to occur in the sperm of older men, and he was 52 when Victoria was born. However it happened, Victoria was a carrier. She had nine children five daughters (two were certainly carriers, two were almost certainly not, and the remaining daughter may or may not have been as she left no children) and four sons (one a hemophiliac—Leopold Duke of Albany—and three normal). In the five generations since Queen Victoria, 10 of her male descendants have had the disease. Virtually all died very young. Those who survived childhood often died in their 20s or early 30s, usually from excessive bleeding following injuries.

The most famous of Victoria's affected male descendants is undoubtedly her great-grandson Alexis, the son of her granddaughter Alix (Empress Alexandra of Russia) and Tsar Nicholas II. Alexis was Alexandra's first born son and heir to the Russian throne. Unbeknown to Alexandra, she was a carrier of the hemophilia-A allele, and her son had inherited the disease. Anna Viroubova, one of Alexandra's favorite ladies-in-wating, recounts:

The hair was born amid the wildest rejoicings all over the Empire. After many prayers, there was an heir to the throne of the Romanoffs. The Emperor was quite mad with joy. His happiness and the mother's, however, was of short duration, for almost at once they learned that the child was affected with a dread disease. The whole short life of the Tsarevich, the loveliest and most amiable child imaginable, was a succession of agonizing illnesses due to this congenital affection. The sufferings of the child were more than equaled by those of his parents, especially of his mother.

The parents became preoccupied with the boy's health. At one point the Tsar observed in his diary how difficult it was to live through the worry resulting from Alexis's excessive and worry resulting from Alexis's excessive and life-threatening bleeding from minor injuries and bruises that all children unavoidably experience. The boy survived his childhood, but some historians have argued that the Tsar's preoccupation with Alexis's health contributed to the neglect of the empire that ultimately bought on the Bolshevik Revolution in 1917. During the revolution, the Tsar, Alexandra, Alexis, and his four sisters disappeared. The fate of the family is unknown, but they are thought to have been machine-gunned to death in Ekaterinburg fortress on July 17, 1918, just 13 days before what would have been Alexis's seventeenth birthday.

LESCH-NYHAN SYNDROME (HGPRT DEFICIENCY)

As a final example of X-linked recessive inheritance we consider the rare condition known as *Lesch-Nyhan syndrome*, which is due to a deficiency of the enzyme HGPRT. HGPRT refers to (*hypoxanthine guanine phosphoribosyl transferase*). Persons with this conditions, virtually all male, have two groups of symptoms. One results from excessive accumulation of *uric acid* in the blood. Recall from Chapter 4 that one normal function of HGPRT is to route certain cellular metabolities into DNA via the minor pathway of DNA synthesis. (A *metabolite* is any compound produced during the course of chemical processes in the cell; the totality of all these processes is called *metabolism*). In the absence HGPRT, these metabolites accumulate and are eventually broken down by other enzymes into uric acid. Accumulation of excess uric acid in the blood), bloody urine, crystals in the urine, urinary tract stones, severe inflammation of the joints (*arthritis*), and the extremely painful swelling and inflammation of joints in the hands and feet (particularly the big toe) known as *gout*. (Although gout is always associated with elevated levels of uric acid, the inheritance of most forms of gout is multi factorial; only aminority of patients with excessive uric acid and gout have HGPRT deficiency.)

Symptoms of excessive uric acid can be treated with appropriate drugs, but Lesch-Nyhan syndrome has another group of symptoms that are of unknown origin and are not alleviated by treatment for excessive uric acid. These symptoms involve the nervous system and are associated with jerky, unwilled, and uncoordinated muscular movement. The most bizarre symptoms of Lesch-Nyhan syndrome is extreme aggressive behaviour, most often expressed as self-mutation of the hands and arms, usually by biting. At present, such self-mutilation can be prevented only by appropriate binding of the hands and arms. Lesch-Nyhan syndrome is an extremely serious condition. Most patients die before the age of five, and almost all die before adulthood. Though rare, the Lesch-Nyhan syndrome is important because it involves HGPRT, which allows us to understand the basis of some of its symptoms. The condition also illustrates the profound influence that genes can exert on behaviour, even though the biochemical basis of this influence is not yet understood.

SEX DETERMINATION

Sex confers the great advantage of making it possible for sexually reproducing eukaryotes to reshuffle their DNA during meiosis by crossing over and independent assortment of chromosomes. This is a prime source for the tremendous variety we see in the living world. Factors controlling male and female gamete formation have been found to be complex, involving genetic as well as other internal and external factors. Our objective in this section is to explore the process of sex determination in several plant and animal species in order to show the genetic complexity and species uniqueness involved in this aspect of differentiation and development.

Two questions with regard to sex, however, have not yet been broached: (a) What determines the sex of the individual? (b) How do the secondary sexual characters of individual develop? These two questions will be answered in the present chapter.

The question as to what determines whether an animal shall be a male or female is a very ancient one, and it is only during the present century that we have solved the puzzle.

A great many theories of sex determination have been proposed, some of which are as follows:

(a) Hippocrates and some subsequent theorists believed that the sex of the offspring depended on the relative vigor of the parents, the more vigorous parent giving his or her sex to the offspring.

(b) Thury thought that the sex of the offspring depended on the degree of ripeness of the ovum at the time of fertilization.

(c) Various writers claim that statistics show that germ cells from the right ovary produce males and those from the left ovary females.

(d) *The nutrition theory*. The egg is a much more highly nourished cell than the spermatozoan, and the idea seems natural that high degrees of nourishment of the mother produce female offspring and lower degrees of nourishment male offspring. Professor Schenk of Vienna gained a huge reputation by controlling the diet of certain royal prospective mothers and predicting the sex of the offspring accordingly. He was correct in his predictions several times, but his success was short-lived. His early predictions were merely lucky, just as one might be who could guess heads or tails correctly several times in succession.

SEX CHROMOSOMAL MECHANISM OF SEX DETERMINATION

In dioecious diploidic organisms following two systems of sex chromosomal determination of sex have been recognized:

(a) Heterogametic males.

(b) Heterogametic females.

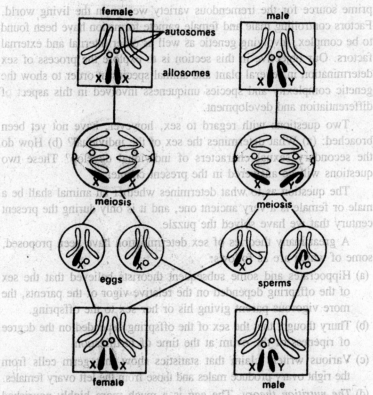

Fig. 5.7. Distribution of sex chromosomes and sex determination in Drosophila.

Heterogametic Males

In this type of sex chromosomal determination of sex, the female sex has two X chromosomes, while the male sex has only one X chromosome. Because, male lacks a X chromosome, therefore, during gametogenesis produces two types of gametes, 50% gametes carry the X chromosomes, while the rest 50% gametes lack in X chromosome. Such a sex which produces two different types of gametes in terms of sex chromosomes, called heterogametic sex. The female sex, because, produces similar types of gametes, is called, homogametic sex. The hetrogametic males may be of following two types:

(i) XX-XO system

The somatic cells of a female grasshopper contain 24 chromosomes, whereas those of the male contain only 23 chromosomes. Thus, in grasshopper (and in many other insects), there is a chromosomal difference between the sexes; females referred to as XX (having two

X chromosomes) and males as XO ("X–oh", having only one X chromosome). The X chromosome is called a *sex chromosome*, the remaining chromosomes are called *autosomes*. Thus in XX-XO system, all the eggs have one X chromosome whereas the sperms are of two types, X and O, that is half the sperms have one X chromosome and the other half have none.

(ii) XX-XY system

In mammals, *Drosophila* and some plants (e.g. the angiosperm genus *Lychnis*) etc., the females are generally referred to as XX (having two X chromosomes) and males as XY (having only one X chromosome and another one called Y chromosome). In *Drosophila* there are four pairs of chromosomes; three pairs of these chromosomes (that is, two pairs of V-shaped chromosomes and a pair of small dot-like chromosomes) in both sexes are called *autosomes*. The fourth pair of chromosomes is different in the two sexes; these are *sex chromosomes*. In female *Drosophila* both the sex chromosomes are identical and each is called X chromosome, in male one of the sex chromosomes is straight (X chromosome) but the other is bent having two unequal arms (Y chromosome). In man, the females have 44 autosomes and two X chromosome (44+X.X) whereas the males have 44 autosomes and one X chromosome and a Y chromosomes (44+X+Y). For further details of the human chromosomes. In the XX-XY system, all the ova have one X chromosomes whereas the sperms are of two kinds, X and Y. In both the XX-XO (*vide supra*) and XX-XY types, the male is the *heterogametic sex* (producing two types of sperms whereas the female is the *homogametic sex* (producing only one type of ovum).

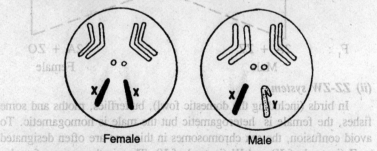

Female   Male

Fig. 5.8. Diagram showing the chromosomes of Drosophila melanogaster.

Heterogametic Females

In this type of sex chromosomal determination of sex, the male sex possesses two homomorphic X chromosomes, therefore, is homogametic and produces single type of gametes, each carries a single X chromosome. The female sex either consists, of single X chromosome or one X chromosome and one Y chromosome. The female sex is, thus, heterogametic and produces two types of eggs, half with a X chromosome and half without a X chromosome (with or without a Y chromosome). To avoid confusion with that of XX-XO and XX-XY type of sex determining mechanisms, instead of the X and Y alphabets, Z and W alphabets are generally used respectively. This kind of sex determination mechanism is called Abraxas mechanism of sex determination, (*Kuspira* and *Walker*, 1973).

The heterogametic females may be of following two types:

(i) ZO-ZZ system

This system of sex determination is found in certain moths, butterflies and domestic chickens. In this case, the female possesses single Z chromosome in its body cells (hence, is referred to as ZO) and is heterogametic, producing two kinds of eggs, half with a Z chromosome and half without any Z chromosome. The male possesses two Z chromosomes (hence referred to as ZZ) and is homogametic, producing single type of sperms, each of which carries a single Z chromosome. The sex of the offspring depends on the kind of egg as shown below :

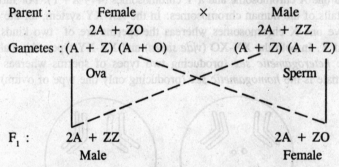

Parent :   Female   ×   Male
                   2A + ZO   2A + ZZ
Gametes : (A + Z) (A + O)   (A + Z) (A + Z)
                   Ova   Sperm

F₁ :   2A + ZZ   2A + ZO
             Male   Female

(ii) ZZ-ZW system

In birds (including the domestic fowl), butterflies, moths and some fishes, the female is heterogametic but the male is homogametic. To avoid confusion, the sex chromosomes in this case are often designated as Z (instead of X) and W (instead of Y). Thus in these cases females are ZW (or XY) and males are ZZ (or XX).

Sex chromosomes in monoploid (haploid) organisms

The sporophyte of liver-wort *Sphaerocarpos* (phylum Bryophyta) contain seven matching pairs of chromosomes plus an eighth pair in

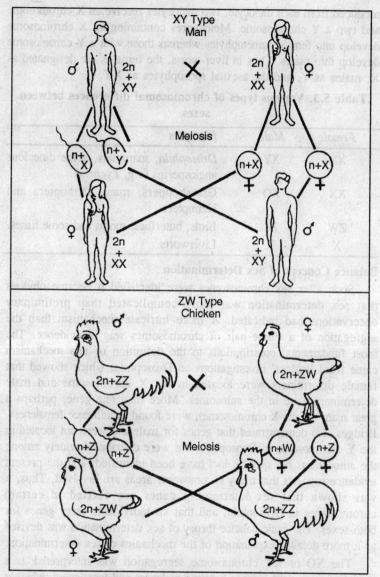

Fig. 5.9. The XX-XY and ZW-ZZ type determination of sex in man and chicken.

which one of the two chromosomes is much larger than the other. The larger member of this eighth pair of chromosomes is called the X chromosome, its smaller partner the Y chromosome. Meiosis terminates the diploid sporophyte generation. At meiosis, the four meiospores are produced from each meiocyte; two meiocytes receive an X chromosome and two a Y chromosome. Meiospores containing an X chromosome develop into female gametophytes whereas those with a Y chromosome develop into males. Thus in liver-worts, the females are designated as X, males as Y, and the asexual sporophytes as XY.

Table 5.3. Various types of chromosomal differences between sexes.

Female	Male	Examples
XX	XY	*Drosophila*, mammals, some dioecious angiosperms (e.g. *Lychnis*)
XX	XO	Grasshoppers; many Orthoptera and Hemiptera.
ZW	ZZ	Birds, buterflies, moths and some fishes.
X	Y	Liverworts.

Balance Concept of Sex Determination

Soon after sex chromosomes were identified it became obvious that sex determination was more complicated than preliminary observations had indicated. A more intricate mechanism than the segregation of a single pair of chromosomes was in evidence. The most fundamental contributions to the definition of this mechanism came from Bridges' investigations on Drosophila, which showed that female determiners were located in the X chromosome and male determiners were in the autosomes. More than one gene, perhaps a great many (in the X chromosome), were found to influence femaleness. Bridges also demonstrated that genes for maleness were not located in the Y chromosome of Drosophila, but were distributed widely among the autosomes. No specific loci have been identified, and the present evidence suggests that many chromosome areas are involved. Thus, it was shown that sex-determining genes are carried in certain chromosomes in Drosophila, and that all individuals carry genes for both sexes. The genic balance theory of sex determination was devised as a more detailed explanation of the mechanics of sex determination.

The XO or XY chromosome segregation was interpreted as a means of tipping the balance between maleness and femaleness, whereas more deep-seated processes were involved in the actual determination. Bridges experimentally produced various combinations of X chromosomes and autosomes in Drosophila. The first irregular chromosome arrangement resulted from nondisjunction, the failure of

chromosome composition	chromosome formulation	ratio of X chromosomes to autosome sets	sex
	3X/2A	1·5	metafemale
	3X/3A	1·0	female
	2X/2A	1·0	female
	2X/3A	0·67	intersex
	3X/4A	0·75	intersex
	X/2A	0·50	male
	XY/2A	0·50	male
	XY/3A	0·33	metamale

Fig. 5.10. Chromosomal composition and ratio of X chromosomes to autosomes in Drosophila.

paired chromosomes to separate in anaphase of the reduction. X chromosomes, which ordinarily came together in pairs in meiotic phase of oogenesis and separated to the poles in anaphase of the reduction division, remained together and went to the same pole. As a result, some female gametes received two X chromosome and some received no X chromosomes.

Following fertilization by sperm from wild-type males, all zygotes had 2n autosomes. Some received two X chromosomes from the mother and a Y from the father. These XXY flies, which in appearance were normal females, were mated with wild-type (XY) males. All progeny had two sets of autosomes, whereas some received XXX, others XXX, XY, or YY sex chromosomes. XXX flies, now called meta-females, were sterile and highly inviable. The XXY combination resulted in females that were normal in appearance and reproductive function, XY equated with normal males, and YY zygotes did not survive. Experimentally produced XO males were similar in sex manifestations to XY males, but the XO males were sterile. XXY females were similar to XX females. These results indicated that, in Drosophila, the Y chromosome is not involved in sex determination but that it does control male fertility.

Flies produced experimentally with three whole sets of chromosomes (3 genomes or 3n triploids) were then included in the studies and, later, some with four genomes (tetraploids) were added. On the basis of many experimental combinations of autosomes and X chromosomes, Bridges established a standard by which various sets of autosomes and X chromosomes were compared with reference to the relative potency of a male-and female-determining capacity. Two sets of autosomes (AA) were found to have enough male-determining potency to overbalance the female-determining capacity of one X chromosome. The chromosome combination AAX(Y) thus gave rise to a normal male. In the presence of two X chromosomes and two sets of autosomes (AAXX), a normal female was produced. Bridges showed that equal numbers of X chromosomes and sets of male-determining autosomes occurred only in females. When the number of sets of autosomes was greater, maleness was expressed. A large over-balance of X chromosomes resulted in metafemales. An overbalance of autosomes was associated with metamales. When the difference in proportion was not great, intersexes with characteristics of both males and females were produced. The various demonstrated chromosome combinations and sex expressions are summarized in Table 5.4.

No other animals or plants have been investigated with equal thoroughness, but indirect evidence suggests that, in many organisms, some such balance is involved. Intersexes can be produced experimentally in some animals by upsetting this balance during the developmental stages. In nature, a margin of safety exists which makes intermediates between the two sexes uncommon.

Table 5.4. Different combinations of X chromosomes and autosomes and corresponding sex expressions in Drosophila (after Bridges)

X Chromosomes	Sets of Autosomes	Sex
1	2	Male
2	2	Female
3	2	Metafemale
4	3	Metafemale
4	4	Tetraploid female
3	3	Triploid female
1	1	Haploid female[a]
3	4	Intersex
2	3	Intersex
2	4	Male
1	3	Metamale

[a] Determination based on patches of tissue in individual flies which show female traits.

GYNANDROMORPHS

In some animals such as insects, upsets in the chromosomal behaviour result in sexual mosaics called gynandromorphs. Some parts of the animal express female characteristics while other parts express those of the male. Some gynandromorphs in Drosophila are bilateral intersexes, with male colour pattern, body shape, and sex comb on one half and female characteristics on the other half of the body. Both male and female gonads and genitalia are sometimes present.

Bilateral gynandromorphs have been explained on the basis of an irregularity in the chromosome mechanism at the first cleavage of the zygote. Infrequently, a chromosome lags in division and does not arrive at the pole in time to be included in the reconstructed nucleus of the daughter cell. If one of the X chromosomes of an XX (female) zygote should lag in the center of the spindle, one daughter cell would get only one X chromosome and the other would get XX. The baisi for a

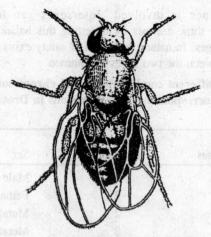

Fig. 5.11. Bilateral gynandromorph in Drosophila.

mosaic pattern would thus be established. One cell in the two-cell stage would be XX (female) and one would be XO (male). In Drosophila, the right and left halves of the body are determined at the first cleavage. One cell gives rise to all the cells making up the right half of the adult body and the other give rise to the left half. If the chromosome loss should occur at a later cell division, a smaller proportion of the adult body would be included in the male segment. The position and size of the mosaic sector would be determined, therefore, by the place and time of the division abnormality.

Gynandromorphs were described in Drosophila by Sturtevant, Morgan, and Bridges beginning in 1919. Following the original descritions, a few conspicuous examples were reported in flies, but the condition was considered extremely rare. More extensive observations have since shown that a gynandromorph of some kind is produced in every 2000 to 3000 flies; many of these represent small sections of tissue involving only a few cells. Spencer Brown and Aloha Hannah-Alava devised a technique to increase experimentally the frequency of gynandromorphs by making use of a ring X chromosome first discoverd by L. V. Morgan.

Bilateral Gynandromorph

In a bilateral gynandromorph the body parts of one side (right or left) shows female secondary sexual characters and another side shows male secondary sexual characters. The bilateral gyandromorph have been observed in butter fly, Colias philodices and in fruit fly, Drosophila melanogaster.

Anterio-posterior Gynandromorph

In an anterio-posterior gynandromorph, the anterior side of animal body shows characters of one sex and posterior side of body shows the characters of opposite sex. The anterio-posterior gynandromorph has been reported in beette, *Lucanus cervus*.

Sex Piebalds

In sex piebalds, the body of gynandromorph consists of female tissues having irregularly distributed patches of male tissue. Such sex piebalds have been reported in *Drosophila*.

ORIGIN OF GYNANDROMORPHS

The gynandromorphs of different organisms are originated by following methods:

1. Degenerates of X Chromosome

In insects and other invertebrates, the first mitotic division of zygote determines the future right and left halves of the embryo. A bilateral gynandromorph of Drosophila, for example, begins its development with a normal diploid zygote having two X chromosomes. During first cleavage due to anaphase lag two kinds of blastomeres are formed : One blastomere (XO) has single X chromosome while other blastomere (XX) has two X chromosomes. The blastomere with XO blastomere with XX chromosomal constitution develops into a female phenotype of gynandromorph.

2. Retention of Polar Nucleus

In silkworms which have a heterogametic (XY) female sex and homogametic male sex (XX), during oogenesis the XY chromosomes normally disjoin or separate and one of them goes to the polar body while another is retained by the egg nucleus. But sometimes the polar body having one sex chromosome does not leave the egg and retained by ooplasm along with egg nucleus. The egg becomes binucleate and has one nucleus with X chromosome and other nucleus with Y chromosome. During fertilization, when X bearing sperm nuclei fuse with each of the egg nucleus to give XX and XY nuclei. The XX egg nucleus develops into male phenotype and XY egg nucleus gives origin to female phenotype.

The gynandromorphs of bees have analogously similar origin. Bees also have binucleate eggs which are originated either due to retention of polocyte nucleus by egg or pre-fertilizic (parthenogenetic) division of zygote nucleus. During fertilization only one sperm enters in the egg and its pronuclei fuses with one of the nucleus of binucleate egg.

The resultant diploid nucleus develops into female tissues, while haploid (unfertilized) nucleus develops into male tissues to form a gynandromorph.

SEX DETERMINATION IN PLANTS

In plants as also in case of human beings the sex is mainly controlled by the Y chromosome. Consequently, irrespective of the number of X-chromosomes and the number of sets of autosomes, if Y-chromosome is present, the individual would be male while if Y-chromosome is absent, it would be female. The mechanism of sex determination has been studied in a large number of plant materials.

Coccinia indica and Melandrium album (Lychnis)

The mechanism of sex determination in Coccinia indica, a member of family Cucurbitaceae has recently been studied in some detail by Prof. R.P. Roy and his co-workers at Patna University. They studied the sex in diploid, triploid and tetraploid plants with and without Y chromosome and observed that irrespective of the number of X-chromosomes and/or autosomes, the presence of a single Y chromosome gave a male individual.

Table 5.5. The relation between chromosome constitution and sex in Coccinia indica.

Chromosome constitution	X/A ratio	Sex
2A+XX	1.00	female
2A+XY	0.50	male
2A+XYY	0.50	male
3A+XXY	0.67	male
3A+XXX	1.00	female
4A+XXXX	1.00	female
4A+XXXY	0.75	male

A similar case earlier worked out by H.E. Warmke in 1946 refers to *Melandrium album*. In case of *Melandrium*, diploids, tiploids and tetraploids having different doses of X and Y chromosomes were studied with respect to their sex. Thus, in *Coccinia* as well as in *Melandrium* a plant is male when one or more Y chromosomes are present and is female when Y chromosome is absent. The female potentialities showed some expression only when the ratio of Y:X reached 1:4. The number of autosomes did not visibly affect the sex expression.

In *Melandrium*, the Y chromosome is longer than the X-chromosome. Plants having different individual fragments of Y chromosome were studied as a result, it was possible to divide the Y and the X-chromosomes into five different segments. These segments are known to control different stages of the development of sex organs. The X and the Y chromosomes have a common segment IV, which helps in pairing and the regular disjunction of X and Y chromosomes during meiosis. The remainder of Y chromosome has three segments, namely I, suppressing femaleness; II, initiating anther development and III, controlling the late stages of anther development. The X-chromosome also has a differential segment V, which should promote femaleness in the absence of female suppressing segment I on Y chromosome.

Table 5.6. Expression of sex in Melandrium with different numbers of X-chromosomes and autosome sets.

Chromosome constitution	X/A ratio	Sex
2A + XX	1.00	female
2A + XY	0.50	male
2A + XXY	1.00	male
3A + XXY	0.67	male (occasional ♂)
4A + XXY	0.50	male
4A + XY	0.25	male
4A + XXXY	0.75	male (occasional ♂)
4A + XXXXY	1.00	hermaphrodite (occasional ♂)

Therefore, while comparing *Drosophila* with *Coccinia* and *Melandrium*, we find that the male determining genes are present on autosomes in *Drosophila* but on Y-chromosome in plants.

2. Mistletoes (Viscum)

Several species of *Viscum* are dioecious, which are found in Africa, Madagascar, Europe, Asia and Taiwan. Sex is determined in this case through multiple translocations as determined only recently. In *Viscum fischeri*, for instance, male plants have 2n = 23, out of which, at meiosis, 14 chromosomes form seven bivalents and the remaining nine chromosomes form a ring (7" + 1.9) Seven bivalents disjoin normally but the ring of nine chromosomes disjoins in 4:5 thus giving rise to two types of gametes, one with 11 and the other with 12 chromosomes. The female plant has 2n=22 forming 11 bivalents (11") disjoining normally and giving only one type of gametes with 11 chromosomes each. Thus male is heterogametic due to translocations without any sex chromosomes involved. Two types of male gametes will give rise to two sexes. This phenomenon is also common in several other species of *Viscum*.

Table 5.7. Chromosome constitutions of two sexes in some dioecious plant species.

Mechanism	Examples
1. Male heterogametic ($♀$ XX; $♂$ XY)	*Human lupulus*
	Melandrium album, M. rubrum,
	Rumex angiocarpus
less well	*Populus* spp., *Salix, Smilax,*
established	and *Cannabis*
2. Male heterogametic	*Vallisneria spiralis*
($♀$XX; $♂$XO)	*Dioscorea sinuata*
3. Male heterogametic	*Phoradendron flavescens*
($♂$ with an extra	*P. villosum*
chromosome)	
4. Female heterogametic	*Fragaria elatior* and
($♀$XY; $♂$ XX)	other *Fragaria species*
5. Compound chromosomes	*Rumex acetosa*
(e.g. $♀$XX; $♂$Y$_1$XY$_2$)	*Humulus japonicus*
6. No sex chromosomes	*Spinacia oleracea*
(perhaps gene controlled)	*Ribes alpinum*
	Vitis cinerea
	V. rupestris
	V. vinifera
	Carica papaya
	Asparagus officinalis
	Bryonia dioica
7. No sex chromosomes	*Viscum fischeri*
in male	
(translocation heterozygosity)	

SEX DETERMINATION IN HUMANS

In early human embryonic development, the gonads are neuter, that is, neither ovary nor testes are differentiated. The neuter embryonic gonad has an outer region called the cortex and an inner region called the medulla. In an XY embryo, the cortex degenerates and the medulla forms the testes. In an XX embryo, the medulla degenerates and the cortex forms the ovaries. Thus, it is apparent that the X and Y chromosomes must contain genes that determine which of these developmental pathways will be followed.

Recently it has been determined that the human and mouse Y chromosomes have genes coding for a protein called the H–Y antigen. This protein acts upon the cells of the undifferentiated gonads and tilts them in the male direction so that they become testes.

Hormones produced by the ovary and testes also play an important role in influencing the development of sex characteristics. For example, once the testes or the ovaries have been formed, the effects of the different hormones produced by them cause degeneration of several ducts and the eventual formation of the external genital organs. Later in life, hormones play an important role in the determination and maintenance of secondary sexual characteristics, such as breast and pubic hair formation.

An unusual hormonal-cellular interaction has been found to be controlled by an X-linked recessive gene. The presence of this mutant gene in a genotypic male leads to a condition referred to as the testicular feminization syndrome. Such individuals are sterile females with male testosterone levels.

6

ENDONUCLEASE

Richard Roberts, a senior investigator at the Cold Spring Harbor Laboratory on Long Island, New York, is a collector. Not of stamps, or butterflies, or even beermats, but of enzymes. And the enzymes he collects are no ordinary enzymes; they are the machine tools of the genetic engineer, the precision cutters that allow the researcher to slice DNA cleanly at any known point. From time to time Roberts publishes his list in one of the learned journals; in 1978 he had about 160, and by 1980 the list had grown to 212. The list is now published each year in January, and Roberts fully expects the 1982 edition to top 300.

The published list grew out of a series of informal versions that Roberts circulated, which molecular biologists all over the world found enormously useful. They now help to keep the catalogue up to date by sending Roberts the information whenever they discover a new cutting enzyme. But what are these enzymes? Where did they spring from and how do they work?

Made in *E. Coli*

Back in 1952, at the University of Illinois, Salvador Luria and his assistant Mary Human began to investigate a very interesting problem. The targets of their curiosity were bacteriophages, the so-called T phages, that infect the bacterium *Escherichia coli*.

Spread on to a nutritive agar jelly and kept warm, a thin suspension of *E. coli* cells will double every 30 minutes or so, quickly forming a smooth greyish yellow carpet over the surface of the jelly. But if the suspension is deliberately infected with bacteriophage, about one virus for every 10000 cells, and then grown as before, the bacterial lawn looks very different. Instead of being smooth and flawless, it is pockmarked by several small round holes. Each of these is called a plaque, and represents the site where a bacterial cell that was infected by virus came to rest. The DNA of the virus, injected through the virus's tail into the cell, subverts the bacterial machinery and forces it to obey the coded instructions of the viral genetic message, producing not bacterial components but viral components. These are assembled into new viruses and some time after infection, usually about an hour, the cell bursts and releases 200 or so new viruses. These infect neighbouring cells and repeat the process. By the end of 24 hours the myriad offspring of each successful virus have radiated out in a circle, destroying the bacteria around them and creating a clear plaque in the bacterial lawn.

There are many different sorts of phage, some labelled T2, T4, T6, T7 and so on, and many different strains of *E. coli*. Some strains of *E. coli* seemed to be protected against infection by certain of the phage types. Luria and Human discovered that growing T2 phage in one host often altered its properties so that it could no longer infect strains that it was usually quite at home in. But the altered phage was able to grow in dysentery bacteria (*Shigella dysenteriae*) and, most mysteriously, the offspring after growth in *Shigella* had regained their full infective power. The change that had come over the phage, whatever it was, was completely reversible, so it was certainly not a genetic mutation. It seemed to depend more on the host machinery that the previous generation had used to create the present viruses than on any property of the phage itself. Further experiments by Guiseppe Bertani in Luria's lab, and Jean Weigle at the California Institute of Technology, confirmed this strange discovery and added more details.

Bertani worked with a different phage, called lambda, which also attacks *E. coli*. Lambda grew beautifully on *E. coli* strain C, but the daughter phages coming out of strain C could not infect strain K. At least, not usually; one in 10,000 of the daughter phages from C did produce a plaque in a lawn of K cells, and everyone, rather than 1 in 10,000, of the viruses recovered from that plaque would now grow freely in strain K. They would also grow in strain C, but a single cycle of growth in C immediately changed the virus back so that it was again unable to grow properly in K.

At that stage, it looked as if there were two separate processes involved in the fight between bacteria and their virus parasites. Some

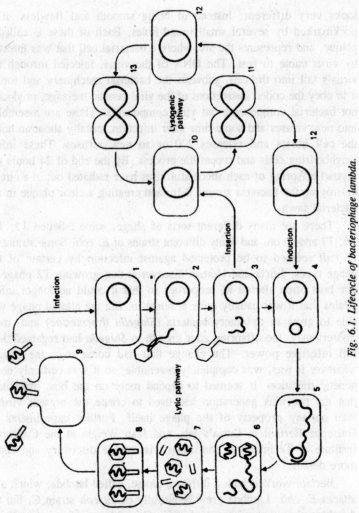

Fig. 6.1. Lifecycle of bacteriophage lambda.

strains of bacteria could successfully prevent virus attack. They were said to restrict the growth of certain types of phage. But if the phage could escape the restriction process, the survivors were somehow modified and able to infect the restrictive host freely. The infectiveness of a virus apparently depended on its most recent host. The systematic observations of Luria, of Bertani, and of Weigle introduced a measure of regularity to the strange phenomenon that came to be called 'host-controlled restriction'. These observations made sense, too, of other results that had been noticed, but not pursued, by earlier workers,

Public health workers need to identify disease-causing bacteria quickly and accurately to prevent epidemics. Different strains of bacteria are resistant to different antibiotics, require different vaccines and so on, and a valuable advantage can be gained by knowing the exact identity of the culprit before trying to treat the disease. One of the identification methods bacteriologists use is so-called 'phage typing'. They infect a lawn of the suspects strain with a set of 25 or more different sorts of bacteriophage and see which types of phage are able to grow and which are restricted. This alone will often tell the bacteriologist what strain he is dealing with. But sometimes things go wrong.

Ephraim S. Anderson and A. Felix worked at the Public Health Service's Central Enteric Reference Laboratory and Bureau in Colindale, north London. The major part of the laboratory's work was to identify the culprits behind various gastric upsets, often in cases of food poisoning. Prompted by Luria and Bertani's revelations of the mysteries of T2 and lambda, Anderson and Felix announced that in 1947, five years earlier, they had noted a similar thing with *Salmonella typhi*, one of the bacteria that causes food poisoning. Certain phages, called 'Vi-typing phages', were restricted by some strains of *S. typhi* and could grow on others. But if a phage was forced to grow on a restrictive host, it produced new phages that were no longer restricted on the original host. For Anderson and Felix this was a nuisance, because it meant that they had to keep their stocks of Vi-typing phages separate if they were to identify the *S. typhl* strains correctly; but in the light of the later work their observations made a great deal of sense. Anderson is, perhaps not unnaturally, a little bitter that he is seldom recognized as a pioneer in the field of restriction, but it is not that easy to make the connection between changing specificity – at that time thought to be a property of the virus – and restriction, a property of the host.

Some time after these events, Luria produced an explanation of the whole curious phenomenon of host-controlled restriction. He couched his account in literary terms. The genetic code, he said, was a universal language, each distinct triplet of bases along the DNA representing the same amino acid in all living things. So if one was looking at the code simply as a reader, the meaning would be the same regardless of who was doing the reading. Now suppose that, instead of regarding the code as a mere reader, one looks at it with the eye of a bibliophile. Little marks might, like the typeface or design of this book, reveal who constructed the code, who printed the book. Restricting bacteria were able to scrutinize all the DNA inside their walls, including that of the infecting phage. As a result they could tell that the phage DNA was foreign, and destroy it. To protect themselves, they would have to be able to recognize their own DNA, perhaps by modifying its structure in some way, and prevent it being destroyed. Occasionally a stretch of viral DNA would escape scrutiny and, while being replicated by the cell, would be modified and protected in the same way that the cell's own DNA is modified and protected. Instead of reading' made in *E. coli* (not strain K)', the DNA would now read 'made in *E. coli* strain K', and the vigilant restriction enzymes would be fooled. What the printer's marks might be, and how the foreign DNA was destroyed, remained mysteries.

Protection and Destruction

For roughly ten years from Luria's description of host-controlled restriction, the mechanics of restriction and modification remained unknown. Then, in 1962, Werner Arber, a Swiss biochemist at the University of Geneva, revealed what was going on. Arber had been inspired by a period spent with Jean Weigle in California, and he and Daisy Dussoix, a student working for her PhD, concentrated their efforts on a variant of phage lambda and two strains of *E. coli*, K12 and KP1. Their lambda phage would grow well in K12, but hardly at all in P1; less than 2 in 10,000 K12 phage particles survive P1, but those that do will breed equally well both in K12 and in KP1. Arber and Dussoix redid the experiment carefully, allowing the phage from KP1 to infect and burst just one K12 cell each, with no continued infection by the resulting daughter phage. The result was rather a surprise. Instead of just 2 particles in 10,000 being able to infect KP1, Arber and Dussoix got 1 in every 100 or so. Because the number of daughter viruses produced in a single cell before it burst was about 100, Arber and Dussoix argued that one progeny phage in each cell literally inherited the physical modification that had protected its parent.

This is complicated, so it is worth going through it again. Most phages grown on KP1 will not grow on K12, because they lack the made-in-K12 mark, but those that do grow will later grow in KP1 and K12. If you take a phage that grew first on KP1, then on K12, and allow it to infect a single KP1 cell, one in a hundred of the particles you get is able to infect K12. This may seem odd, but can be explained simply. The phage that grew in K12 picked up a made in K12' mark, and that mark is present when it infects KP1 again, and enables that particular phage to infect K12 in the future. Arber and Dussoix argued that one progeny phage in each cell inherited the physical modification that had protected the parent particle. Indeed, the infective 1 in 100 is the parent DNA, complete with its previously acquired 'made in K12' mark, repackaged into a new coat. On 8 December 1978, when his contribution to science was recognized by a Nobel prize, Arber explained their idea to an elegant Stockholm audience: 'We were convinced that this [modification] was transferred from the infecting parental phage particle. But was it a diffusible internal phage protein or was it perhaps carried on the parental DNA molecule?'

It turned out to be on the DNA, and to be a stable alteration to the molecule, not affected by the some times violent chemical procedures used to purify DNA. Finding out that the modification - which, as Luria had said, affected the substance of the DNA but not the spelling of the genetic message – consisted of tacking a small chemical group, a so-called methyl group, on to specific nucleotides in the DNA, took a little longer – until the early 1970s, in fact. When Arber grew *E. coli* on a medium deficient in methionine, the amino acid that cells use as a source of methyl groups, the bacteria lost their ability to modify DNA. Indeed, other experiments suggested that cells would not survive long without methionine because their own DNA was unprotected and so, in a sort of inevitable suicide, the cell's restriction enzymes turned on the very DNA that had created them.

While Arber was working out that modification involved changes to the DNA, Dussoix and another colleague, Grete Kelenberg, tried to find out what restriction really was. They grew phages on strain

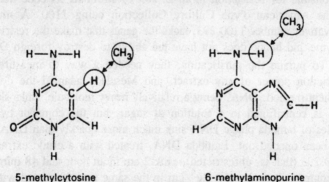

5-methylcytosine   **6-methylaminopurine**

Fig. 6.2. Modified bases. The substitution of a methyl (CH₃) group for one of the hydrogen atoms in a base marks that base out and protects the DNA from restriction enzymes.

K12 bacteria which had in turn grown up in a medium that contained ^{32}P, a radioactive isotope of the element phosphorus. As a result, the phage DNA contained a radioactive label and could be traced. Dussoix and Kellenberg infected various strains of *E. coli*, some restrictive and others not, with the labelled phage. After an interval of 3, 7 or 15 minutes they stopped all chemical reactions in the cells and looked to see what happened to the radioactive label. On strain K12, which of course did not restrict the growth of phage that had been grown on K12, over 90 per cent of the hot phosphorus was in the form of large insoluble molecules inside the bacteria. On P1, which did restrict phage growth, more than half the phosphorus was floating freely in solution and obviously no longer part of a DNA molecule. Even after as little as three minutes, unmodified DNA injected into restrictive cells was completely ineffectual, having been broken down into tiny bits.

The Enzyme Isolated

After Chicago and California, where he had pioneered density gradient methods for separating large molecules, and had been part of the team that isolated messenger RNA, Matthew Meselson found himself with his own lab at Harvard. In 1966 Robert Yuan, a Fellow of the Damon Runyon Memorial Foundation, arrived as a postdoctoral fellow. Meselson offered Yuan a choice of two projects. Either he could investigate the enzymes involved in the recombination of phage T4, or he could search for the host restriction enzymes. Undaunted by previous failures, and encouraged by Meselson, Yuan decided to make a frontal attack on restriction enzymes. They chose to purify the enzymes responsible for restriction in an *E. coli* of strain K, its code number in the American Type Culture Collection being 1100. A mutant derivative, number 1100.293, lacks the genes that make the restriction enzyme and hence does not have the ability to destroy foreign DNA.

To pursue the purification, they needed a way to measure the restriction power of any extract, and Meselson adapted the density gradient method. DNA, being a relatively heavy molecule, sinks slowly if it is centrifuged in a solution of sugar, but the compact twisted circles of lambda phage DNA sink much more quickly than DNA that has been opened out. Lambda DNA, treated with a crude extract of 1100.293 (that is, unrestricted), sank 2 cm in an hour and 48 minutes; by contrast, it sank only 1½ cm in the same time if treated with an extract of the restricting strain. Clearly, the restricting strain did have the power to open up the DNA and make it sink more slowly. The assay method was a bit tedious: labelled DNA had to be tracked through the density gradient by counting the particles emitted by each successive millimeter of sucrose solution; but it worked, and revealed when DNA had been broken up by enzymes and when it had not.

Purification began, as it almost always does, with a technique called 'dialysis'. The rag-bag mixture of proteins and everything else from the cells is put into a sack made of a special material and submerged in a mixture of solvents. The small impurities pass through the membrane and the dialysate, as it is called, that is left behind is a purer solution of the large proteins. (Dialysis, essentially, is like washing; the technique is in everyday use to clean kidney patients' blood of harmful impurities.) Unfortunately for Meselson and Yuan, the dialysate of *E. coli* K seemed to have no restriction activity. DNA was untouched by it. This stumped them for a while and caused a frustrating delay, until they discovered that two other chemicals, so-called 'co-factors', were needed for the restriction enzyme to work. One of these was ATP, the molecule that stores and transports energy in the cell. The other was S-adenosylmethionine, SAM for short. As SAM provides methyl groups, and is needed for good restriction in living cells, it was no great surprise that the cell extract also needed it. ATP and SAM provided the crude cell extract with quite a powerful destructive effect on lambda DNA.

With the requirements of the reaction all worked out, Meselson and Yuan proceeded to the business of purification. They grew *E. coli* in vast amounts, until the stock broth was a soup containing 600 million cells in every millilitre. The stock culture was spun down 'in a centrifuge, the spent broth thrown away, and the cells stored at − 20°C. From the frozen mass, they took 120 grams of cells and whirled them in a blender with tiny glass beads. The beads, like a miniature crushing mill, broke open the cells and released the cytoplasm. Two hours at 35,000 r.p.m. separated the empty cell walls from the cytoplasm, which tests showed was able to degrade DNA.

Cytoplasm contains a great deal more than restriction enzyme; apart from all the other enzymes, there are assorted other chemicals that are not wanted. The 300 millilitres of crude extract now had to be cleaned up. The first stage was to separate the proteins from the other chemicals. Ammonium sulphate is gentler than phenol and does this nicely, making the proteins precipitate out of solution. Meselson and Yuan collected and precipitated protein and dissolved it up in a special mixture, which they dialysed to get rid of small impurities. Then they purified the dialysate by column chromatography.

The principle of column chromatography is simple. A mixture in this case of proteins, is poured on to the top of a column of some absorbent material. Meselson and Yuan used chemically treated cellulose. The proteins tend to stick to the cellulose, but they can be washed off again by the buffer solution they are dissolved in. Each protein has a characteristic stickiness that determines the speed at which it will travel through the column. Stickier proteins get left behind, while not so sticky ones are the first to drip out of the end of the column.

Meselson and Yuan poured the dialysate, 100 ml of it, on to a column, 6 cm across and 11 cm deep, of specially prepared cellulose. The proteins sorted themselves out, and the two researchers washed the column with a litre of buffer solution, taking care to collect separate 50 ml samples, or fractions, as they dripped through. The restriction activity was sure to have collected in one or more of those 200 samples, but to find out which they had to go through the tiresome business of incubating some of each sample with DNA, putting the DNA on to a sucrose gradient, and seeing whether the DNA had been attacked. When it was all done the results were clear. All the activity was concentrated in just two of the fractions. The rest could be thrown away.

The two fractions were mixed together, dialysed again, and put through the chromatographic separation once more. This time the column was taller and thinner, 1 cm by 15 cm, and made of slightly different cellulose, all of which combined to enhance the separation yet further. Washing the samples out now used only 300 ml, and each fraction was only 9 ml; but again, each fraction had to be tested to see whether it had the power to restrict DNA. The restriction activity was concentrated into just three adjacent 9 ml fractions. The fractions were pooled, dialysed, and concentrated down to 7.5 ml by removing water. Chromatography now was too insensitive to separate the constituents of the mixture, because if there were several proteins they were essentially all equally sticky. But they might be of different density, so the final step was a purely physical separation using a density gradient.

The 7.5 ml was divided into three portions and each was placed on top of a test-tube containing a density gradient of glycerol. The tubes were spun at 25000 r.p.m. for 20 hours and gingerly removed from the centrifuge. A pin-prick in the bottom of each tube allowed the glycerol and layered proteins to drip out each millimeter of liquid in the tube collected as a separate fraction and tested. Three fractions had the power to break up DNA; they were over 5000 times more active than the crude cell extract.

Those days, Yuan recalled, formed 'one of the most exciting periods in my life. 'The long hours, made the finding of open eating places an added complication.' At the end of it, with 'great joy', he and Meselson published their work in *Nature*. From the 8 grams of protein in the original extract, Meselson and Yuan had obtained something like, half a thousandth of a gram, but that tiny amount contained practically all the restriction activity of the 120 grams of *E. coli* cells. With pure enzyme, they could look in detail at how it worked.

Destroyer and Protector

Meselson and Yuan's enzyme was technically an endonuclease. That is, it acted within a double helix of DNA to break it, rather than attacking the ends of the helix. When they attacked labelled DNA with the enzyme, very little of the radioactive phosphorus found its way into the solution. Most of it stayed bound up in the DNA, which proved that the enzyme did not just break up the DNA molecule by chomping away at one end. Also, the enzyme worked perfectly well on the closed circles of DNA that comprise the genetic message of lambda phage. So it attacked double- stranded, whole DNA.

The product of the pure enzyme was also double-stranded DNA, though obviously in shorter lengths. Incubating a mixture of DNA and enzyme extensively and then adding more enzyme did little to alter the pattern of settling of the DNA in the sucrose gradients, a pattern that resembled the one that would be obtained if the entire lambda DNA were divided into four quarters. Another' trick proved that the degraded DNA was double-stranded. Normal double helices settle at the same speed in strong and weak salt solutions, whereas single-stranded DNA curls up in strong salt solution and settles three times more quickly than in a weak solution. Meselson and Yuan found that the enzyme-treated DNA settled at the same speed regardless of salt concentration; it was double-stranded. Furthermore, there are no single-strand breaks, or nicks, in the treated DNA. Separating the two chains does not alter the settling pattern, as it would if some of the strands were nicked into shorter pieces.

It looked as if the restriction enzyme from *E. coli* K worked in two stages. It made a break in one strand and then, some 30 seconds later, the second strand broke. Meselson and Yuan couldn't tell whether the same enzyme molecule made both breaks, nor were they sure whether the enzyme was attacking a specific sequence along the DNA.

The pattern of fragments that they got suggested that the enzyme might recognize just a few sites that it then attacked, but they couldn't be certain that this was so.

Perhaps the most interesting result was that a modification on just one of the two strands protected the molecule from the enzyme. DNA molecules from phages grown in K were modified and protected against the enzyme of K. Those grown in C were not. Meselson and Yuan separated the DNA strands in samples from the two types of phage and then mixed the single strands. Some of the DNA from K-grown phage came together with strands from C-grown phage to form hybrid double helices, known as heteroduplexes, on which one strand, the K strand, was protected and the other not. The enzyme did not attack these hybrid strains, not even to make a nick in just the unmodified strand. This finding was extremely important, as Meselson and Yuan realized:

The resistance of heteroduplexes may serve to protect newly replicated bacterial DNA from attack by the cells' own restriction enzyme, allowing time for modification of the newly synthesized chain. Indeed, if restriction and modification are accomplished by the same enzyme, the choice between the two reactions may normally be governed by' whether the substrate is an unmodified homoduplex or a heteroduplex, respectively.

Perverse Complexity

The achievements of Matthew Meselson and Robert Yuan in isolating and purifying the restriction enzyme of *E. coli* and working out how it operated were enormous. But it was only in 1979 that we gained a understanding of how it works. The reason for the delay was, as the writers of one textbook put it, that the enzyme Meselson and Yuan chose to work with is 'perverse in the complexity of its behaviour'. The final story is astounding.

The enzyme is large, and is made of three parts. One recognizes a specific sequence of bases on the DNA. The second cuts the DNA if, and only if, the recognition site contains no protective methyl groups. The third part adds methyl groups to one strand if the other strand already has one. The recognition site is 13 nucleotides long:

5′ —A—A—C—N—N—N—N—N—N—G—T—G—C— 3′
3′ —T—T—G—N—N—N—N—N—N—C—A—C—G— 5′

The middle section of six N's indicates that the exact identity of those nucleotides is irrelevant, but the flanking sequences of three and four are vital. How the enzyme recognizes the site is a mystery, although it looks as if the recognition part of the molecule fits inside the groove of the double helix and reads its way along. If, when it comes to a recognition site, it finds a methyl group on one strand (the exact location of the protective methyl is still unknown), it acts as a methylase and adds protection to the other strand. If it finds both strands methylated, it stops reading and falls off the helix. If it finds no methyl groups it destroys the helix.

The exact details of destruction still aren't known for the enzyme from *E. coli* K, but a very similar enzyme from strain B is better understood, John Rosamond worked it out with some colleagues while he was a visiting researcher at Berkeley, using direct observation with an electron microscope, and a series of cleverly contrived stretches of DNA (manufacture of which, ironically, had to await developments in the technology of restriction enzymes). The DNA in question had target sites for the enzyme at different distances from the end of the molecule. Only if the site was more than 1000 bases from the end of the DNA did the enzyme cut it. And it never cut the DNA at the recognition site; the damage was always at least 1000 bases from the site.

The enzyme becomes bound to the recognition site and undergoes some sort of transformation, perhaps losing one of its subunits. Then, while still attached at that site, it begins to pull the DNA through itself. It always pulls in DNA from the same side of the sequence, the side with three recognition bases, holding on to the four-base site and effectively, travelling along the DNA. Looking at the complex of DNA with enzyme in the electron microscope, Rosamond could see loops at the end of the molecules. These loops show the enzyme frozen in the act of walking along the DNA. When it has pulled in a certain amount of DNA, somewhere between 1000 and 5000 nucleotides, it stops. Nobody knows why it stops where it does; certainly, the site of the break is not fixed either with respect to the recognition site or with regard to the sequences of bases there. Perhaps it is as simple as a kink in the DNA. In any case, regardless of the reason why the enzyme stops tracking along the molecule, once it has stopped it makes a nick in one of the strands. Other enzymes come along and attack the exposed DNA in the nick, dissolving away a stretch of about 75 nucleotides before the second strand is broken. The result is two fragments of DNA that can be swiftly degraded by yet more enzymes. And long after the DNA has been severed the restriction enzyme remains bound to the recognition site, where it breaks down large amounts of ATP. Some ATP is used to power the hauling in of the DNA through the enzyme, but why the cell continues to waste energy molecules with such profligacy is not clear; it might be a man-made artefact caused by lack of some vital regulatory molecule in the test-tube cell substitute, or it may represent a specific extra function for the restriction enzyme that is at present unknown.

There are undoubtedly further twists to be unravelled in the byzantine knot of restriction enzyme activity. And all that complexity, while undoubtedly fascinating, hardly seems worth all the effort. What use is a cutting tool that, while it recognizes a specific site, nevertheless makes itself felt at some random point 5000 bases away from that site? The answer, quite simply, is that, aside from its intrinsic interest, the restriction enzyme that Meselson and Yuan purified from *E. coli* K prompted a search for other restriction enzymes, and the vast majority of these turned out to be much simpler. They recognize a sequence and, without any need for ATP or SAM, break the DNA right there and then. No tracking, no randomness, just a nice clean slice. And tools like that are very handy indeed.

A Whole New Class

Sharing the Nobel platform with Werner Arber in December 1978 were Hamilton Smith and Daniel Nathans. Smith and Nathans are both professors of microbiology at the prestigious Johns Hopkins University School of Medicine in Baltimore, Maryland. Where Arber had pioneered the detailed investigation of the enzymes that lay behind host-controlled restriction, Smith was honoured for discovering a whole new class of restriction enzymes, and Nathans for putting those enzymes to work in the service of fundamental molecular biology.

It began, as success stories often do in science, with a lucky chance. Smith, at the time a recently arrived member of the Johns Hopkins faculty, was working with bacteria called *Haemophilus influenzae* strain Rd. This had the useful property of being very changeable, and Smith began to investigate some of the transformations that the bacteria underwent as they swapped bits of DNA with other bacteria. With a young graduate student, Kent Wilcox, Smith used a viscometer to measure the extent to which cell extracts broke up DNA. Long strands of DNA from a very viscous solution, while smaller ones are less viscous; a decrease in viscosity mirrors the break-up of DNA. As another part of the study, Smith allowed the *H. influenzae* cells to take up radioactively labelled DNA from various sources and then tried to recover this donor DNA to see what had happened to it.

One day, Smith and Wilcox offered the bacteria labelled DNA from a phage called P22, a virus that Smith had long been familiar with. To their surprise, when they came to look for the labelled DNA in the cells, they couldn't find any.

When he received his Nobel prize Smith continued the story for his audience in Stockholm, trying hard to conceal the emotion involved:

With Meselson's recent report in our minds, we immediately suspected that the phage DNA might be undergoing restriction, and our experience with viscometry told us that this would be a good assay for such an activity. The following day, two viscometers were set up, one containing P22 DNA and the other, *Haemophilus* DNA. Cell extract was added to each and we quickly began taking measurements. As the experiment progressed, we became increasingly excited as the viscosity of the *Haemophilus* DNA held steady while that of the P22 DNA fell. We were confident that we had discovered a new and highly active restriction enzyme.

Their confidence, needless to say, was not misplaced, but it took a considerable amount of effort to find out what they had and how it worked.

Smith and Wilcox went through more or less the same stages that Meselson and Yuan had gone through; there is really no alternative, and the purification of almost any protein from a cell would be bound to involve many of the same procedures. The starting point was a culture of *H. influenzae*, growing in a 12 litre vat of sustaining brain and heart broth. Instead of glass beads, Smith used ultrasonic vibrations to break open the cells and release the cytoplasm. Put in the viscometer with P22 DNA, just ten-millionths of a litre of the crude cell extract was enough to start breaking up the DNA and reducing the viscosity. The crude cell extract was washed, separated chromatographically, washed again, and separated again. At the end, having left out the purification by density gradient that Meselson and Yuan had used, Smith and Wilcox had an enzyme that was 200 times more active than the raw cytoplasm.

This restriction enzyme needed neither ATP nor SAM, though it would not work unless there were magnesium ions present. It was smaller than the *E. coli* K enzyme, with a molecular weight of only about 70,000. It attacked foreign DNA with alacrity, reducing the genome of T7 from a single length of molecular weight 26,400,000 to about 40 bits with an average molecular weight of 1,450,000. The bits were all double-stranded, and no nucleotides were removed from the chain. The enzyme appeared to chop through the DNA in one go producing nicks in the two strands at almost the same time and place. They christened the enzyme 'endonuclease R'; endonuclease because, like Meselson and Yuan's enzyme, it attacked nucleic acid molecules from within (that is, it could break the middle of a chain – exonucleases attack at the tips of the molecules), and R for restriction.

Meselson and Yuan had guessed that their enzyme recognized a specific sequence of bases. For similar reasons, namely the relatively small number of breaks produced, Smith and Wilcox felt the same way about their enzyme. But they went further and estimated the length of the recognition site. T7 DNA is about 40,000 bases long, and the *Haemophilus* enzyme broke this into 40 pieces about 1000 bases long. On a stretch of randomly organized DNA a particular unique sequence of, say, four bases would occur roughly every 256 bases; clearly, four bases is too small a site. To occur every 1000 or so bases, a site would need to be five or six bases long. At the very end of their paper announcing the new restriction enzyme, Smith and Wilcox derived this estimate and then had the satisfaction of stating: 'In the accompanying paper ... the base sequence recognized by endonuclease R is completely identified and provides confirmation of this estimate.

Recognition

At the same time as he had been working on the properties of the *H. influenzae* restriction enzyme, Smith was also tackling the question of its recognition site. Kent Wilcox was in on the early stages of this project too, but could not continue because the army had sent him his draft notice of induction. His prime preoccupation therefore become to complete the formal requirements of his master's degree. Smith continued alone for a time, and then was joined by Thomas Kelly Jr.

All the evidence pointed to a specific recognition site. Of the 40000 sugar–phosphate links in each chain of the viral DNA, the enzyme broke only 40. There had to be some sort of guidance mechanism to get the enzyme to cleave just there. The strategy Smith and Kelly adopted sounds simple. They would look at the ends of the fragments and identify the nucleotides there. If the site was specific, they would find a specific pattern of nucleotides ending each and every fragment. Putting it into practice required a battery of other enzyme systems, two sorts of radioactive label and a great deal of ingenuity.

The starting point was purified endonuclease R and T7 DNA labelled with ^{33}P. This is a radioactive form of phosphorus that is less energetic than the usual ^{32}P; it was used as a general label to tell them where the DNA was. Smith and Kelly attacked the single nucleotide at the 5' end of the fragments first. An enzyme called alkaline phosphatase removes the phosphate group from the end of a fragment. This done, the fragments were incubated with ATP labelled with energetic ^{32}P and another enzyme, polynucleotide kinase. This enzyme transfers the labelled phosphorus from the ATP to the nucleoside. After an hour at blood heat the doubly labelled DNA – ^{33}P throughout and ^{32}P at the 5' end – was extracted, purified and analysed.

Snake venom is the source of yet another enzyme, this one called snake venom phosphodiesterase. This has the useful property of breaking DNA into its component nucleotides, leaving the phosphate group attached to the 5´ carbon of the sugar. When the venom enzyme had done its work Smith and Kelly had a mixture of four different nucleotides, all radioactively labelled but some – the nucleotides that were at the 5´ end of the restriction fragment – labelled with ^{32}P while all the others carried only ^{33}P. The problem now was first to separate the four nucleotides, and then to identify the ones that had the hotter ^{32}P label. Separation was routine, using electrophoresis. Similar to chromatography, electrophoresis is a process in which an electric current frog-marches the molecules through a thin layer of cellulose. Molecules that are small, or highly charged, move faster than those that are large, or not so highly charged. Once separated, the nucleotides had to be identified. This is where the differential labelling came in. ^{33}P is not very energetic, and the particles it gives off as it decays are easily blocked ^{12}P, on the other hand, gives off more energetic particles. Smith laid a sheet of Kodak X-ray film on either side of the cellulose gel that had been used for electrophoresis. As the phosphorus decayed it gave off particles, which collided with the silver grains in the film and left a permanent record of their position. The radioactive phosphorus essentially takes a picture of itself; hence the name autoradiography. One side of the gel was in direct contact with the film. Strong and weak particles could get to the silver, so ^{33}P and ^{32}P each made their mark. On the other side of the gel was the gel's thin supporting plastic. Flimsy though this was, it was enough to stop the weaker decay products of ^{33}P. Only the hotter label of the terminal nucleotide would show on this film.

Conceptually simple, this intellectual breakthrough was absolutely fundamental to the work that was to follow. But after the very first run, when they looked at the films and compared the exposed positions with the pattern they got with known nucleotides. Smith must have been a bit disappointed. The hot label was present in two nucleotides 63 per cent attached to the adenine and the remaining 37 percent to guanine. So the cleavage site was 'not absolutely specified'. All was not lost, however, for adenine and guanine are both purines; the enzyme made a break on the 5´ side of a purine, but didn't distinguish between adenine and guanine.

What was the penultimate nucleotide on the fragment? As before, the phosphorus on the end was replaced with a hot phosphorus, but instead of using snake venom, an enzyme called exonuclease I was brought in. This nibbles away at DNA fragments from the 3´ end, but stops when there are just two nucleotides left. Again, the dinucleotides were separated and auto-radiographed. The label was again in two places. One, with 62 per cent of the radioactivity, could have been either AA, or CG, or GC. The other was either GA or AG. Snake venom separated the first pair into single nucleotides; all the hot label was on adenine, so the pair was definately AA. The second pair's ^{32}P was also on the adenine, so this one was GA. The site was specific. The 5´ base could be either A or G, but the next base along was always an adenine.

The final three bases on the 5´ end of the fragment turned out to be AAC and GAC, so the specificity was holding up. What about the other side of the break, the 3´ end of the fragments? Here another bit of thought enabled Smith and Kelly to take a shortcut. There were, logically, only two ways that the enzyme could work. It could either break the DNA duplex evenly, producing fragments with flush ends, or it could break unevenly, so that the fragments had one longer strand at the end. Only if the break was even, and the ends flush would the sequence of bases at the 3, end of the fragment be exactly complementary to the sequence at the 5´ end. Yet another enzyme – micrococcal nuclease – was brought in. This enzyme breaks whole DNA into single and double nucleotides, those from the 3´ end being double nucleotides joined by a single phosphate. Smith and Kelly separated these out from all the other nucleotides by chromatography and found that they were of two different sorts. Breaking them up and looking at the individual nucleotides revealed that one was TC and the other TT. This was exactly what they would predict if the break is even. They had almost all the details of the recognition site: it was

$$5´ -G-T-Py-Pu-A-C- 3´$$
$$3´ -C-A-Pu-Py-T-G- 5´$$

with the break coming between the two unspecified bases in the middle. (Notice that the sequence is a palindrome. It reads the same on the two strands, just as the sentence 'able was I ere I saw Elba' reads the same forwards or backwards. The vast majority of subsequently identified recognition sites turned out likewise to be palindromic: the consequences of this are extremely important.) Such a sequence of six bases would occur in a random genome once every 1024 base-pairs. The fragments T7 DNA produced by endonuclease R were about 1000 base-pairs long, while those of P22 were 1300 base-pairs long. As Kelly and Smith noted:

These facts suggest that the sequence [above] contains sufficient information to account fully for the observed degree of specificity of endonuclease R. However, since strictly speaking neither the T7 nor the P22 DNA molecule represents a truly random collection of nucleotides, the possibility remains that the recognition region for endonuclease R might be larger

They had to look at the fourth nucleotide from the end; if that too was specific, the recognition region was longer than six base-pairs. Fortunately, it was not.

The recognition site of a restriction enzyme had been fully identified, and the pace of progress was speeding up. Thirty years from the first phage-typing to Luria's experiments; ten years from Luria to Arber; eight years from Arber to Meselson and Yuan; and two years from them to Smith. Host-controlled restriction, which Hamilton Smith described as 'an apparently insignificant bacteriological phenomenon', had yielded an enzyme that, he saw, had 'unexpectedly far-reaching implications'.

Things Get Easier

Almost as soon as Smith had discovered the first specific restriction enzyme, his colleague Daniel Nathans was putting it to work in the service of molecular biology. Nathan's target was a little virus that infects the cells of monkeys, hence its name simian virus 40, or SV40. SV40 can, when conditions are right, transform the cells it has infected and make them grow like cancerous tumours, so it has not unnaturally been the subject of intense interest by many groups of researchers. But before examining the developments, in SV40 and elsewhere, that followed Smith's work with the *Haemophilus influenzae* enzyme, it is worth looking at the way in which interest in restriction enzymes took off.

Meselson and Yuan had an enormously hard job demonstrating that the various fractions they collected were, or were not, possessed of restricting activity. They had to use modified DNA labelled with one type of radioactive isotope and unmodified DNA with a different label. Then, after incubating a mixture of the two with the putative enzyme, they had to spin the products down a sucrose density gradient. Dividing the gradient into portions and counting the different types of radioactivity in each took yet more time, and at the end the results had to be examined carefully to see which fractions were able to destroy unmodified DNA. It worked, but it took time.

Smith and Wilcox went one better. No longer were they dependent on tedious, density-gradient separations and radioactivity assay (though they still used those for confirmation); they had the viscometer, which gave a purely physical indication of whether the DNA was being broken or not. In the right hands, this was a much speedier process for testing the various fractions, and enabled Smith and his helpers to progress rather rapidly. Still, the techniques were not as fast as they were to become, and it was Nathans and his SV40 who pushed the speed up another notch.

Nathan's intention was to divide the DNA of SV40 up into manageable fragments, the better to understand how the entire virus worked. He quickly established that Smith's restriction 'enzyme did indeed break open SV40's circle of DNA, and that it created several fragments, The next goal was to resolve the mixture of fragments into its component parts, and for this Nathans enlisted the help of Kathleen Danna, a graduate student in his laboratory. The technique they used was electrophoresis, but rather than using cellulose as a supporting medium for the mixture of fragments they used a gel containing polyacrylamide. This is a long thread like molecule that links to form a mesh permeated by small pores. The amount of polyacrylamide sets the average size of the pores, which in turns restrict the passage of molecules through the gel. Small molecules always travel faster, but by adjusting the amount of polyacrylamide in the gel the biochemist can fine -tune his molecular sieve to sort out a particular size most efficiently: Nathans and Danna put the sample of radioactive SV40 DNA, digested by the restriction enzyme, at one end of a 13 cm strip of polyacrylamide gel. The DNA, of course, is completely invisible, so to keep track of it they added a dye, bromophenol blue, that moved little faster than the smallest chain of DNA. Sixty volts from one end of the gel to the other provided the motive power to separate the fragments of DNA, smaller fragments racing ahead of larger ones, and at the end of eight hours the blue band of dye had travelled 13 cm and reached the end of the gel. The problem now was to make the invisible visible, and see what had become of the DNA.

Danna froze the 13 cm strip of gel to make it easier to handle and then cut it into about a hundred bands, each just 1.2 mm wide. Each band sat for a while in solvent, and then the amount of radioactivity that had leaked out into the solvent was counted with a superior sort of geiger counter. The results showed clearly that the fragments of nucleic acid had indeed separated out. The column of numbers counts of radioactivity from 100 or more samples, produced a clear pattern of peaks and troughs; nine peaks and ten troughs. Two of the peaks contained more than their fair share of DNA, an anomaly that autoradiographs of the gels explained by showing two bands close together at each of the two positions. The restriction enzyme from *H. influenzae* chopped the DNA from SV40 into 11 chunks, and a whole series of different measurements proved that the amount of DNA in the 11 fragments added up to the total amount of DNA in the whole virus. 'We conclude,' wrote Danna and Nathans, 'that every molecule of SV40 DNA yields one of each of these fragments. That was why each of the fragments formed a band in the polyacrylamide gel. They were always the same set of fragments, and they lined up in the gel according to size. It was just the result Nathans needed.

It was also ideal for identifying new restriction enzymes. If some portion of purified cell extract gave evidence of breaking DNA, the products of the digestion could be layered on a gel and separated by electrophoresis. If the enzyme was truly a restriction enzyme, breaking the DNA at a set number of specific sites, then it would produce the same set of fragments from every molecule of DNA, and the fragments would line up to form the tell-tale bands. One had to use radioactive DNA, it's true, and follow up the electrophoresis by slicing up the gel and counting the radioactivity, or else by allowing the fragments to photograph themselves; but Danna and Nathans had made it possible to look for restriction activity even more efficiently than had Smith and Wilcox.

Another advance came a couple of years later, in 1973, from Cold spring Harbor Laboratory. Phillip Sharp, Bill Sugden and Joe Sambrook streamlined the search for restriction enzymes still further. Their breakthrough was in two parts. First, they changed the electrophoresis gel, from polyacrylamide to agarose. DNA fragments are large molecules, and a polyacrylamide gel with holes large enough for the DNA to get through contains so little polyacrylamide that it forms an impossibly mushy gel. Agarose, a long chain polymer rather like starch, can provide additional support for a weak polyacrylamide gel and is better than polyacrylamide because agarose is not as sensitive to the concentration of electrically charged particles in the solution. When a protein mixture of enzymes has been separated chromatographically the different components are washed out of the column with different concentrations of solvent. Previously, each fraction had to be adjusted to the same concentration before being tested with DNA and electrophoresed. With agarose, the fractions could be taken straight from the column, incubated with DNA, and put through electrophoresis.

The second improvement was perhaps even more important, for, it got rid of the lengthy procedures needed to make the DNA in the gel visible. Slicing and counting, staining with dyes (which needed to be removed again before anything else could be done with the DNA), and autoradiographs were all time-consuming and tedious. Sharp added a simple chemical, ethidium bromide, to the gel and the mixed fragments of DNA. Ethidium bromide inserts itself between the bases of the DNA and stretches the helix out slightly, but that is neither here nor there. Much more important, the DNA, makes the ethidium bromide glow in ultraviolet light. No staining, no radioactivity, no lengthy wait for autoradiographs; you simply, take the agarose gel into a darkroom, switch on an ultraviolet light, and there it is. Bands containing as little as 50 billionths of a gram (0.05 microgram) of DNA light up yellow-orange; to the eager researcher the glowing bands can seem as bright as neon signs and just as conspicuous. Sharp's technique made searching for restriction enzymes a dream Or, in the dry prose of a scientific paper: "the lengthy staining and destaining or autoradiographic procedures which are an integral part of most of the techniques that are used for electrophoresis of DNA are eliminated ... In our hands the technique has proved to be a very useful and flexible tool for assaying restriction enzymes."

Sharp's method made everything much easier; separating and seeing DNA was now relatively simple, and the community adopted the method with alacrity. 'Agarose gel electrophoresis did not originate with our *Biochemistry* paper, 'Sharp has told me, 'but was certainly popularized by it'. The DNA detection was another matter. Sharp had spent a year with a postdoctoral fellowship at the California Institute of

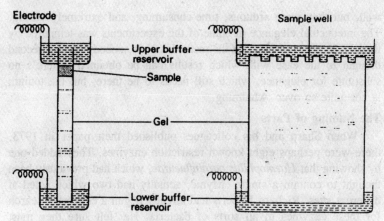

Fig. 6.3. Electrophoresis apparatus. The sample mixture is carried through the gel by an electric current, which separates out the fragments according to size.

Technology, where he had seen how the dye ethidium bromide fluoresced much more brightly when bound to DNA. He remembered this at Cold Spring Harbor when he wanted to visualize DNA fragments.

I decided to try to stain gels with ethidium bromide as a means of detecting the bands formed by different length fragments. The minimum concentration of ethidium bromide necessary for saturation of DNA was calculated and within 3 hours I had successfully detected DNA bands in gels with ethidium bromide.

Another conceptual leap came from Camil Fuchs, a statistician at Wisconsin university. Fuchs made it vastly easier to discover the recognition site of a new restriction enzyme. Working from the starting point that the enzymes recognize a palindromic site, Fuchs wrote a computer program to detect 4-, 5- and 6-base palindromes, and set the program to work on the complete sequences of two viruses, SV40 and ΦX174, both of which were known in their entirety. The computer told Fuchs how many fragments would be generated, what length they would be and so on for every palindrome in the two genomes. To discover the enzyme's most likely recognition sequence, the researcher had only to use the new restriction enzyme on SV40 and ΦX174, measure the fragments so easily separated and visualized, and simply read the tables that Fuchs published in *Gene*. It was a simple matter then to confirm that sequence by more pedestrian methods.

The contrast between then and now, between sucrose gradient separation and fluorescent bands, is hard to imagine. Robert Yuan remembers that in those early days, such assays served their function well, but they were arduous, time-consuming, and extremely boring. The intellectual elegance of some of the experiments was tempered by the laboriousness of many of the methods'. Now, nobody gives a second thought to the ease with which results can be obtained. There's no substitute for elegance, which still needs to be there, but the tedium is not quite so over- whelming.

The Naming of Parts

When Sharp and his colleagues published their paper in 1973, there were perhaps eight known restriction enzymes, They added one by showing that *Haemophilus parainfluenzae*, which had previously been thought to contain a single enzyme, actually had two which acted at different sites. Richard Roberts had already begun a concerted search for these enzymes in all sorts of bacteria. He 'felt sure they must exist...This was a somewhat heretical view at the time, in that most of my colleagues told me that it was unlikely that there would be more enzymes of this sort.' Roberts's conviction proved correct; a steady stream of new restriction enzymes with new recognition sites followed, and with them a similar' continuous stream of visitors with DNA samples who wished to see which enzymes would cut them'. This led to the first, private catalogue, in 1974, and by the published list of 1976 Roberts had documented more than 80 restriction enzymes. The number now is above the 300 mark.

The plethora of enzymes could have become a source of confusion, but very early on Smith and Nathans, with remarkable prescience, saw where they were heading and polled many of their colleagues in the field to bring some order to it all. Every restriction enzyme would have a specific name which would identify it uniquely. The first three letters, in italics, indicate the biological source of the enzyme, the first letter being the initial of the genus and the second and third the first two letters of the species name. Thus, restriction enzymes from *Escherichia coli* are called *Eco*; *Haemophilus influenzae* becomes *Hin*; *Diplococcus pneumoniae Dpn*; and so on. Then comes a letter that identifies the strain of bacteria: *Eco* R for strain R (strictly for *E. coli* harbouring a plasmid called R), *Eco* B for B. Finally there is a roman numeral for the particular enzyme if there is more than one in the strain in question; *Eco* RI for the first enzyme from *Escherichia coli* R, *Eco* RII for the second.

The enzymes, having been named, can also be divided into three groups. Class I enzymes are the troublesome ones like Meselson. *Eco* K, which recognize a specific sequence but don't cleave the DNA at a specific point: they walk a random distance from the recognition site and break the DNA there. Class II enzymes are the workhorses of the genetic engineer, Like Smith's *Hin* they recognize a specific site and break the DNA at a particular place within that site, A very few class II enzymes are a bit odd; like all restriction enzymes, they recognize a specific sequence, but they don't cleave the DNA within the recognition site; instead, they make a break a set number of nucleotides away. *Mbo* II, for example, from the bacterium *Moraxella bovis* (which causes pinkeye in cattle), recognizes

$$5´ —G—A—A—G—A— 3´$$
$$3´ —C—T—T—C—T—5´$$

but makes its break some way down stream of this, to create a fragment with

$$5´ —G—A—A—G—A—N—N—N—N—N—N—N—N— 3´$$
$$3´ —C—T—T—C—T—N—N—N—N—N—N—N— 5´$$

at the end. These 'odd' class II enzymes used to be placed, by European molecular biologists in particular, into a third class, class III. But American workers, and Roberts in particular, adopted a slightly different classification. Their class III contained enzymes like Eco PI, which 'have characteristics intermediate between those of the Type I and Type II restriction endonucleases'. 'The original classification made more sense,' says one European biologist, 'but Roberts has become pre-eminent and so ... we have adopted the current usage'. For practical purposes, the random effects of class I and class III restriction enzymes means that they don't find much use in applied genetic engineering. The real stars are the class II enzymes.

What they Do

By making a wise choice from the catalogue of known enzymes, the genetic engineer can find one to perform practically any task. Almost any sequence of bases can be located and cut at will. Some enzymes recognize a long sequence, six or seven bases long: they are often useful for opening a circular strand of DNA at just one point. Others have a much smaller site, four or even three bases long: these will 'produce small fragments that can then be used to determine the sequence of bases along the DNA. Enzymes from different sources often recognize the same site. They are called isoschizomers, and while some cleave at the same place in the site, others cleave at different places. Nobody knows whether isoschizomers are 'the same' enzyme, in terms of their exact structure; it seems unlikely. Enzymes such as Hin dII, the first to be characterized, allow some flexibility within a rigid site and are very useful. So cuts can be made anywhere along the DNA, dividing it into many small fragments or a few longer ones, and in an utterly repeatable fashion. The cuts made by a type II enzyme on a given sort of DNA will always be the same.

Strictly speaking, an enzyme qualifies as a restriction endonuclease only if the bacteria also has a specific modification enzyme to protect its own DNA; but in many cases the restricting activity is all that the genetic engineers are interested in. Nevertheless, some of the modification enzymes have been isolated and characterized, and they inevitably do mirror the recognition site of the restriction enzyme, possibly because the two sorts of enzyme share a subunit that is dedicated to seeking out a particular sequence of bases along the chain. But there are some oddities in the restriction-modification pattern. *Diplococcus pneumoniae* has two enzymes, *Dpn* I and *Dpn* II, that recognize the same four-base site, GATC. *Dpn* II is completely normal, and works like any other type II enzyme, but *Dpn* I will break the strand only if the site is modified by having a methyl group attached to the adenine. This is extremely odd. Why should the normal run of events be upset in this way? And how does *Diplococcus pneumoniae* protect itself from its two potentially devastating restriction enzymes? Perhaps the bacteria don't use this enzyme as a restriction enzyme. As Hamilton Smith says,' it is different to rationalize this reversal of the normal role of methylation.

Like the recognition site, the cut that each enzyme makes varies from enzyme to enzyme. Some, like *Hin* dII make a clean cut straight across the double helix, Fragments from *Hin* dII have ends that are flush. Others make a staggered break, Eco RI, for example, recognizes

$$5' \ -G-A-A-T-T-C- \ 3'$$
$$3' \ -C-T-T-A-A-G- \ 5'$$

but makes its cut between the G and the A in each strand. This leaves each fragment with a protruding single strand at the 5' end. *Pst* I, from the gut living bacteria *Providencia stuartii*, does the reverse. It recognizes the sequence

$$5' \ -C-T-G-C-A-G- \ 3'$$
$$3' \ -G-A-C-G-T-C- \ 5'$$

and cuts between the A and G, leaving the protruding end at the 3' end of the double helix.

Enzymes that make a staggered cut-are especially important, because the single strands that they leave protruding are complementary in base sequence. Under the right conditions, the complementary bases will pair up again, so if you cut two different sorts of DNA with one of these enzymes and mix all the fragments, the chances are that fragments from the two sorts of DNA will come together in a new hybrid molecule. You will have made a new combination of genes – recombinant DNA.

What's it all for?

There are two ways to answer this simple question. One is the answer that occupies much of the rest of this book, that restriction enzymes are 'for' genetic engineering. Certainly it would be impossible without them. But they didn't evolve to help us manipulate DNA. So what, in the evolutionary sense of 'what good', are restriction enzymes really for'?

The obvious answer would seem to be that they are a defence against viral infection. This certainly seems reasonable enough. After all, that is how the phenomenon was first uncovered. Unmodified bacteriophages cannot grow very well in hosts that possess restriction enzymes, so restriction enzymes do protect cells from viruses. But is that all? Probably not, because if restriction really is a, defence against viruses it is a very inefficient one. There is no defence against viruses that carry the modification, and it seems a little far-fetched to say that the whole elaborate mechanism evolved to protect bacteria of one strain from viruses that had most recently grown on a different strain. In any case, a far better evolutionary defence against viruses would be to lose, or modify, the sites on the outside of the bacteria that the virus recognizes and attaches to before inserting its DNA into the host. And if restriction were a protection against infection, we should expect to see far more of it in higher organisms, which are just as prone to viral attack as bacteria. In fact, there still very little evidence of any restriction activity in any eukaryote cell.

So it looks as if restriction did not evolve to protect bacteria from invading phage DNA, although it incidentally serves that purpose now. What is left in the way of invading DNA? DNA from other bacteria. When bacteria mate, they exchange DNA. If different strains were to mate, restriction enzymes in the recipient would usually ensure that the DNA from the donor was from a cell with the same restriction modification complex. The system would act to keep strains pure, by destroying DNA from different strains. The same could be true of higher organisms. A single-celled green alga, *Chlamydomonas*, does have a restriction-modification enzyme system, but the enzymes do not seem to have anything to do with attack by viruses. Instead, they destroy *Chlamydomonas* DNA after mating, The DNA in the chloroplasts from the male partner is not methylated, and is destroyed by the female's restriction enzyme, ensuring that the offspring inherit their chloroplasts exclusively in the maternal line. Salvador Luria, talking about bacteria, says:

The branding-and-rejection system facilitates the evolution of bacterial strains in diverging directions, in the same way that isolation mechanisms in cross-fertilization play a role in the evolution of plant and animal species.

Table 6.1. A sample of restriction enzymes

Source organism	Abbreviation	Recognition and cleavage site $(5' \rightarrow 3')$ $(3' \rightarrow 5')$
Bacillus amyloliquefaciens H	Bam HI	G|GATCC CCTAG|G
Escherichia coli RY13	Eco RI	G|AAT|TC CTTAA|G
Haemophilus aegyptius	Hae II	Pu GCGC|Py Py|CGCGPu
Haemophilus aegyptius	Hae III	GG|CC C|GG
Haemophilus haemolyticus	Hha I	GCG|C C|GCG
Haemophilus influenzae R$_d$	Hin dII	GTPy|PuAC CAPu|Py TG
Haemophilus influenzae R$_d$	Hin dIII	A|AGCTT TTCGA|A
Haemophilus parainfluenzae	Hpa I	GTT|AAC CAA|TTG
Haemophilus parainfluenzae	Hpa II	C|C|GG GGC|C
Providencia stuartii 164	PstI	CTGCA|G G|ACGTC
Streptomyces albus G	Sal I	G|TCGAC CAGCT|G

More important than the evolution or purity of strains and species is the restriction modification complex itself. By destroying DNA associated with any other modification enzyme, the recognition part of the complex ensures the survival of copies of itself, regardless of what species or strain they may be in.

Restriction enzymes pose fundamental questions, not only about their evolutionary *raison d'eter* but also about the mechanics of how they work. The interaction between protein, the recognition portion of the enzyme, and nucleic acid, the DNA it cleaves, is at the heart of understanding how cells regulate the expression of their genetic material. Not all the genes are being listened to at once, and proteins play a vital role in controlling and orchestrating the operation of the whole genome. Restriction enzymes, as models of more general protein-nucleic acid systems, will doubtless provide fascinating insights to those prepared-to pursue them. But for the vast majority of molecular biologists, restriction enzymes are of importance not because they might provide fundamental insights or anything like that: they cut DNA, and that's what counts.

7

MOLECULAR GENETICS OF MAN

The study of human genetics is complicated by the fact that, unlike other species of animals and plants, humans are not bred experimentally, therefore, we can not apply the type of genetics analysis that have been discussed in previous chapters. There is difficulty in the study of human genetics due to two reason (1) Geneticist is not able to arrange the matings of the human individuals he is studying. (2) The long life-cycle of man, production, relatively small number of offspring; are unfavourable factors in terms of certain standard research techniques. However, the study of human genetics not impossible. In this chapter, we will discuss briefly how family studies can be used to discover the genetic basis of human traits. This involves *pedigree analysis* where the phenotypic records of families extending over several generations are compiled so that gave segregation patterns can be hypothesized. Naturally the more complex the pedigree, the more accurate the genetic analysis. A modern application of pedigree analysis is called *genetic counseling* in which a human geneticist makes predictions about the probabilities of particular traits occurring among the progeny of a couple in whom or both show evidence of that trait in their family.

Though the branch of human genetics was established as early as 1901, no significant work has been done in the early years as man was found to be an unfavourable object for genetic studies because of the following hindrances:

1. The life span of man is so long that it does not permit the geneticist to study more than five or six generations in a family. In *Drosophila*, several generations can be obtained and studied in a few months and in Bacteria, in a week.

2. The number of offspring produced by man is far less than that produced by most insects and plants. In man, thus, very few samples of the various genetic possibilities can be obtained for study.

3. Man does not live in a uniform environment throughout his life. His varying natural and emotional environments greatly influence his inherited characters, making the study of the later somewhat complicated.

4. Marriages cannot be "controlled" by a geneticist who wishes to study the offspring of a specific mating.

5. Majority of human beings are genetically heterozygous for many characters. Therefore, it is difficult to get homozygous or pure strain.

PEDIGREE ANALYSIS

The pedigree analysis is the study of traits as they have appeared in a given family line for several past generations. These days pedigree records are properly maintained and the inheritance of many human traits like polydactyly, syndactyly, idiocy, intelligence, skin colour, haemophilia, colour blindness and so many other diseases have been studied by pedigree analysis. A family pedigree chart conventionally has circles for female individuals and squares for a male individuals. The unshaded circle and squares designate the females and males exhibiting normal characters, while the shaded circle and squares are used for those females and males who exhibit the abnormal character or the diseases. A marriage is indicated by a horizontal bar connecting a circle and square end the symbols for offspring are shown suspended from a line drawn perpendicular to the marriage bar. Individuals on the same aline are from the same generation. Heterozygous customarily are designated by colouring half of the symbol block. Carrier of a sex-linked recessive gene is designated by a black dot in the middle of the symbol.

Identical twins are indicated by a where as fraternal twins by or where as fraternal twins or.

Occasionally, an arrow pointing at a particulars affected individuals indicated that the disease was brought to the notice of geneticists by the person indicated by the arrow. Such a person is known as *proband* or *propositus* (for male) and *proposeta* if female. There are other specialization symbols, but they do not concern as here. The important symbols are put together in the pedigree as shown in the figure.

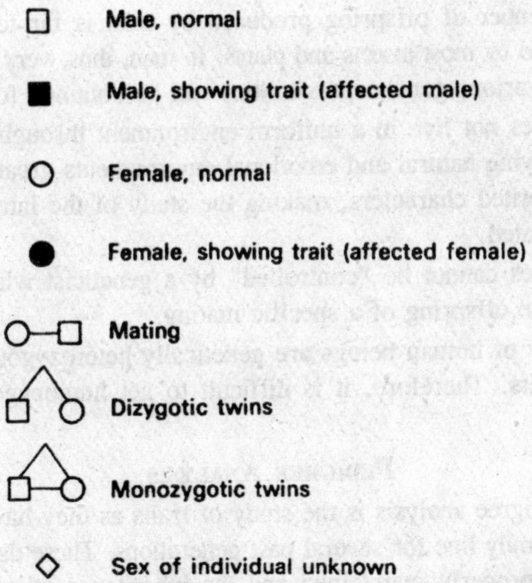

☐   Male, normal

■   Male, showing trait (affected male)

○   Female, normal

●   Female, showing trait (affected female)

○—☐   Mating

△/☐○ Dizygotic twins

△/☐○ Monozygotic twins

◇   Sex of individual unknown

Fig. 7.1. Examples of symbols used in human pedigrees.

Examples of Human pedigree

1. The pedigree inheritance pattern that is characteristic of a *Y-linked* (holandric) trait, which presumably is the result of mutation on the Y chromosome. Y-lined traits should be readily recognizable since they show father-to-son transmission and no females should ever express them. The pedigree is the conventional pedigree given for the *Lambert* family of England that involves the so-called porcupine men. In 1716, *Edward Lambert* was born to two normal parents, *Edward* was one of many children, and all but *Edward*, remained normal throughout their lives. At 7-8 weeks of age, *Edward's* skin begin to turn yellow, and it gradually became black and thickened until his whole body, with the exception of head, face, palms, and soles, was covered with rough, bristly scales and bristle like outgrowth—hence the name "*porcupine man*".

The pedigree shows that all male descendants of *Edward Lambert* had this trait (called *ichthyosis hystrix gravior*) suggesting that it was Y-linked. Careful scrutiny of the records, however, indicates that the pedigree is not correct. In particular, it seems that only three rather than six generations has affected males, and only four or five rather than 12 persons exhibited the trait. Altogether, the revaluation of the available data rules out this pedigree being a valid example of Y-linked trait and suggested, instead that the trait is the result of a rare autosomal dominant mutation.

One trait form present-day families that is considered to be Y-linked in human is hypertrichosis of the ear. The phenotype is the presence of relatively long hairs on the pinnae of the ears.

One gene that has clearly been localized to the Y chromosome is the H-Y locus, the product of which is the H-Y antigen. (An antigen is any large molecule that stimulates the production of specific antibodies or that binds specifically to an antibody; an antibody is a protein molecule that recognizes and binds to foreign substance—the antigen–introduced into the organism). The evidence that this locus is on the Y chromosome came from work done in 1955 by *E-J. Eichwald* and *C.R. Silmser* to determine whether there were detectable differences between males and females that could be related to the sex chromosomes. Their experimental system was strains or inbred mice. The inbreeding (carried out by making brother-sister matings) was done in so many generations that the resulting individuals had essentially the same genotype. These strains are called *isogenic*. *Eichwald* and *Silmser* reasoned that the only genetic differences between isogenic brothers and sisters would be the result of the sex chromosomal differences between the two sexes. They transplanted skin from females of an inbred mouse strain to male mice of the same strain and vice versa. In the former there was no rejection of the transplant, but in the latter experiment the skin transplanted to the female mice was eventually rejected. Since the only difference in males and females of the strain was the presence of the Y chromosome in the males. They concluded that the antigen responsible for the transplant rejection was coded for the Y-linked genes. Since the acceptance of tissue grafts is called *histocompatibility*, the Y-linked gene involved in this phenomenon is said to be a histocompatibility, locus is a protein found on cell surfaces in many mammals, including humans. It is not known how this protein functions in the sex-determining mechanism in mammals.

2. An example of a *sex linked recessive* trait is haemophilia, a defect in blood coagulation, and the classical pedigree is that of Queen Victoria. Part of her pedigree is presented in Figure. The assumed genotypes, where h is the recessive mutant gene, are given next to the people.

It seems that the h mutation arose in the germline of Queen Victoria. Note that only males show the trait since they are hemizygous h Y. Females would have to be hh to have haemophilia and, since it is a rare gene, this is unlikely as it requires the pairing of a haemophilic male with a carrier (heterozygous) female. Such a pairing does occur from time to time, the characteristics of X-linked recessive inheritance are : (a) males are hemizygous and, therefore, if they express the trait they transmit the mutant gene involved to all their daughters but to none of their sons; (b) for rare X-linked recessive traits, many more males than females exhibit the trait owing to the difference in the number of X chromosomes between the sexes and (c) there should be approximately 1 : 1 ratio of normal individuals with the trait among the male progeny of the heterozygous (carrier) mothers.

3. Not many *sex-linked dominant* traits have been identified. An example is brown enamel. Such traits show the same type of inheritance as sex-linked recessive traits except that heterozygous females express the trait. Since females have two X chromosomes and males have only one X, sex-linked dominant traits are more frequent in females than in males. For rare traits, most affected females in pedigree would be heterozygous.

4. An example of an autosomal dominant trail is *Huntingtion's chorea*, a disease that results in involuntary movements, progressive central nervous system degeneration, and eventually death. The mean age of onset of this genetic trait is between 40 and 45 years, but the disease may appear early in life and sometimes after 60. The American folk singe Woody Guthrie was affected by this disease.

The characteristics of an autosomal dominant trait are : (a) every affected person in a pedigree must have at least one affected parent; (b) each generation in a pedigree should have individuals who express the trait; (c) since the X-chromosome is not involved, father-to-son and mother-to-daughter transmission should occur as frequently as father-to-daughter and mother-to-son transmission; and (d) approximately equal numbers of males and females in a pedigree should express the trait.

5. An example of an autosomal recessive trait is *galactosemia*. Galactosemia is a disease where the biochemical defects known. The disease is manifested in gg babies when they are fed mild; they do not grow well and develop permanent brain damage as well as other problems. If they are removed from a milk diet, the children can develop normally. The defect in individuals with galactosemia is a nonfunctional enzyme galactose 1-phosphate uridy transferase (GUT). This enzyme is essential for the conversion of galactose to UDP-glucose. Galactose is produced when

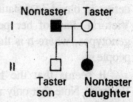

Fig. 7.2. An hypothetical pedigree for the trait PTC nontasting.

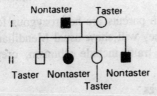

Fig. 7.3. *A second hypothetical pedigree for the PTC nontasting trait.*

the disaccharide lactose in milk is enzymatically cleaved to glucose and galactose. In the absence of the GUT reaction. Galactose 1-phosphate accumulate and this damages cells.

KINDS OF HEREDITARY TRAITS

The hereditary traits can be grouped into six categories on the bases of their visibility or expression. These are :

Dominant Traits

Dominant traits always appear in almost every generation possessing them. Various skin and exoskeletal traits like piebald (white spotted skin); tylosis (thickened skin); ichthyosis (scaly skin); epidermolysis (blistered skin); red, beaded hairs, hypotrichosis (hairlessness) are some of the dominant traits. In the chart these are classified well.

Autosomic Recessive Traits

These are invisible characters characteristic by the irregularity of their appearance in pedigree. These recessive characters when become double (homozygous), only then appear otherwise they may skip one or several generations and appearing when recessive gene becomes

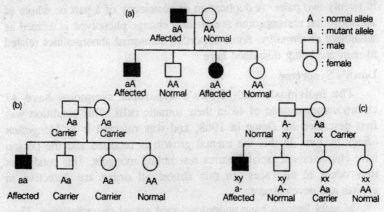

Fig. 7.4. *(a) Autosomal dominant; (b) Autosomal recessive; (c) X-linked.*

homozygous. If both parents are heterozygous for the recessive gene then upon mating they will show usual Mendilian ratio 3 dominant to 1 recessive. These traits include albinism, cretinism, alkaptonuria, etc.

Sex-linked Recessives

These characters pass from generation to generation only through gametes. The colour-blindness, haemophilia and various disease come under this category which have been described in the chapter of sex-lined inheritance.

Physiological Traits

This category includes various excretory trait (lime alkaptonuria) pheny ketonuria) blood groups traits (like erythroblastosis foetalis) and other biochemical disorders.

Mental Traits

These traits affect the development and work of numerous system *feeble mindedness*, *epilepsy*, *idiocy* etc. belong to this category.

Abnormal or Pathological Traits

The pathological traits (concerning itself with the acute diseases) belongs to two categories namely *teratological* in which defects or deformities are due to developmental upset and *nosological* which occurs as diseases of one kind other or the other.

AUTOSOMAL ABNORMALITIES

Autosome are the chromosomes bearing genes for the somatic characters. There are forty-four autosomes in human beings arranged in twenty-two pairs. A duplication or deficiency of a part or whole of an autosomal chromosome results in a change phenotype is termed as *autosomal abnormality*. Some important autosomal abnormalities related to man are being discussed here :

Down's Syndrome

The individuals with Down's syndrome symptoms have 47 chromosomes instead of 46 in their somatic cells. This condition was first described by *Down* in 1968, and was referred it as *Mongolian idiocy* by him, in this the mental growth is retarded and the person have characteristic facial features resembling mongols. This conditions may occur in all races. In this almost all organ are defective in growth and development.

Mongol females have underdeveloped sexual characteristics. They are not sterile. Mongol males have undescended testes and their semen contains a reduced number of sperm count. The life expectancy of mongols is estimated as 18 years by *Collmann* and *Stoller* in 1963.

This syndrome is a congenital originating from the non-disjunction of chromosomes of pair 21 during meiosis. The frequency of production to abnormal eggs per 1500 among mothers under 30, are per 750 at maternal age 30-34, are per 600 at the maternal age of 35-39 and one per 300 among mothers of 40-45.

Patau's Syndrome

Patau et al. (1960) described a trisomy of the chromosome number 13 (D-group) that is why this abnormality is called *Patau's syndrome.* It is characterized by multiple and sense body malformation as well as profound mental deficiency. Hare lip and cleft palate is very common among the suffers. Polydactyly is most conspicuous. The internal organs are severally malformed and the patients often suffer from disorders of kidney and heart. Death usually occurs soon after birth. About one out of 1000 newly born babies exhibit trisomy.

Edward's Syndrome

The syndrome was first described by *Edward* et al. in 1960. It is associated with the trisomy of chromosome number 18 (E. group). This produces receding clin, malformed ears and defective nervous system. The hands are short and show little development of second phalanx. The life expectancy is very poor not mor than a year or so.

CRI-D4-CHAT or Cat Cry Syndrome

This syndrome was first described by *Lejeune* et al. in 1963. This syndrome is due to deletian in chromosome number 5. The most prominent symptom is a curious, faint, mewing cry. The babies have small average birth weight and suffer from considerable mental defect. Cardiovascular anomalies are common. The condition is quite compatible with survival.

Sex Chromosomal Abnormalities in Man

An increase or decrease in number of sex chromosome in the normal complement of female (XX) and male (XY) result in syndrome of sex chromiosome in human beings. The common sex linked chromosomal abnormalities are:

(i) Kleinfelter's syndrome

(ii) Turner's syndrome

(iii) XXX Syndrome or Super female.

These syndromes have already been discussed under separate head— the non-disjunction given elsewhere in the book.

S.No.	Character Dominant	Recessive

A. Autosomal Dominant Trains

S.No.	Character Dominant	Recessive
1.	Brachydactyl	Normal
2.	Syndactyly	Normal
3.	Polydactyly	Normal (5)
4.	Ectodactyly (abortive fingers)	Normal
5.	Cartilaginous growth of bones	Normal
6.	Curly hair	Straight hair
7.	Hairlessness	Normal hair
8.	White forelock	Normal black hair
9.	Ichthyosis (scaly skin)	Normal skin
10.	Dark skin colour	Whit skin colour
11.	Absence of enamel of teeth	Normal teeth
12.	Progressive muscular atrophy	Normal
13.	Hare lip and clefted plate	Normal
14.	Congenital catract	Normal Eye
15.	Glucoma	Normal Eye
16.	Astigamastism (cornea nor spherical)	Normal Eye
17.	Mongoloid fold of skin around eye	Normal, no fold
18.	Long eye lashes	Short eye lashes
19.	Large eyes	Small eyes
20.	Near sightedness and far sightness	Normal vision
21.	Hypertension (high blood pressure)	Normal
22.	Huntingtion's chorea	Normal
23.	Polycystic kidney	Normal
24.	Hypospadias	Normal

B. Autosomal Recessive Characters

S.No.	Character Dominant	Recessive
25.	Red body hair	Non-red-hair
26.	Blond hair	Dark hair
27.	Absence of sweat gland	Normal
28.	Blue or grey eyes	Normal brown eyes
29.	Microphthalmus	Normal
30.	Attached ear lobes	Normal free ear lobes
31.	Sickle cell anemia	Normal
32.	Phenylketonuria	Normal
33.	Schizophrenia	Normal
34.	Alkeptonuria	Normal
35.	Xeroderma pigmentosum	Normal
36.	Retinal glaucoma	Normal

| 37. | Microcephali | Normal |

C. Sex-linked Characters (Recessive)

38.	Diabetes mellitus	Normal
39.	Haemophilia	Normal
40.	Colour blindness	Normal Colour vision

D. Sex linked Dominant Character

| 41. | Hypophosphatemic rickets vit-D resistance | Normal |
| 42. | Xg³ blood group (+) | xg³(−) |

E. Characters Controlled by Multiple Alleles and Multiple Factors

43.	A, B, AB and O blood groups (Multiple alleles)
44.	Skin colour (Multiple factor)
45.	Intelligentia
46.	Hepatoglobin (a blood serum protein)

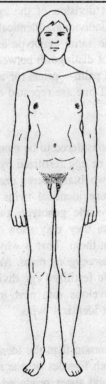

Fig. 7.5. Diagram of an individual with Klinefelter syndrome (XXY).

TWINING

Lower animal usually produce large number of young ones while higher animals show a tendency towards reduction in multiple births. Cats, cattle and dogs etc., vie birth to more than two young ones. This phenomenon of production of many young ones is called *superfetation* while the two young ones produces at a time as called *twins*.

In human being the phenomenon of twins is as it were, a kind of natural experience which permits us to distinguish between the influence of heredity and environment, both of which play essential parts in the lives of all organism.

KINDS OF TWINS

Identical Twins

Such twins are extremely rare. They develop from a single zygote and are also known as *monozygotic* or *one-egg twins*. Each of the two cells resulting from the first division of the zygote, behaves like a zygote and develop into an individual. Identical twins are always of the same sex. They have the same genotype and phenotype and, at times, even the mother cannot distinguish between the two. However, patterns of finger—prints and palm— prints (or sole-prints) that appear on the right hand (or foot) off one are repeated on the left (or foot) of the other and *vice versa*.

Original of identical twins

The identical twins are considered to be *monozygotic* as they have developed from single ovum or egg fertilized by a single sperm. This fertilized egg than divides two blastomeres each of which develops into identical twin. Thus these identical twins originating form the same egg would be of the same genotype and same traits in the beginning. In the later stages they may show variations due to the differences of environment on them. That is why these are also called *monoval twins* (one egg) or *monozygotic twins*. *Newman* and *Patternson* stated that in *Armadio* a single fertilized egg divides in to four or five segments each of which develops into new individual. Thus, this organism develops quadruplet identical twins.

Fraternal Twins

Such twins are more common than the identical twins. Fraternal twins may be both males, both females or one male and one female. They are just like brother and sister produced by the same parents except with the different twins. They show many dissimilarities and are different genotypes.

Origin of fraternal twins

Fraternal twins develops by the chance fertilization of two or by two sperms and are thus also known as *dizygotic* or *two egg twins*. The two eggs develop simultaneously in the uterus and form fraternal twins having similar appearance but differing in various anatomical characteristics.

Siamese Twins

These twins original like identical twins but the separation of the two individuals is incomplete i.e., they remain attached one or more part of the body. They usually do not survive of the birth, though some instances of their survival are well-known. In recent years several cases of successful separation of Siamese twins by surgery, have been recorded.

If the degree of union of twins is symmetrical that is if there is one head and two bodies or two heads and single body resulting in

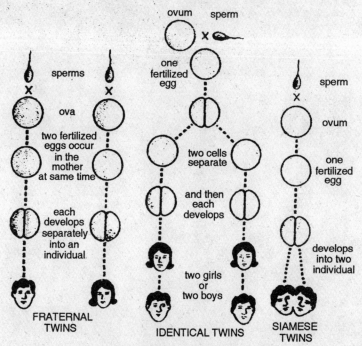

Fig. 7.6. Origin and kinds of human twins.

abnormal traits thus such twins are called *double monster*. They usually do not survive.

Significance of Twins Study

The study of twins give us valuable data regarding the relative importance of heredity and environment. For example, *Muller, Freeman* and *Holzinger* reared apart the identical twins under different environmental and social conditions. They showed that two twins which were originally alike developed different intelligence tests and other traits. It proved that environment plays a dominant role in the heredity of individuals but when environment is similar the twins did not show any major variations. Thus twin studies show if environment is normal, exceptional intelligence is independent largely on exceptional heredity.

8

MOLECULAR GENETICS OF POPULATION

The concept of a population is generally used by demographers simply to denote an assembly of individuals that have a common definition. For instance, the human species can be subdivided into population of cigarette smokers versus non-smokers, a population of cigarette smokers versus non-smokers, a populations of fervors versus man fishers. Each schemed of subdivided could some as a valid cretenion for defining populations in answer to certain types of questions about humans.

Genetics in general concerns the genetic constitution of organisms and the laws governing the transmission of this hereditary information from one generation to the next. Population genetics is that branch of genetics concerned with heredity in groups of individuals, that is, in population. Population geneticists study the genetic constitution of population and how this genetic constitution changes from generation to generation. Hereditary changes through the generations underlie the evolutionary process. Hence population genetics may also be considered as evolutionary genetics. However, these two concepts can be distinguished. It is often understood that population genetics deals with populations of a given species, while evolutionary genetics deals with heredity in any populations, whether of the same or of different species. By these definitions, evolutionary genetics is a broader subject than population genetics—it includes population genetics as one of its parts.

POPULATIONS AND GENE POOLS

The most obvious unit of living matter is the individual organism. In unicellular organisms, each cell is an individual; multicellular organisms consist of many independent cells, many of which die and are replaced by other cells throughout the life of an individual. In evolution, the relevant unit is not the individual but the population. A population is a community of individuals linked by bonds of mating and parenthood; in other words, a population is a community of individuals of the same species. The bonds of parenthood that link members of the same population are always present, but mating is absent in organisms that reproduce asexually. A Mendelian population is a community of interbreeding, sexually reproducing individuals, that is, Mendelian population are those in which reproduction involves mating.

The reason why the individual is not the relevant unit in evolution is that the genotype of an individual remains unchanged throughout of its life; moreover, the individual is ephermeral (even though some organisms, such as confier trees, may live up to several thousand years). A population, on the other hand, has continuity from generation to generation; moreover, the genetic constitution of a population may chance—evolve—over the generations. The continuity of a population through time is provided by the mechanism of biological heredity.

The most inclusive Mendelian population is the species. As a rule, the genetic discontinuities between species are absolute; sexually reproducing organisms of different species are kept from interbreeding by reproductive isolating mechanisms. Species are independent evolutionary units: genetic changes taking place in a local population can be extended to all members of the species, but are not ordinarily transmitted to members of a different species.

The individuals of a species are not usually homogeneously distributed in space; rather, they exist in more or less well-defined clusters, or local populations. A local population is a group of individuals of the same species living together in the same territory. The concept of local population may seem clear, but its application in practice entails difficulties because the boundaries between local populations are often fuzzy. Moreover, the organisms are not homogeneously distributed within a cluster, even when the clusters are quite discrete, as in true of organisms living in lakes or on islands; the lakes or islands may be sharply distinct, but individuals are not evenly distributed within a lake or on an island. Animals often migrate from the local population to another, and the pollen or seeds of plants may also move from population to population, all of which makes local populations far from completely independent of each other.

The concept of a gene pool is useful in the study of evolution. The gene pool is the aggregate of the genotypes of all the individuals in a population. For diploid organisms, the gene pool of a population with N individuals consists of 2N haploid genomes. Each genome consists of all the genetic information received from one parent. Thus, in the gene pool of a population of N individuals, there are 2N genes for each gene locus, and N pairs of a homologous chromosomes. The main exceptions are the sex chromosomes and sex-linked genes that exist in a single dose in heterogametic individuals.

GENETIC VARIATIONS AND EVOLUTION

The existence of genetic variation is a necessary condition for evolution. Assume that at a certain gene locus all individuals of a given population are homozygous for exactly the same character. Evolution cannot take place at the locus, because the allelic frequencies cannot change from generation to generation. Assume now that in a different population there are two alleles at that particular locus. Evolutionary changes can take place in this population: one allele may increase in frequency at the expense of the other allele.

The modern theory of evolution derives from *Charles Darwin* (1809-1882) and his classic, On the origin of Species, published in 1859. The occurrence of hereditary variation in natural populations was the starting point of Darwin's argument for evolution by a process of natural selection. Darwin argued that some natural hereditary variations may be more advantageous than others for the survival and reproduction of their carriers. Organisms having advantageous variations are more likely to survive and reproduce than organisms lacking them. As a consequence, useful variations will become more prevalent through the generations, while harmful or less useful ones will be eliminated. This is the process of natural selection, which plays a leading role in evolution.

A direct correlation between the amount of genetic variation in a population and the rate of evolutionary change by natural selection was demonstrated mathematically with respect of fitness by Sir Ronalad A. Fisher in his Fundamental Theorem of Natural Selection (1930): The rate of increase in fitness of a population at any time is equal to its genetic variance in fitness at that time. (Fitness, in the technical sense used in the theorem, is a measure of relative reproductive rate).

The Fundamental Theorem applies strictly to allelic variation at a single gene locus, and only under particular environmental conditions. But the correlation between genetic variation and the opportunity for evolution is inturitively obvious. The greater the number of variable loci and the more alleles thre are at each variable locus, the greater the possibility for the change in the frequency of some alleles at the expense of othrs. The requires, of course, that there be selection favouring the changes of some trait(s) and that the variation be relevant for the traits(s) being selected.

TWO MODELS OF POPULATION STRUCTURE

Two confliciting hypotheses were advanced during the 1940s and 1950s concerning the genetic structure of population. The classical model argures that there is many little genetic variations; the balance model, that there is a great deal.

Classical Model

According to the classical model, the gene pool of a population consists, at the great majority of loci, of a wild-type allele with a frequcncy very close to 1, plus a few deleterious alleles arisen by mutation but kept at very low frequency by natural selection. A typical individual would be homozygous for the wild-type allele at nearly every locus, but a few loci it would be heterozygous for the wild allele and a mutant. The "normal", ideal genotype would be an individual homozygous for the wild-type allele at every locus. Evolution would occur because occasionaly a beneficial alleles arises by mutations. The beneficial mutant would gradually increase in frequency by natural selection and become of the new wild-type allele, with the former wild-type allele being eliminated or reduced to a very low frequency.

Balance Model

According to the balance modek, there is often no single wild-type allele. Rather, at many—perhaps most—loci, the gene pool consists of an array of alleles with various frequencies. Hence individuals are heterozygous at a large proportion of these loci. There is no single "normal" or ideal genotype; instead, populations consist of arrays of genotypes that differ from one another at many loci but are satisfactorily adapted to most environments encountered by the populations.

The balance model sees evolution as a process of gradual change in the frequencies and kinds of alleles at many loci. Alleles do not act in isolation; rather, the fitness conferred by one allele depends on which other alleles eixist in the genotype. The set of alleles present at any one locus is coadapted with the sets of allels at other loci; hence alllic changes at one locus are accompanied by allelic changes at other loci. However, like the classicla model, the balance model accepts that many mutants are unconditionally harmful to their carriers; these deleterious allles are aliminated or kept at low frequencies by natural selection, but play only a secondary, negative role in evolution.

The Hard-Weinberg Law

It is indeed rare in any science for the fundamental model which it is based to be the first to be developed. But such is the case with the dormulations set forth independently in 1908 by *Hardy* and by *Weinberg*. They were faced with the question of how particulate Mendelian inheritance alone, in the absence of allother forces except segregation, could maintain genetic variability at a locus. At that time, the competing hypothesis to particulate inheritance was that an offspring was a blend of the mother's and father's genetic constitution. This blending hypothesis was alternative to the Mendelian particulate hypothesis that had been recently rediscovered (in 1900). The observations of certain experimental mating that supported particulate inheritance suggested that one half of the genetic variability would be lost in each generation. Such an outcome was also predicted by the blending theory. For example, the cross Aa X Aa on the average yields one half homozygous progeny. This homozygosity was thought to cause a "decay" in the ability of the progeny to generate genetic variability through segregation in the next generation. The key fallacy of this argument, which was exposed in the model developed by these two men, was that the Mendelian population is a mixture of mating types, so that the matings that contribute to a loss of heterozygosity are compensated for by other matings that generate heterizygotes. *Hardy* and *Weinberg* realized that when all possible mating types involved in the producton of the population were considered, the overall ability of the population to maintain segregating alleles (genetic variability) would not "decay" in each generation, as predicted by the blending theory. The *H.W. law* simply states that the genotype frequencies in the parental generation. The law assumes random mating of parents and Mendelian segregation involved in reproduction is very large. If p is the frequency of one allele (A) and q = (1 - p) is the frequency of a second allele (a) in the parental generation, the H-@ laws states that the genotype frequencies expected in the offspring are given by the binomial expansion $(p + q)2$. The result is

relative frequency of AA $= p^2$
relative frequency of Aa $= 2pq$
relative frequency of aa $= q^2$

By defintion, p2 + 2q + q2 equals one. If the H-W laws is an appropriate model for the locus in the population, the progeny will always have H-W equilibrium frequencies. The law assumes a static equilibrium. It must be emphasized that factors that could lead to a change in allele or genotype frequencies throughout the life cycle are not represented in the H-W law.

For convenience, we will use, S, Y and Z as the observed frequencies of the genotypes AA, Aa, and aa, respectively. A population is said to be in H-W equilibrium if these observed frequencies are equal to the expected H-W frequencies of p2, 2pq and q2, respectively. In the interpretation of genotype frequencies, it is important to realize that the H-W equilibrium will result if the H-W law is valid model for the population. But the observation of H-W equilibrium frequencies in a particular population does not prove that the H-W law is the only possible explanation for the reproduction of the population. For example, balancing forces throughout the cycle of reproduction could lead to H-W equilibrium frequencies resulting from a dynamic equilibrium, whereas the H-W law assumes a static equilibrium. In practice, the H-W equilibrium property is used to relate genotype frequencies at some point in the life cycle of a population to alleles frequencies at that point. We will next consider the derivation of the static. H-W equilibrium caused by the operation of the H-W law.

For convenience, we will use S, Y and Z as the observed frequenceis of the genotypes AA, Aa, and aa, respecpctively. A population is said to be in H-W equilibrium if these observed frequencies are equal to the expeced H-W frequencies of p^2, $2pq$ and q^2, respecrivcely. In the iñterpretation of genotype frequencies, it is important to realize that the H-W equilibrium will result if the H-W law is valid model for the population. But the observation of H-W equilibrium frequencies in a particular population does not prove that the H-W law is the only possible explanation for the reproduction of the population. For example, balancing forces throughout the cycle of reproduction could lead to H-W equilibrium frequencies resulting from a dynamic equilibrium, whereas the H-W law assumes a static equilibrium. In practice, the H-W equilibrium property is used to relate genotype frequencies at some point in the life cycle of a population to allele frequencies at that point. We will next consider the derivation of the static H-W equilibrium caused by the operation of the H-W law.

Consequences of the Hardy-Weinberg Equilibrium

A population that reproduces by random mating, in which no forces are disturbing the allele or genotype frequencies during the life cycle, has a number of properties that are consequence of the H-W equliibrium. If we can assume that the H-W law is an adequate description of genetic variation, the properties of the H-W equilibrium can also be used to understand allele and genotype frequencies in that population. Before considering the mathematics of how populations might deviate from the H-W equlibrium, we will review the consequences and uses that can be expected for the H-W equilibrium, as we have defined it here.

Prediction of Allele and Genotype Frequencies

The key consequence of the H-W law is the fixed relationship between allele frequencies and genotype frequencies for the autosomal loci that define the gene pool of a population in H-W equilibriu; that is,

$$p^2 = X (AA)$$
$$2pq = Y (aa)$$
$$q^2 = Z (aa$$

By knowing the allele frequencies we can determine the genotype frequencies, we can determine the allele frequencies in the population. Thus fundamental binomial property of the frequencies of alleles and genotypes in diploid species may also be used to related the allele frequencies in one generation to the genotype frequencies in the next generation.

Conservation of Genetic Variability

The static H-W equilibrium will continue indefinitely as long as there are no disturbing influences that alter random mating and as long as the normal Mendelian segregation ratios occur in the offspring of all mating types. Consequently, any genetic variability that exists in the population will be maintained as long as the H-W equilibrium persists.

Restoration of H-W Equilibrium

If the allele frequency is disturbed at any point in the life cycle by the intervention of mutation, d,rift, selection, or migration, the parental genotype frequenices may not be in H-W equilibrium. But the genotype frequencies in the next generation of parents will return to the H-W equilibrium values after just one generation of random mating if the disturbing forces have been removed from influencing the population.

Dynamic H-W Equilibrium

When there is a static equilibrium, both the allele and genotype frequencies are predicted by the H-W law. When the allele frequencies are disturbed, the population does not return to the former equilibrium, but seeks a new equilibrium in one generation. But an alternative kind of equilibrium may be more typical in natural populations, in which the allele frequencies remain stable from one generation to next even though the genotype frequenies are disturbed during the life cycle. Most natural populations are likely to experience this kind of dynamic equilibrium because a balance of the forces of mutation, genetic drift, selection, and migration is usualy operating in a real population. An idealized population in which these factors do not play a role in reproduction rarely, if ever, exists in nature. Consequently, the consideration of the dynamic equilibrium is important. We will discuss the dynamic equilibrium in more detail later in chapter, when we consider deviations from the H-W law.

Prediction of Heterozygote Frequencies

The assumption that a staic H-W equilibrium holds a population allows us to make a number of inferences about genotype frequencies from allele frequencies. Figure shows a plot of genotype frequencies against allele frequencies for a locus with two alleles. We may note two properties of genotype frequencies as a function of allele frequencies. First, those populations with an H-W equilibrium allele frequency near 0.5 will have higher frequencies of heterozygotes than those populations with allele frequencies of ehterozygotes than those populations with allele frequencies nearere zero or one. Maximum hetrozygosity is achieved when $p = q = 2pq = 0.5$. as the allele frequency moves away from 0.5, the frequencies of the homozygotes increase. If a population is at an H-W equilibrium near zero or one, we know that it has fewer heterozygotes and less genetic variability than a population with an equilibrium frequency near 0.5. In the range of p from 0.33 to 0.66, heterozygotes will have a higher frequency than eithr type of homologote, but when p is less than 0.33 or greater than 0.66, one or the other of the homozygote genotypes will have a higher frequency than heterozyotes.

A second consequenes of the differences in allele frequency between populations is also illustrated. We note that as the recessive allele becomes rarer, an increasing proportion of the recessive allele is carried by heterozygotes (Aa) as opposed to recessive homozygotes (aa). This property helps to explain the persistence of recessively inherited diseases in a population. The consequences of this relationship between allele frequencies and genotype frequencies for removing the recessive allele by section will be discussed in the final section of this chapter. We will then demonstrate what is intuitively apparent from namely, that it becomes increasing difficult to remove a recessive allele from the populations as its frequency approaches zero, because it is being carried more frequency by heterozygotes, who arenot affected by the selective forces that operate on the recessive homozygotes.

USES OF HARDY—WEINBERG EQUILIBRIUM

Testing the H-W Equilibrium

Deviations of the observed genotype frequencies from the expected frequencies predicted by the H-W law are a measure of the failure of a population to reproduce without the influence of mutation, drift, selection, or migration rejection of the H-W equilibrium for a population is the first step in estabishing the presence of forces that are altering allele frequencies from generation to generation.

Prediction of Genotypes for Genetic Counseling

Knowing that the H-W equilibrium is true allows us to compute the probability of a particular genotype's occurring in an unstudied individual. If the individual is known to be a carrier of a deleterious recessive allele, it is possible to use the H-W law to compute the probability that such a person will marry another carrier. If the frequency of the deleterious allele is less than 0.33, we know that it is more likely that the known carrier will marry an individual who is homozygous for the normal allele. The probability that the mate is a carrier ($2pq$) will decrease as the frequency of the deleterious allele approahes zero.

Mathematics of Allele Frequency Changes Owing to Deviations from the hardy-Weinberg Law

Biological evolution depends on the diffrences in allele frequencies that occur (1) among the breeding units of a species that are isolated in space and (2) over the generations within a unit. The Hardy-Weinberg law describes an ideal population of infinite size in which the allele frequency is constant over time. Under these steady-state conditions, evolution could not proceed. In virtually all species, however, the allele frequency is not constant from genertion to genertion and from one population to the next. Biological evolution is measured in terms for the change in the hereditary compositon of population over time. Genetic change within population (called *anagenesis*) or between populations (called *cladogenesis*) over time is a direct outcome of the deviations of a population from the static expectation of the H-W equilibrium. Differential adaptatoin of groups of organisms to new environments cannot take place unless the allele frequencies change. Each of the disturbing forces may operate to influence the allele and genotype frequencies for a given locus in a way that is not predicted by the H-W law, to produce patterns or distributions of allele frequencies in time within populations and in space among populations of a species. Consequently, for most loci the the H-W law alone is an inadequate mathematical model for predicting the behaviour of the allele frequencies of a population from generation to generation.

SOURCES OF GENETIC VARIATIONS AND THEIR IMPACT

Genetic variation is fundamental to the survival of a species. Without inherited variation there is not potential for adaptation to a new of changing environments. The evolution of a species depends on the presence of inherited allelic variations that will be adaptive, will result in a higher reproductive fitness, and will subsequenlty replace the less fit alleles.

As evolution proceeds, the forces of selection tend to reduce the amount of genetic variability. Yet continued evolution depends on a supply of new genetic types. Without a constant renewal of genetic variation, evolution would ultimately grind to a halt, and the species would be at risk for extinction because it could not adapt. It should come as no surprise that the successful populations are those that have an ample storehouse of heritable variations from which to draw as the environment changes.

There are these fundamental sources of genetic variations that are available to a population. They are mutation, recombination, and migration into the population from another population of the species. Because recombination and migration are simply a reorganization of the genotype and a movement of variants, respectively, the ultimate source of all heretible variability is mutation.

Mutation

Although it is the ultimate source of variation, mutation is not strong force in changing the gene pool. A mutation rate of a wild type allele to a mutant from an order of 10^{-5} to 10^{-7} pet generation would require hundreds of thousands of generations for the mutant to replace the wild type.

Migration

Mutations in each generation result in changes in a small fraction of the genetic material of a population. Another source of variation is migraton into the population of an individual who carries an inherited form a gene, chromosome, or genome that is not already present. This process introduces, rather than creates, a new variation in the population. The initial success of this new variation depends on the success of the individual to interbreed with members of the population. A migrant who enters a population but does not contribute to the gene pool of that population would be ineffective in introducing new genetic variants. The contribution of migration to the introductoin of new alleles into a population may vary from about the mutation rate to a substantial contribution, depending on the degree of isolation from other populations.

Selection

The term *selection* is used to include all of the effects occurring during the life cycle that contribute to differential survival of an allele in the reproduction of the population. Selection may occur as differential survival of different alleles during gametogenesis or of genotypes during embryogenesis and development. It may also occur as differential fecundity (capability to reproduce) of genotypes during the reproductive span of the organism. The sum of all the selective differences among alleles during the reproduction of the population is the fitness value of an allele. The fitness value summarizes the differential contribution of each allele in the parental gene pool to the gene pool of the next generation.

One of the most convincing examples of the power of selection to change the genetic make up of a population was established by Kettlewell. He investigated the phenomenon of industrial melanism in the English peppered moth, Biston betularia. All samples of this species collected before the mild-1800s were grayish-white with black spotting. These moths typically perch for long periods on light-grayish lichen-covered bark that closely resembles their own colouration. But in some populations of moths vary a different, totally black from occurs that was first identified in Manchester, England, about 1850. Studies have established that the difference in colouration between the two forms is controlled by a single locus with two alleles. The allele that determines the black (or melanic form is dominant to the allele that determines the typical grayish colouration that resembles the lichen-covered bark. It was found that in the smoke-polluted woods around certain English factoreis, the lichen was absent and the trees had become darkened by soot. In this environment, the dark melanic form was considerably more prevalent than the lighter form. The two types of moths. The moths with the typical lighter colouration were found to be most prevalent in the unpolluted countryside, where lichen covered bark was common. But in the wodded areas where the liches were killed by the industrial soot, the black form was found in highest frequency. Further investigation showed that the selection pressure in this case was prediation by birds. Birds that feed on the moth use vision to locate their prey. As a consequence, melanic forms have a higher survial rate in the industralized environments and a lower survival rate in the nonpolluted areas where lichens create a lighter background. It was hypothesized from this work that it took less than 40 years for the moth do adapt genetically to the industrial revolution by developing the dark colouration.

Genetic drift

The theoretical population consideral at the outset of this chapter to be in Hardy -Weinberg equilibrium was of infinite size. Even though natural population are smaller than that, many of them are large enough for random mating to occur in effect, and genetic equilibrium is maintained through the generations. On the other hand, if the sample of alleles contributing to the zygotes for the next generation is not representative of the overall allelic composition of the population's gene pool, deviations from genetic equilibrium can occur. This will be observed either as chance variatons of allele frequencies in the population or possibly as chance fixation of an allele (i.e. P or q = 1) in the population. Such a random change in allele frequencies is called genetic drift. The effect of genetic drift is very small in large population but can be large in a small population. Fixation of one allele or the other becomes more likely the smaller the population is.

In natural population, the risk of loss of an allele from a population as a result of genetic drift is very high for alleles that are present at very low frequencies. This result is fixation of the frequent allele. Clearly, if the rare allele is lost in the sampling cprocess in one generation, it cannot be replaced by a compensating variation of sampling in another generation. Instead, it can only be replaced by mutation. When the occurs, the new allele is again very rare in the population and is again subject to loss through genetic drift. Those alleles that remain in the population may spread through a population as a result of genetic drift, regardless of their selective advantage or disadvangate. Further, in small populations, genetic drift, will action all loci represented by two or more alleles, but the direction and magnitude of the effect is likely to be different at each locus.

There can be other effects of population size on allele frequencies. For example, in human populations, rare alleles are often found in particular areas at relatively high frequencies. The reason for this is that small isolates (self-contained breeding units) within a larger population are particularly susceptible genetic derift. A good illustration of this is found in the Dunkerys' population of eastern Pennsylvania, USA. The Dunkers are a small religious sect who are descended from 28 West German immigrants who arrived in the United States over 250 years ago. The current population consists of about 300 individuals, of whom about 90 are parents in each generation. This is undoubtedly a very small breeding population and one which is isolated from other populations because of their religious beliefs. From studies of a variety of genetic traits, it has been concluded that the frequencies of some genes are very different in the Dunker population compared with either the United States or West German population. This illustrates what is called the isolate effect or founder effect; that is, the present allele frequencies reflect a chance sampling of alleles in the original immigrants and pairing occurring inly within the population.

Conclusion

We have seen in this chapter a little of how genes in populations are distributed and the effects of various factors, such as mutation, selection, and migration, on the gene pool of a population. All fo the genes of an organism, in association with the environment, are responsible for the phenotype of that organism. Therefore, as the environment changes, different combinations of gene frequencies in the population will result over many generations by the forces described. This is the process of evolution, at least in simple terms. However, evolution is an extremely complex process in which numerous factors are intertwined, and a lot remains to be learned about it. This chapter has presented a simplified view of the genetics of population and it is hoped that the reader will extrapolate the basic concepts that have been discussed to natural populations and to the evolutionary process.

9

IMPROVEMENT OF HUMAN RACE

The science of eugenics was founded in 1883 by *Sir Francis Galton*, a cousin of *Charles Darwin*. The idea itself is very ancient and can be found in the works of *Plato* and the sages of antiquity. It as much as many diseases, defects, and abnormalities are hereditary and some are regularly transmitted by parents to children, it was not unreasonable to propose that children unfit for life should not be brought into the world. This, of course, amounts to preventing persons who are seriously defective from reproducing.

Legislation to sterilize such persons exists in many countries in the United States the first law of this kind was adopted in 1907 by the State of Indiana. By 1940 similar laws existed in thirty states, being more strict in some than in others. In all thirty states mental deficiency is subject to sterilization; in twenty-nine mental diseases are liable to the same treatment. In twenty-three states there are laws controlling epilepsy. In other states sterilization can be applied in certain cases of physical malformation and nervous diseases. From 1907 to 1950 more than 50,000 such operations were performed, two fifths of the sterilized being men. It is still difficult to weigh the results of these eugenic experiments which have not in all cases been based on sufficiently solid genetic and medical grounds. Similar legislation has been proposed in certain provinces of Canada, in Tasmania, and in New Zealand.

In Europe sterilization laws were first introduced in 1929 in the Swiss canton of Vaud, and in the same year in Denmark, Norway, Sweden, Finland, and Iceland. In Germany and in Estonia the law, after being blindly applied, has been repealed. Laws have been proposed, without being passed, in England, Holland, Hungary, Czechoslovakia and Poland. At the moment such laws are retained only in the Scandinavian countries and in some Swiss cantons.

The Scandinavian laws provide that the patient himself can ask to be sterilized and that he operation cannot be performed without his freely given consent. During the period 1929–1950 more than 6,000 operations took place in Denmark, two-thirds of those sterilized suffering from mental deficiency, and two-thirds of these being women. In Sweden, for the period 1935–1948, some 15,650 people were sterilized, women again outnumbering men. The number of those sterilized continues to rise and Professor *Kemp* estimates that in Denmark today there are 600 operations a year, distributed equally between the mentally deficient and those suffering from other afflictions. At this rate an increasingly rapid elimination of mental deficiency may be anticipated. Denmark not only has laws providing for sterilization but also others covering legal abortion, the prevention of certain marriages, and eugenic measures such as isolation, the obligatory declaration of disease etc.

Of course, these various measures encounter moral, social, and religious opposition, and the question arises whether their efficacy is genuine. The answer will vary according to the way in which the gene responsible for the affliction is transmitted.

Eugenics can be studied under two heads:

(i) Negative eugenics.

(ii) Positive eugenics.

NEGATIVE ENGINES

In this the defective germ plasm is not allowed to mix. This restriction can be brought about in the following ways:

By Controlling Immigrations

Most of the advanced nations are very selective in permitting foreigners to enter their lands and mingle with their populations. They believe in encouraging only the *cream* of other nations, i.e. people with high intellect. This is an attempt to shut out germplasm which may be undesirable.

It is compulsory to get vaccinated and injected as an immunity measure, against certain contagious and epidemic diseases before travelling to a foreign country.

But these measures are not sufficient to check undesirable germplasm because a person may have high intellect and may possess sound health but in his genome he may be carrying an undetected recessive gene which when homozygous may be fatal.

Marriage Restrictions

Every country or society has the customs or laws which tend to restrict marriages. According to biological aspects marriage is an experiment in breeding, not human courtship as described by various novels. In several countries the marriages of mental defectives, habitual drunkards, idiots, feeble-minded, insane persons, epileptics, alcoholics and persons having venereal diseases are prohibited. As a result of these regulations the genes necessary for these defective traits do not have chance to mix in the generation. Only marriages between undefective persons should occur. Even the cousin marriages are extremely useful if they are without set-linked diseases.

Sexual Separation of the Defective

The defective persons may have various sex-linked diseases such as night blindness, haemophilia, colour blindness, etc., and various other defective traits which may be regulated by dominant or recessive genes. The increase of germplasm of the persons having such defective traits in the population can be checked by keeping them away and separated from the society. Different states have wisely adopted the restricted measures in segregation the mental defectives from the society and to place them in mental hospitals.

Sterilization

It is a drastic step of restricting defective germplasm from meeting with the other germplasm. By this method, ducts carrying sperms or eggs from gonads are removed surgically thus blocking the way of undesirable germplasm to external world. This is of two types :

Vasectomy

It is minor operation in males in which **vasa** deferentia (sperm ducts) are surgically removed or rendered **ineffective** by some means. In the castration complete testes are removed **thus** putting the sexual life to an end.

Salpingectomy

In this type oviducts are gutted or removed surgically in females and thus avoid the chance of fertilization due to non-availability of ovum.

Thus, these operations fall into two categories namely temporary and permanent. In the temporary sterilization, vasa deferential or fallopian tubes are tied-off with the help of surgical thread in males or females. In the latter method, these ducts are cutted permanently.

Criteria for Negative Eugenics (Genetic Variables)

In practice the effectiveness of marriage restrictions, segregation, control on immigrations and sterilization as eugenics measures depends on several genetic variables like:

(a) The mode in which undesirable trait is inherited;
(b) The rate of frequency of the gene or genes concerned in the populations;
(c) The age at which the defective trait makes its appearance; and
(d) The extent to which environment may check or inhibit the expression of the gene. Regarding the mode of inheritance of these trails the following possibilities may exist; (i) The trait may be due to dominant gene. (ii) It may be due to a gene without dominance (i.e. heterozygote intermediate). (iii) Sex-linked recessive gene may bring about it. (iv) Finally, a trait may be produced as a result of cumulative genes.

POSITIVE EUGENICS

Subsidizing the Fit and Sperm Banks

Because the highly endowed persons lead a well-planed life and to avoid unnecessary difficulties in nursing the children they often prefer to have small number of children. Therefore, the selected young men and women of best eugenic value should be encouraged to increase their birth rate. Moreover, *H.J. Muller* has suggested that such persons not only should increase their family size but through artificial insemination the outstanding man can serve as fathers to many more children than would be otherwise possible. The artificial insemination is already widely practiced to permit those women whose husbands are sterile or have some serious hereditary afflictions to bear children. The sperms and eggs of outstanding persons can be stored for future use by quick freezing and storing them in deep freeze. These germ cells thus can be stored for 100 or more years.

Recently in U.S.A., a "sperm bank" was floated, primarily for collection and preservation of sperms of Nobel Prize laureates and probably other exceptionally gifted intellectuals. Its aim is to produce children of "high mental quality" through artificial insemination. The initial response to the sperm bank was poor but recently *Robert Graham* has claimed that the response is now fairly good. It is also claimed that about 15 children have already been produced with the help of sperms thus acquired. However, it is yet to be seen how far this revolutionary idea succeeds in its aim.

Promotion of Genetic Research

The mechanism of inheritance of many specific traits can be clearly understood provided basic principles of heredity and distribution of genes are known. The physiological action of genes is another problem and with its complete knowledge, many diseases can be cured. The nature of mutation, their effects and possible control may bring about the better offsprings having high learning capacity.

Besides, genetic research on plants and animals is receiving much support from different state government. By this encouragement, good varieties of plants and animals highly beneficial to man have been produced.

Early Marriage of those having Desirable Traits

It is most commonly observed fact that the highly placed persons of the society often have great ambitions for the future life. In achieve their ambitions goals, they often devote the best part of their youth and they are able to marry in their mature egg (i.e., 30 to 35 years). The biological and psychological investigations have revealed that the aged persons often lack in necessary amount of emotional warmth for the sexual activities and moreover, their germplasm also lost its vigour. Therefore, some laws should be formulated to prevent the late marriages of highly endowed persons by applying high taxation on them and at the same time the young persons having best hereditary traits should encouraged for early marriages.

Genetic Counselling

To produce healthy progeny should be the endeavour of man as this alone can ensure a better future for humanity. Genetic counselling can make a significant contribution in this direction. For families with history of genetic diseases, genetic counselling can provide the much needed relief.

By careful examination the genetic counseller can detect genetic abnormalities like *Down's syndrome* and even recessive genes for disease like *sickl-cell anaemia*. Knowledge of the possibilities of transmitting these diseases to offspring can help a person in choosing a marriage partner.

Genetic counselling is equally useful after marriage. An Rh^- woman with an Rh^+ partner, when aware of the implications in advance, can go in for suitable medical aid well in time. The study of the amniotic fluid (obtained by a technique called *amniocentesis* involving withdrawal of the fluid with the help of a hollow needle) can reveal the sex of the foetus as well as *congenital diseases* (like Down's syndrome) and metabolic disorders that it may possess. This information can help the couple to decide whether or not retain the pregnancy, or at least be mentally prepared for the inevitable.

Protection against Mutagens

We now know that mutagens can induce mutations, some of which may be deleterious and even lethal. Harmful mutations can result in deformed offspring and increase human misery. It is, therefore, essential to check exposure of human germ cells to mutagens like high-energy irradiations, chemicals, etc. Medical X-ray should be advised and carried-out with utmost care. Chemical mutagens should be experimented, with, and handled with all possible precautions. The December 3, 1984 gas tragedy in Bhopal (M.P.), India, (leakage of MIC–methyl isocyanate) and the subsequent discovery of "dangerous" experiments carried out in Bhopal should be sufficient to warm world governments of the possible hazards of chemical warfare in which chemical mutagens may be used. These hazards will in no way be less then those of exposure to high-energy irradiations frigerred by atomic bombs.

Improvement of Environment Conditions

Environment plays a dominant role in the heredity of man. Better facilities of training, schooling, living and studying should be given. These all are euthenic programs for the benevolence of human race.

Generally sexual fertility is correlated with intellectuality reaching maximum very rapidly in idiots and stupids while more slowly in intelligent and genius persons. A shown earlier idiots as well genius are homozygous genes responsible for particular traits while average are heterozygous having greater fertility. Their selection may yield good eugenic results.

EUPHENICS

Euphenics deals with the treatment of genetic diseases of man. The credit for the goes to A.C. Pai (1974). More specifically it deals with the control of several inherited human diseases especially in born errors of metabolism in which the missing of defective enzyme has been identified. The excellent example of two category is the *phenylketonuria* or PKU. In the abnormally the patients are unable is metabolize an amino acid–the *phenylalanine* properly, the resulting

186   Molecular Biology of Genetics

product causes severe mental retardation. Such patients are advised to take phenylalanine free diet.

Although a number of inherited diseases can be treated in a similar euphenic manner, but these constitute only a small fraction of known inherited diseases. For the most part, biochemical geneticists could not identified the biochemical errors of many genetic diseases. In other cases, such as *albinism*, even though the metabolic block leading to an abnormality is known, but, it is not possible to correct it.

10

PROKARYOTIC GENE REGULATION

Transcriptional control requires a three-component system : a regulatory gene, a control sequence of DNA (the operator) where the regulatory gene product binds and the regulated structural gene or operon (group of adjacent structural genes governed by the same transcriptional regulatory system). The whole transcriptional control system can be either *negative* or *positive*. The system in which the regulatory gene product binds to inhibit transcription are called *negative transcriptional control* systems. The regulatory gene in a negative transcriptional regulatory system is coding for a repressor protein. The positive transcriptional control system is one in which the regulatory gene codes for an expressor protein, one necessary for the gene to be expressed. There is evidence that a number of operons are controlled by both positive and negative transcriptional control systems. In such cases, the two different regulatory genes produce their repressor and expressor products. There are separate control sequence for each of these products. The genes under such control are expressed only when both systems are "go"—repressor is not bound to its control sequence and expressor is bound to its control sequence.

The simple distinctions that have been given are each further subdivided into inducible and repressible operons within each category. An inducible operon is normally not expressed but can be induced (turned on, make to begin transcription of mRNA) when the right environmental signal is received. A repressible operon is normally expressed but can be repressed (turned off, stopped from transcribing mRNA) when the right environmental signal is received. Repressible operons can sometimes be depressed (expressed more than usual) as well as being repressed. A small molecule usually serves as the environmental signal ; this small molecule is called the *inducer* for inducible operons and the corepressor for repressible operons. The role of the small molecule signal is to bind to the regulatory gene product (the repressor protein or expressor protein), changing the ability of the regulatory protein to bind to its control sequence or operator.

Small molecule signals are almost always input or output compounds from the biochemical reactions catalyzed by the proteins coded by the operon. Occasionally they are compounds belonging to other pathways, for example, pathways whose use is preferred to those of the regulated operon, or compounds whose concentration must be balanced with those in the pathway.

NEGATIVE TRANSCRIPTIONAL CONTROL

The negative transcriptional system is one in which the regulatory gene produces a repressor protein, and the system may be either inducible or repressible. The *E. coli* lactose i (lac i) gene interaction with the lactose (lac) operon is the classic example of a negative inducible system.

Lactose operon of *E. coli*

Function in the wild type

The sugar lactose cannot be used as an energy source of *E. coli* unless it is first broken down into its glucose and galactose components. This reaction is catalyzed by the enzyme β-galactosidase, which has a tetrameric structure of identical 135,000-daltons polypeptides.

In a wild type cell growing in a medium that does not contain lactose, there are only a few molecules of *β-galactosidase*. However, if the cell is growing in a medium containing lactose as the sole carbon and energy source, there are about 3000 copies of the enzyme. In other words, induction of enzyme synthesis occurs as a result of the presence of lactose. Lactose itself is not the actual inducer in this system, but rather induction is brought about by the action of *allolactose* which is produced from lactose by the enzyme activity of the few molecules of β-galactosidase will remain high, but once the lactose runs out the enzyme level will diminish rapidly. This

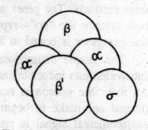

Fig. 10.1. A model for the structure of prokaryotic RNA polymerase showing association of five polypeptides ($\alpha_2\beta\beta'\sigma$).

is not an all-or-none phenomenon; the amount of enzyme produced is directly proportional to the amount of inducer present (up to the maximum amount found in the cell).

The addition of lactose to the cell not only brings about the increase in β-galactosidase levels has but also a rapid increase in the synthesis of *β-galactoside permease* and *thiogalactoside transacetylase*, two enzymes also needed for lactose breakdown. Genetic experiments have shown the genes for all of the three proteins are linked on the chromosome and adjacent to them are two regulatory sites, the operator and the promoter. A short distance away is the *i* gene, which codes for a repressor gene involved in the regulation of the system. As a result of the phenotypic properties of regulatory mutations, *F. Jacob* and *J. Monod* proposed their classical operon model for the control of gene express bacteria, a more up-to-date description of which will be given here. By definition, an operon is a genetic unit consisting of contiguous genes that function coordinately under the joint control of an operator and a repressor.

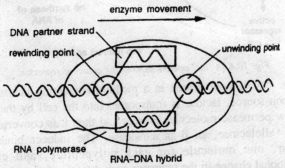

Fig. 10.2. Active centres in bacterial RNA polymerase enzyme.

The z^+, y^+, and a^+ structural genes code for *β-galactosidase*, *permease*, and *transacetylase*, respectively. Genetic experiments with mutant strains lacking enzyme activity showed that the three genes are adjacent on the chromosome. The i^+ gene (repressor gene) codes for a repressor molecule, which is a protein. The expression of this gene is constitutive; that is, the product is synthesized all the time. Control of the amount of gene product, then, is a function of the rate of which RNA polymerase can bind to the i gene promoter (pi^+) and initiate message produces a polypeptide that aggregates to produce the functional repressor tetramer. If the cell is growing on a medium lacking lactose, the repressor will bind to the operator (o^+) region,

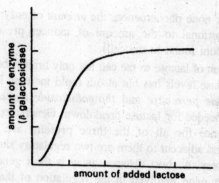

Fig. 10.3. Induction of β galactosidase synthesis by lactose.

which is located adjacent to the z^+ gene. When this complex is formed, RNA polymerase cannot bind to the structural gene promoter (p^+) region, and thus transcription of the gene is prevented.

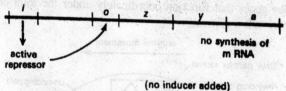

Fig. 10.4. A 'lac' operon showing the action of repressor.

If the cell is now placed in a medium containing lactose as the sole carbon source, lactose is transported into the cell by the activity of the few permease molecules present and then it is converted to the inducer, allolactose, an β-galactosidase. The inducer binds to the repressor, one molecule for each polypeptide, and causes a conformational change in the repressor such that it no longer has affinity for the DNA. As a consequence, the repressor falls of the operator and once that has occurred. RNA polymerase can bind to the structural gene promoter and initiate transcription of the operon. The lactose operon is a single transcriptional unit so that the RNA polymerase transcribe the z, y, and a genes, in that order, into a single polygenic (polycistronic) mRNA. This mRNA is translated by ribosome attaching to the 5' end (z gene end) and moving down the molecule. Thus the β-galactosidase is made fit and, after the stop codon of that region, the ribosome continues moving toward the 3' end of the message. Then after recognizing the initiation sequence for the permease gene, the ribosome begins to translate the part of the message to produce permease. The process is repeated at the boundary between the permease

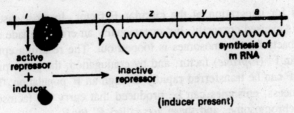

Fig. 10.5. A 'lac' operon showing induction by inducer.

and transacetylase gene sequences. The general principle that pertains here is that ribosomes can only initiate translation at the end of a polycistronic mRNA. (This makes the coordinate production of proteins of related function easy to control.) It is not possible for ribosomes to bind and initiate translation at the start regions of the permease or transacetylase sequences, presumably because the correct initiation sequence only found at the 5' end of the message.

Elucidation of the Regulation of the Lactose Operon by Studies of Mutants

The Jacob-Monod operon model of control of gene expression was based on studies of a number of regulatory mutants in which the control of the expression of the lactose operon was abnormal. An important part of the Jacob and Monod's mutant studies involved partial diploid strains, and the construction of these strains will be described before the properties of the mutants themselves are discussed.

In the discussion of Hfr strains of *E. coli*, it was shown that Hfr strains could revert to the F+ state if there was a reversal of the

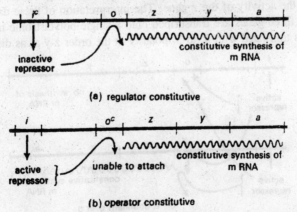

Fig. 10.6. Constitutive strains resulting due to mutations in regulator gene and operator gene.

process for integration of the circular F factor. In most cases the F factor is excised correctly, but occasionally an error is made and part of the bacterial chromosomes is looped out. The resulting episome is called an F' (*F-prime*) factor, and by conjugation, the genes picked up by the F can be transferred rapidly through an F⁻ population. Thus, by this process, episomes can be produced that carry the lactose region of the chromosome, and these are called *F' lac*.

Mutants of the structural genes

Both missense and nonsense mutants have been isolated for the three structural genes. Mapping these mutants provided evidence for the order z-y-a on the chromosome. A missense mutation in one of the genes results in the loss of activity of the enzyme for which the gene codes but does not affect the activities of the other two enzymes in the system.

On the other hand, the *nonsense mutations* have some interesting properties. For example, a nonsense mutation in the z gene (z⁻), providing it is not too near the end of the gene, will not only abolish z gene activity but also reduce or abolish the expression of the y and a genes. This is called *polarity*, or the polar effect, and thus the nonsense mutations are sometimes called *polar mutations*. Indeed there is a gradient of polarity of the effect of chain-terminating mutants in the z gene on the expression of the other two genes. The closer the mutation is to the operator, the more severe the polar effect; that is, the less likely permease and transacetylase will be produced. Polar mutations in the y gene effect the activity of the y gene and a gene but not the activity of the z gene. The interpretation of these data was that the three genes are transcribed onto a single polycistronic mRNA, which is translated with 5'-to-3' polarity in the order z-y-a, as discussed

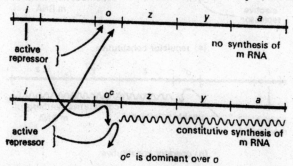

Fig. 10.7. *Check on enzyme synthesis in a partial diploid, heterozygous for regulator gene (I/Iᶜ).*

previously. The polar effect of chain-terminating mutations is the consequence of the distance ribosomes have to travel before recognizing a new translation initiation sequence–the farther it is, the more likely the ribosome will fall off the message.

Operator mutants

A series of mutants were isolated that were constitutive for enzyme production. In other words they had lost regulatory control such that the enzymes were produced whether or not the inducer was present. When the mutations were mapped, it was found that several were clustered next to the z gene in a region that is now called the operator. These so-called operator-constitutive (o^c) mutants have lost the ability to bind the repressor protein such that transcription cannot be prevented. This latter point is supported by genetic and biochemical evidence. We will discuss the former here.

The effect of oc mutations on the contiguous structural genes and on z, y, and a genes located on a different piece of DNA was examined by haploid and partial diploid strains. In these studies, mutant strains were constructed with various combinations of operator and structural gene alleles, and the production of the enzymes was monitored in the absence and presence of the inducer, lactose.

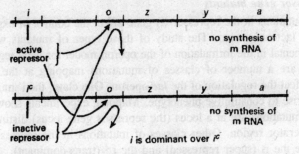

Fig. 10.8. *Constitutive enzyme synthesis in a partial diploid, heterozygous for operator gene (O/O^c).*

Class 1 is the wild type where neither enzyme is produced until lactose is added as the inducer. *Class 2* is a haploid strain carrying on oc mutation that leads to constitutive production of the enzymes. *Class 3* is a partial diploid carrying oc and y$^-$ mutations on one chromosome and the o$^+$ and z$^-$ alleles on the other chromosome. In this case β-galactosidase (z gene product) was produced constitutively, but permease (y gene product) was produced only in the presence of lactose. Class 4 is a similar case, with oc and z$^-$ on one piece of DNA and the o$^+$ and y$^-$ alleles on the other DNA. Here the permease is produced constitutively and the β-galactosidase is inducible. The two latter cases show that the effect of the oc mutation is limited to those genes adjacent to it on the same piece of DNA ; that is, it is a cis-dominant mutation. Using class 3 as an example, z^+ is on the same DNA as oc and hence is transcribed constitutively. The y^- mutation results in a nonfunctional permease. In the strain, the wild type y^+ allele is on the chromosome that also carries the o^+ allele. This DNA, then, is under normal regulatory control, and hence the y^+ is inducible. All of these data are consistent with the thesis that the operator region does not produce a diffusible product. Further, biochemical experiments showed that DNA form o^c strains will not bind the repressor, thus showing that the operator is the site of repressor action. The operator, then, is a controlling region that in the wild type can bind the repressor, which then prevents transcription. In the o^c mutants, the region has been altered (e.g. nucleotide pair change or deletion) so that the required protein—nucleic acid interaction does not occur and transcription cannot be stopped. Finally, since the o^c mutants do not affect the properties of β-galactosidase, it has been concluded that the operator is most probably a region distinct from the z cistron.

Repressor gene mutants

Mutations in the repressor (i) gene affect the control of expression of the lactose operon. The study of these types of mutants was also instrumental in the formulation of the operon model for gene regulation. There are a number of classes of mutations mapping at the i locus that affect the regulation of the *lac* operon. One class, the i^- mutations, gives rise to constitutive phenotype. Mapping experiments showed that these mutations are at a locus (the repressor gene locus) distinct from the operator region. Other classes of mutations in the repressor gene include the is (super repressed) and the i^{-d} (trans-dominant).

Class 1 is the wild type as before and *class 2* shows the constitutive nature of i^- mutations. *Classes 3* and *4* involve partial diploids in which a z^- mutation is on one DNA any a y^- mutation. In both cases normal, inducible production of the enzymes is the case showing that the i^+ is dominant to i^- for genes either on the same or a different DNA. This is called *trans-dominance* and is interpreted to mean that the i^+ gene codes for a diffusible product that acts to prevent transcription in the absence of lactose. This we now know to be the repressor protein that binds to the operator. The i^- mutations produce an inactive repressor that cannot bind to the operator, and this results in constitutive enzyme production in haploid cells. In the i^+/i^- partial diploids, there are enough repressor molecules produced from the i^+ gene to bind to the two operators present and thus normal regulation is in effect.

An i^s mutations results in a complementely negative phenotype with respect to *lac* enzyme production. In partial diploids, i^s is transdominant to the i^+ allele. The interpretation is that i^s mutations result in the production of an altered repressor molecule (a super-repressor), which binds to the operator normally but is not capable of recognizing the inducer molecule, lactose. Hence transcription cannot be initiated since the defective repressors remain stuck on the operators.

The last class of i mutations are the i^{-d} mutations. Like the i^- mutations, these result in constitutive enzyme production in haploids, but unlike the i^- alleles, they are transdominant to the wild-type i^+ allele. These i^{-d} mutants are very rare, and their phenotype is believed to be related to the tetrameric nature of the repressor. That is, the wild type produces a repressor protein of four identical polypeptides. This repressor molecule has only one binding site for the operator. In i^{-d} mutants the subunits appear nor to combine normally so that no operator-specific binding site results. In the i^+/i^{-d} strains there is a mixture of normal and defective repressor subunits and the trans dominant of i^{-d} is thought to be because repressor made from combinations of the two cannot bind to the operator. Only purely wild-type repressors could bind, and statistically, they would be quite rare. With this in mine, the i^- mutations discussed previously must either be nonsense mutations, which produce short polypeptides, or missense mutations, which result in polypeptides that do not participate in tetramer formation.

In summary, the i mutations provide evidence that the i gene produces a diffusible product—the repressor—which prevents transcription of the *lac* operon. The site of action of the repressor is the operator region. Also, the i mutations show that the lactose repressor has three recognition reactions coded into its structure :

1. With the inducer, lactose ; this presumably alters its shape causing it to dissociate from the DNA.
2. With the operator region.
3. With itself in that it acts as a tetramer.

Promoter mutants

These mutants map to the left of the operator region and are characterized by the lack of mRNA production in the presence or absence of lactose. The date show that p^- mutations are cis-dominant to p^+ in that their effect is limited only to the genes on the same piece of DNA. This is shown especially clearly by classes 5 and 6, where inducible enzyme production resulted for the wild-type gene on the p^+ DNA whereas no enzyme was produced from the wild-type structural gene on p^- DNA. Classes 3 and 4 also indicate that the properties of p^- mutations are not affected by oc or i^- constitutive mutants. These facts are interpreted if we assume the p^+ region is the binding site for RNA polymerase. If it is altered so that polymerase cannot bind, no transcription will occur.

The trp regulatory gene and tryptophan operon

The *E. coli* tryptophan operon is controlled negatively by the *trp* regulatory (*trp R*) gene. This regulatory system is negative and repressible. Notice that this operon codes for catalysts of the biosynthesis of tryptophan, a vital amino acid needed to make proteins. We can expect that biosynthesis of tryptophan will usually be needed; only when there is an influx of tryptophan into the bacterial environment will transcription of these genes by superfluous. The transcription is thus usually occurring, but shut off when conditions permit. Making mRNA and proteins requires a lot of energy, so the cell spares itself the synthesis when the enzymes being coded are not needed.

The *trp R* gene is not near the trp operon in *E. coli*. It codes for a repressor protein that will not bind to the *trp* operator (*trop O*) unless the end product, tryptophan, is bound to it. Tryptophan is the corepressor, and serves as a signal for turning off transcription of these genes. This system is clearly beneficial, since the bacteria need not make catalysts for tryptophan biosynthesis if tryptophan is already in excess. Notice that, in this case, unlike the case of the *lac i/lac* operon interaction, the promoter (RNA polymerase site) is between the operator and the structural genes. The promoter is the site adjacent to the site for mRNA initiation, so the *trp O* region is not transcribed into RNA, whereas the *lac O* region is transcribed. The *trp O* and *trp* promoter (*trp P*) regions overlap, like the analogous regions in the *lac* operon, and the repressor function *in vitro* by blocking the access of RNA polymerase to the transcription initiation site, as in the *lac* operon.

A feature of this repressible operon that was unexpected is the attenuator region. The *attenuator* is a region of the mRNA leader near gene E where transcription usually terminates in the absence of regulatory input. This regulatory input probably involves the transfer

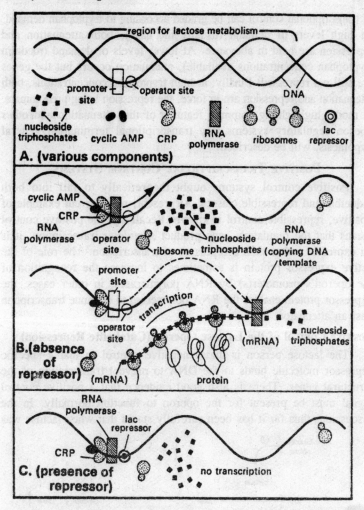

Fig. 10.9. Mechanism involved in the positive control system for the regulation of gene activity in E. coli lac operon.

RNA (tRNA) for tryptophan. If there is insufficient tryptophan to keep the cognate tRNA^{trp} acylated for protein synthesis, the RNA polymerase continues past the attenuator to transcribe the entire *trp* operon. Otherwise, transcription ends in a block of G-C pairs, a block of A-T pairs, and a region of two-fold symmetry (palindrome), having produced 160 base pairs of the *trp* operon leader but no trp structural gene mRNA coding sequences. Thus, even the relatively coarse mechanism of transcriptional control can be graded according to tryptophan demand. At high levels of demand (usually the case), both attenuation and repression are held in abeyance. At lower levels of demand (medium tryptophan concentrations available), attenuation occurs but the genes are still not repressed. Finally, at high tryptophan concentrations, both attenuation and repression are in force, the repression being predominant. A model highlighting common features of this attenuation and other operon regulatory systems, the transcriptional termination general hypothesis, will be described.

POSITIVE TRANSCRIPTIONAL CONTROL SYSTEMS

Positive control systems ought theoretically to fall into both inducible and repressible classes. At present, no clear cut example of positive, repressible control is known. Recall that the positive control means that the regulatory gene product *stimulates* transcription; it is an expressor rather than a repressor of transcription. The role of the active expressor protein is sometimes to increase the recognition of the operon's promoter(s) by RNA polymerases; in other cases, the expressor protein enables the RNA polymerase to continue transcription past an attenuator.

Positive Control of the Lactose Operon (Catabolite Repression)

The lactose person is under negative control in that a specific repressor molecule binds to the DNA to prevent transcription of the structural genes. There is also good evidence that a positive control signal must be present for the operon to function normally. In the discussions thus far it has been carefully stated that when lactose was

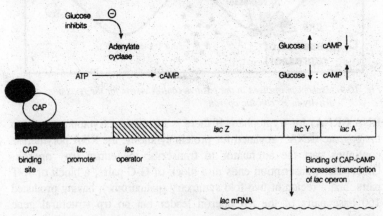

Fig. 10.10. Catabolite repression of lac operon.

present, it was the *sole* carbon and energy source. If both glucose and lactose are present in the growth medium, the cells will preferentially catabolize glucose and the lactose operon in not transcribed. A similar situation applies to a number of other operons involved in the catabolism of other sugars, for example arabinose and galactose. These are called *glucose-sensitive operons*, and the phenomenon is commonly called *catabolite repression* (the *glucose effect*).

The effect of glucose on transcription of the operon in question is the result of the action of a breakdown product of that sugar to lower the intracellular amount of cyclic AMP (cAMP : 3', 5'-cyclic adenosine monophosphate). This molecule is made from ATP in a reaction catalyzed by adenyl cyclase and is broken down with the aid of the enzyme phosphodiesterase. Thus the (unknown) catabolite of glucose could bring about the decrease in cAMP levels either by inhibiting adenyl cyclase or by stimulating phosphodiesterase or perhaps by doing both.

The importance of cAMP to the transcription of the lactose and other glucose-sensitive operons is that a complex of cAMP with a *catabolite gene activator* (GCA) protein (a dimer of molecular weight 44,000) must bind to the promoter before RNA polymerase can bind and initiate transcription. Schematically the events shown are needed for transcription of the operons. If insufficient cAMP is present to make the complex, transcription is blocked at the various operons.

Molecular Details of Lactose Operon Regulation

Information has been obtained about the sequence of nucleotide pairs involved in the promoter and operator regions of the lactose operon.

The actual sequencing involved nucleic acid fingerprinting techniques. The repressor binding site was determined by sequencing the stretch of DNA protected from DNase digestion when the repressor protein is bound to the operator. The exact limits of the cAMP-CGA binding site and RNA polymerase interaction sites are not known, but genetic mutations that affect the level of expression of the lactose operon, and which presumably are in the promoter, show the promoter region to be about 80 nucleotide pairs long. It is noteworthy that the end of the *i* gene is immediately adjacent to the promoter sequence. Comparison of the sequence of the lactose operon mRNA with the DNA sequence shows that transcription begins in the operator region within the region protected by the repressor. This is shown in more detail which also shows the region of the mRNA protected by the ribosome (the ribosome binding site) during the initiation step.

As can be seen, the first 38 bases of the mRNA are not translated, the codon for fmet starting at position 39. The first part of the mRNA is a copy of most of the operator region. The ribosome binding site was determined by sequencing the part of the mRNA remaining after RNase digestion while the ribosome is bound in its initiation configuration. This latter arrangement was achieved in vitro by having only fmet-tRNA in the reaction mixture so initiation but not elongation could occur. The ribosome binding site of the lactose operon covers 50 nucleotides of the mRNA and includes the codons for the first seven amino acids of the β-galactosidase. The boxed nucleotides in the diagram indicate sequences that have also been found in ribosome binding sites of other prokaryotic mRNAs. Specifically there is a nonsense codon (UAA here), a purine-purine-UUU-X-purine (where X is usually a purine), an AGGA sequence, and the start codon AUG.

The ara Gene and the Arabinose Operon

This operon (genes *ara B, A* and *D*) was first described as a simple, positive transcriptional control, regulatory system, inducible by the alternative sugar arabinose. The evidence obtained by *Lee, Englesberg*, and colleagues showed that deletions or nonsense mutations in the regulatory gene, *ara C⁻*, shut off expression in the operon, rather than making it constitutive. Thus, the *ara C* product could be viewed as an expressor rather than a repressor. These are *C⁻* mutations were found to be recessive in merodiploids. This finding makes sense because a mutant expressor protein, which no longer bound the inducer arabinose, would not bind to the operator. Then, the alternative *ara C⁺* expressor could bind to both arabinose and the operator, and its function would dominate the phenotype.

Later, the model was revised in the light of a more complete study of possible mutant phenotypes. The *ara E* gene, not in the operon, was found to be co-regulated with the operon. A class of *ara C* constitutive mutants was also found. By itself, this finding need not have disturbed the model, since the constitutive version of the expressor protein could simply bind to its control regions even when arabinose was lacking. The *ara C^c* mutants should be dominant if so, but the *ara C^c* mutants were recessive to *ara C⁺* in merodiploids. This result was probably found because the *ara C⁺* expressor acted as a repressor when arabinose was absent. When arabinose bound to the repressor, it converted the repressor into a positive control expressor.

COMPLEXITIES OF TRANSCRIPTIONAL REGULATION IN PROKARYOTES

The prokaryotic systems that operate via transcriptional control often utilize different control systems that respond to different signal molecules in the environment. This level of complexity can yield very sophisticated responses in the bacterial cell, as in the case of the catabolite repression system. Nevertheless, there are even more complex transcriptional control systems acting in bacterial. The example presented can be considered a *regulatory cascade*—that is, one regulatory event precipitates a chain reaction on more than one set of genes.

Flagellar Phase Variation

In many species of *Salmonella*, there are two nonallelic structural genes for *flagellin*, the main flagellar protein. These genes are called H1 and H2 (from the German *hauk*). Although both H1 and H2 genes are present in a cell, only one is usually expressed—flagellin in phase 1 is produced from transcription and translation of gene H1, whereas in phase 2, the flagellin is produced by transcription and translation of gene H2. Cells change from phase 1 to phase 2 at a measurable rate on the order of one change per 1000 cells per bacterial generation. The change can be detected using whole cells, by means of antibodies to H1 and H2 flagellin, or the flagella can be isolated and their proteins characterized.

The structure of the regulatory system involved. First, look at the H1 gene regulation. When the *ah* 1 (operator) is open, the mRNA is produced and H1 flagellin is made. The *ah* 1 operator can be turned off or blocked by a repressor coded by the gene *rh* 1 in the operon with the H2 gene. This finding was confirmed by *in vitro* translation of isolated mRNA. The complexity lies in the fact that the repressor of H1 is not regulated by a small molecular signal. Instead, the repressor itself is regulated by transcriptional control. Whenever the repressor is made, it evidently acts as a repressor of H1 without being activated or inactivated by signal molecules. But, when the repressor is made, H2 flagellin is made at the same time, since the H2 gene and the *rh* 1 gene are in the same transcription unit (operon). Thus, the two types of flagellin are alternatives : either one or the other is produced.

The next problem is not the H2, rh 1 operon is regulated. The operator (or perhaps promoter) for this operon is ah 2. The ah 2⁻ mutants lose the ability to make H2 flagellin and also lose the ability to repress H1 flagellin simultaneously. Their phenotype is stable H1;

they are no longer diphasic. The region labelled *vh* 2 is the region
that regulates expression of the H2-rh 1 operon. There is no evidence
that vh 2 codes for a protein. Instead, *vh* 2 may be a sequence that
undergoes spontaneous inversion at the measurable rate. The region *vh*
2 may allow H2-*rh* 1 expression when it is inserted in one direction
but disallow transcription when it is inserted backwards. This idea is
proposed because H2 DNA from a diphasic *Salmonella* stock has been
subjected to molecular cloning attached to 1 phage. The DNA was
denatured and a heteroduplex analysis showed what appeared to be an
inversion loop adjacent to H2 on the molecule. The proportion of
these inversion loops correlated with the ratio of *Salmonella* in the
two different phases. This evidence suggest (but does not prove) that
vh 2 may control the expression of the H2 operon depending on its
own insertion polarity.

TRANSCRIPTIONAL TERMINATION CONTROL VIA mRNA ALTERNATIVE CONFORMATIONS

General Transcriptional Termination Hypothesis

Several bacterial operons are subject to a control mechanism,
transcriptional termination control, that takes advantage of the tight
coupling between transcription of mRNA and its translation into protein.
In these operons, transcription is terminated and the new RNA is
released before the structural genes have been transcribed, unless the
newly formed mRNA assumes a particular conformation which allows
transcription to continue. This permissive conformation is achieved by
interaction with the translation apparatus. Both ribosome binding and
a subnormal level of a particular aminoacyl tRNA are necessary in
order for transcription to continue into the structural genes.

A general hypothesis is to explain this phenomenon has been
presented by *Keller* and *Calvo*. This hypothesis involves two stable
mRNA leader conformations. Figure shows schematically the two
conformations for the leader of the *leucine* (*leu*) operon mRNA. The
first, when transcription continues and the operon is on, involves
translation of a short peptide, called the *leader peptide*, by a ribosome.
When this ribosome arrives at a group of leucine codons, it becomes
arrested due to a limited supply of leucyl tRNA. This arrested state
allows the formation of the mRNA conformation containing the
preemptor helix and loop. This preemptor helix blocks the formation
of the terminator helix that shuts off transcription. The entire operon
is transcribed under these conditions. Notice that the supply of leucyl

tRNA in normal cells is a very good indication of the supply of the end product, leucine, formed by enzymes encoded by the *leu* operon. When leucine is low, the transcription will occur so more leucine can be made.

When leucine is high, the transcription is terminated, since a ribosome will not be frozen at the leucine codons of the leader peptide. The mRNA leader will form the most stable base-paired interactions it can, which are those of terminator and terminator protector helices. These helices will result in the termination of RNA transcription in the leader, without continuation into the *leu* operon structural genes. Since these helices, the termination helix and its protector helix, are the most stable conformation for the leader mRNA, only a block to their formation can allow transcription.

Notice that this mechanism cannot apply to eukaryotes, because transcription and translation in eukaryotes are separated into different cell compartments by the nuclear envelope. It is a major control on pathways for synthesis of the amino acids leucine, threonine, phenylalanine, tryptophan and histidine in bacteria. In mammals, these pathways are not found. In lower eukaryotes such as fungi, these genes are for the most part widely separated in the genome.

Histidine Operon Control

The *histidine* operon of *Salmonella* has long been a regulatory enigma. There is an apparent operator, his *O,* with cis dominant constitutive mutations. Five unlinked genes also can be mutated to cause his operon constitutive expression : *his U* (tRNA^his), *his R* (histidyl tRNA synthestase), *his W, his T,* and *his S* (genes for enzymes which modify bases of tRNA^his). The operon is expressed except in histidine excess, so it was viewed as repressible operon with histidyl tRNA as its small-molecule signal. But where was its repressor or expressor protein? Exhaustive searching did not reveal any additional regulatory genes, though it did reveal that RNA polymerase recognizes the two promoters of this operon better when ppGpp (3'-diphospho- 5'-diphosphoguanosine) is bound to it. This strange nucleotide is known to be high when the general level of amino acids is low, probably being the product of some type of idling reaction at the ribosome.

The transcriptional termination mechanism may be the only control responding specifically to histidine levels in this operon. *Johnston* and collaborators have characterized events at the his O region and found that this region is translated, since it contains nonsense mutants responsive to suppression. The leader peptide contains 16 amino acids,

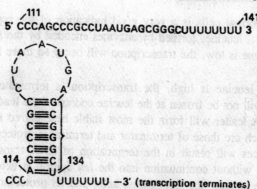

Fig. 10.11. *Termination structure.*

including 7 adjacent histidines. The run of histidine codons in the mRNA is evidently the sensor for histidyl tRNA concentration.

Two conformations, (*a*) and (*c*), for the histidine leader mRNA that lead to termination at the attenuator helix followed by a run of Us. It also shows a conformation, (*b*), leading to continued transcription into the histidine structural genes. The arrest of the ribosome at a histidine codon allows two preemptor helices to form in this case. *Johnston* and coworkers sequenced the operator DNA of a constitutive mutant, his O 1242, and found a deletion preventing the formation of the attenuator helix—thus the termination conformation could not form. They also found *his O* mutations which cause a *his C* phenotype. These resulted from termination in the leader peptide before the ribosome reached the histidine codons. It is possible that additional areas of the histidine leader sequence participate in conformational control, since it is 151 nucleotides long—an unusually lengthy leader even among transcriptional termination—regulated operons. Identified portions of *his O* regions are shown schematically.

Post-translational Control via Noncovalent Binding of Signal Molecules

The two mechanisms by which prokaryotes generally control the activity of a protein after it has been translated from the corresponding mRNA are (1) non-covalent interactions with signal molecules and (2) covalent modification of the protein itself, for example, phosphorylation of one or more amino acids in the backbone of the protein. This section is concerned with the first alternative, non-covalent signal mechanisms.

The noncovalent binding of a molecule to a protein can have an activating effect or an inhibiting effect on the normal action of the

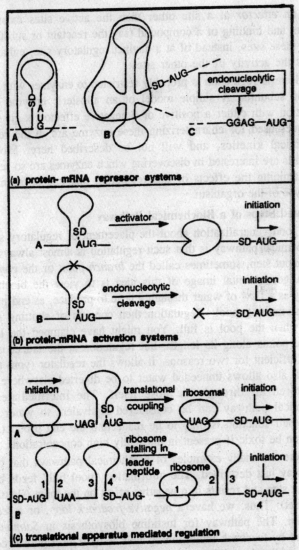

Fig. 10.12. *Some models of translational regulation in prokaryotes.*

protein. If we consider an enzyme, an activator would increase the rate of reaction catalyzed by the enzyme, whereas an inhibitor would decrease the rate. In many cases, these activations and inhibitions operate via allosteric mechanisms. By definition, *allosteric* regulation is an effect on enzymatic rate caused by binding of a small molecule called an *effector* at a site other than the active sites exist in an enzyme, and binding of a compound (say the reactant or substrate) at one of these sites, instead of at a distinct regulatory site, enhances or inhibits the activity of the other sites.

Allosteric regulation is probably restricted to enzymes with several catalytic subunits. A simple model of an allosteric enzyme and its interaction with either a positive or a negative effector is given. The techniques used for characterizing these enzyme are in the realm of biochemical kinetics, and will not be described here. Molecular geneticists are interested in discovering which enzymes are so regulated and examining the effects of this regulation that can be seen in the phenotype of the organism.

Regulated Steps of a Biochemical Pathway

A good generalization about the placement of regulatory steps in a biochemical pathway is that such regulation is almost always found at the input step, sometimes called the *branch point* or the *committed step*. A good mental image of this idea is to view the biochemical pathway as a flow of water through a hose to produce, as end product, a full swimming pool. Regulation then consists of shutting off the faucet when the pool is full. You might have clamped the hose at multiple points along its length, but regulation at the faucet is more energy efficient for two reasons. It allows the regulator (you) to save work. It also allows unneeded water to be diverted elsewhere rather than stored all through the hose itself. The intermediates in a biochemical pathway can be considered equivalent to water in the hose : their function is only to be made into the end product. They may even be toxic if present in unusually high concentrations.

There are many examples of biochemical pathways that operate in the way just described. The information "pool full" feeds back to the input step and results in a negative effect on the input (shutting off the faucet). Thus, we have a *negative feedback loop*, or a *feedback inhibition*. The pathway for histidine biosynthesis in *Salmonella* is regulated by feedback inhibition as well as by transcriptional control. When histidine is made as the end product, it inhibits the first enzyme in the pathway, phosphoribosyl-ATP synthetase, coded for by the *his G* gene. The pathway to the aromatic amino acids (tryptophan, phenylalanine, and tyrosine) is regulated by feedback inhibition as well, but the design of the inhibition varies in different bacteria. The pathway exhibits *sequential feedback inhibition* in *Bacillus subtilis*. The regulation is sequential because phenylalanine, tyrosine, and tryptophan excesses

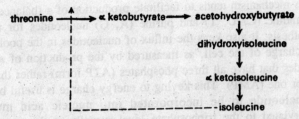

Fig. 10.13. Feedback inhibition in the synthesis of isoleucine in E. coli.

cause buildups of the intermediates chorismate and prephenate. These intermediates in turn inhibit the input step, as well as another step in the pathway.

An alternative regulatory scheme for this pathway, as found in *E. coli*, is an isozymic feedback pattern. There are three isozymes (alternative enzyme catalyzing the same reaction) of the first input enzyme, DAHP synthase. Each of these is feedback inhibited by one of the three major end products. Each end products also shuts off its own input step at or near the branch of the pathway leading to it, via feedback inhibition. There are isozymes of chorismate mutase as well, and the phenylalanine inhibits chorismate mutase P, the isozyme leading towards phenylalanine. In addition, phenylalanine inhibits the next step, prephenate dehydratase, which is in a complex with the chorismate mutase P. Tyrosine inhibits prephenate dehydrogenase; although this enzyme is also complexed with its isozyme of chorismate mutase, the tyrosine does not inhibit the chorismate mutase T activity. Tryptophan inhibits anthranilate synthase, its committed step.

Effects of Noncovalent Interactions with Signal Molecules

One of the most important functions of the signal mechanisms that act after translation is to coordinate the proper allocation of resources within the prokaryotic cell. This coordination results in optimal use of carbon, nitrogen, and energy for the survival of the organism. A mechanism that illustrates the balance of resources is the regulation of the first step in pyrimidine nucleotide biosynthesis, catalyzed by aspartyl transcarbamyolase (ATC). This enzyme is responsible for production of pyrimidine nucleotide precursors from central metabolites and is feedback inhibited by one of the end products, CMP. Even in insufficient amount of CMP, UMP, and TMP are present, the reaction catalyzed by this enzyme will not proceed quickly unless ATP concentration is high. ATP serves as an activator (positive allosteric effector) for the enzyme ATC, whereas CMP serves as an inhibitor negative allosteric effector).

This mechanism tends to facilitate production of a (balanced pool of pyrimidine (C, U, T) and purine (A, G) nucleotides for nucleic acid synthesis. It also keys the influx of nucleotides in the pool to the energy charge of the cell, as measured by the production of adenine nucleotides that have all three phosphates (ATP form) rather than two (ADP) or one (AMP). This keying to energy charge is useful because each nucleotide to be incorporated into nucleic acid must be phosphorylated to the triphosphate level, usually at the expense of ATP.

Another example of metabolic integration via noncovalent signaling can be seen in the inhibition scheme for *E. coli* glutamine synthetase (GS). This enzyme has a three part post-translational regulation scheme. It is stabilized in a more active state by divalent cations, it is inhibited by a variety of compounds, most of which are end products, and it is regulated by covalent modification in response to nitrogen demand. Glutamine produced by GS is a precursor of all the compounds listed below it; one or both of the nitrogens of glutamine are especially important in synthesizing these end products. These six end products serve as separate, independent feedback inhibitor of GS. Their effects are additive; all are required to approach complete inhibition.

Also, glycine and alanine inhibit GS in similar fashion. Although these two amino acids are not made from glutamine, they share the input nitrogen pool with glutamine synthetase, so they are signals relating to the amount of nitrogen already in use by the biosynthetic pathways shown. When the glutamine-dependent and glutamine-independent nitrogen-assimilation pathways all have low levels of products, the GS works fast. Otherwise, the enzyme is slowed by inhibition to an extent. The extent depends on how many important nitrogenous signal compounds are already at high concentrations. Again, a balance (this time between various nitrogen compounds) is achieved by the noncovalent signals. In addition, the GS regulation point switches off nitrogen assimilation, catalyzed by GS and other biosynthetic enzymes, to allow the nitrogen elimination required when nitrogenous compounds are in excess.

The effects of the feedback systems on the phenotype can be summarized by saying that this type of regulation results in vigor by avoiding waste. What is meant can be illustrated by the feedback-resistant type of mutations. In the biosynthesis of histidine in *Salmonella*, for example, the input enzyme, phosphoribosyll ATP synthetase, in feedback inhibited by histidine. Mutants in *his G*, the gene for this input enzyme, sometimes simply abolish the activity of the enzyme.

There is also a class of *his G* mutants that has normal activity for the phosphoribosyl ATP synthetase, but the enzyme is resistant to feedback inhibition by histidine. Such as feedback-resistant mutant wastes energy making excess histidine. One might expect that repression would override this wasted synthesis and turn it off at the transcription level, but in at least one well-characterized feedback-resistant missense mutant of *his G*, repression by histidine also fails to occur. The mechanism of this effect is not yet clarified.

In *Salmonella typhimurium*, the input step for leucine biosynthesis is α-isopropyl malate synthase (IPMS). In wild type cells, this enzyme is strongly inhibited by leucine, which tends to dissociate IPMS into dimers and monomers rather than the uninhibited major form, tetramers. The *Calvos* discovered that a mutant, which can grow in 5, 5, 5,-triluoro-Dl-leucine (unlike wild type), possessed a leucine-feedback-resistant IPMS. This mutant, flr 191, excreted small amounts of leucine. Its growth rate and yield of cells per volume of medium were normal, however. A second flr mutant, flr 19, was resistant to the same leucine analog because of a tenfold increase in the *leu* operon mRNA transcription. This strain also excreted a little leucine but grew normally.

The interesting experiment of the Calvos was to combine these two mutations in the double mutant strains, CV 241. This doubly mutant strain excreted leucine heavily, and, in addition, its yield of cells was reduced by 43%. CV 241 took 84 min for each cell division, whereas the comparable wild type and each of the single flr mutants took only 56 min per division. Clearly, this regulatory failure had serious negative effects on the mutant's ability to survive. We can infer from the two examples described that wasteful production of metabolites, even when they can be deposed of (into the medium), is deleterious to an organism. The system for leucine control is particularly illuminating in that we see how an organism can be protected by having two separate regulatory mechanisms for the same pathway. Redundancy is thus a protective device in some cases.

Post-translational Control via Covalent Modification

The second major protein-level regulatory system in prokaryotes is covalent modification. *Covalent modification* of proteins is catalyzed by specific enzymes. Although the covalent bonds formed are usually more stable than the noncovalent binding discussed in the previous section, these bonds can be broken by specific enzymes, which thus reverse the regulatory effects caused by the modification. Covalent modification is typically used to control bacterium-wide processes responding to environmental signals, rather than to control individual biosynthetic pathways.

Glutamine Synthetase of *E. coli*

Glutamine synthetase (GS) is feedback inhibited by at least eight different nitrogenous compounds. In addition, it is regulated by covalent attachment of adenylates (AMPs) to each of its 12 subunits. The GS is most active when it lacks adenylylation, and when all 12 AMPs are attached (GS) It is slightly active only when MN^{2+} replaces Mg^{2+}. It can still be easily detected because, although GS will not make much glutamine, it still catalyzes a rather rapid glutamyl transferase reaction. The general effect of the covalent modification scheme is that, when there is plenty of α-ketoglutarate and not much glutamine, the enzyme is as GS, unmodified. This form is more active, and furthermore, it resists feedback inhibition by the usual inhibitors except for glycine (not feedback since it is not an end product). When there is little α-ketoglutarate and plenty of glutamine, the GS is adenylylated to form GS. This form of the enzyme is not very active; the more of the 12 subunits that have AMPs attached, the lesser the activity. In addition, this GS is regulated by feedback inhibition, as shown. As you can see, the previous, section contained a description of GS rather than GS, which is not feedback inhibited.

The control of the adenylylation and dedenylylation is rather complex. The same protein, adenylyl transferase (A Tase) adds or removes the AMPs depending on the α-ketoglutarate, ATP, and glutamine concentrations and also on its small regulatory protein, PII. PII also favours the adenylylation or deadenylylation depending on conditions. When α-ketoglutarate and ATP are high but glutamine is low, uridine transferase adds a UMP to PII, another covalent modification, to form PII. PII bound to A Tase favours clipping the AMPs off from GS to regenerate GS. When conditions change, auridylyl-removing enzyme (possibly the same protein as the uridylyl transferase) clips the UMP from the regulatory protein. PII, thus reformed, causes the A Tase to adenylylate GS to for GS.

This covalent modification system is a global system because the influx of nitrogen into metabolism is made to respond to the form in which nitrogen is presented to the cell. Medium with ammonia (NH_3) as nitrogen source results in GS being the predominant form, whereas the slower, more regulated GS predominant when glutamate is the nitrogen source.

Chemotaxis in *E. coli*

E. coli swim by moving their flagella. When the flagella beat counterclockwise (ccw), the bacteria swim smoothly in one direction. When the flagella beat clockwise (cw), the bacteria tumble (change direction drastically). When bacteria are in a homogenous medium, they alternate between cw and ccw beating, generating a pattern of movement called a random walk. *Chemotaxis*, movement in response to a chemical signal, is generated by using more of one or the other direction. For example, a sudden large increase in an attractant chemical or a sudden large decrease in a repellent chemical results in smooth swimming (ccw beat) for several minutes. The response is transient; after a few minutes, the bacteria adapt to the new conditions and return to random walk behaviour. Decrease in attractant or increase in repellent increases cw beat transiently, increasing tumbling for a short period. The combined effect of this system is to bias the random walk so that a bacterium moves toward an attractant and away from a repellent.

The system for chemotaxis consists of flagellar components, signal transduction components, and signal receptor components, all of which are proteins. The genes that are known to code for these proteins. The signal receptors tend to be special transport proteins or permeases for the chemicals eliciting the response. They are often located either in the periplasmic space (between the cell wall and the cell membrane of the bacterium) or in the cell membrane itself. The signal transduction system consists of three known proteins, coded for by the genes *trg*, *tar*, and *tsr* (equal to *che* D). Mutants in these genes swim normally but lose response to certain chemicals. The *trg⁻* mutants, for example, do not respond to ribose or to galactose. The *trg⁺* protein probably is the signal component that interacts with the ribose binding protein coded for by *rbsᴾ* and the galactose binding protein coded by *mglᴮ*.

This concept is supported by the fact that saturation of the ribose receptor will inhibit responses to galactose. The tar⁻ mutants are unable to respond positively to aspartate or maltose or to respond negatively to hydroxyl ion (OH⁻) or divalent metal ions. The tsr⁻ mutants are not attracted by serine or repelled by hydrogen ions (H⁺), fatty acids, indole, or hydrophobic amino acids. Both tar⁺ and tsr⁺ code for membrane proteins of about 60,000 daltons molecular weight. The *fla* I gene mentioned in the transcriptional control section as a positive regulatory gene, controls both tar⁺ and tsr⁺; fla I⁻ strains make neither *tsr* nor *tar* gene product.

Changes in the level of covalent modification in this system serve as a switch. A protein methyl transferase, probably coded for by *che* X, transfers methyl groups from S-adenosyl methionine to the *tar* and *tsr* gene products. The role of the methylation and demethylation of these proteins is to allow stimulus transduction and adaptation. Methionine starvation, which prevents methylation of membrane proteins, prevents tumbling (cw rotation); responses to stimuli that either enhance or decrease tumbling frequency cannot occur under these conditions.

During an increase in attractant, methylation of membrane proteins increases. Methylation is decreased (evidently by demthylation) during increases in repellent. A model of methylation changes during responses to attractant concentration changes. The implication of the data is that changes in methylation state occur during response and during adaptation. For example, that normal behaviour or random walk behaviour is characteristic of cells with three different extents of membrane protein methylation. The current idea about these findings is that it is a change in methylation, rather than the extent of methylation itself, that results in the behavioural switch. Mutants that are *che* X⁻ exhibit only smooth swimming like *met–* strains starved for the S-adenosyl methionine precursor, methionine. In view of model, you might find this phenotype surprising, since smooth swimming is shown as characteristic of methylated proteins.

Again, it is evidently a change-sensing mechanism that results in starting or inhibiting tumbling; without the protein methyl transferase action, the change is not sensed. The smooth swimming may well be the state of lesser interaction between flagellum and switching molecules. The smooth state would then be thought of as a basal or turned off response, whereas tumbling would be the turned on response. Consistent with this hypothesis is the phenotype of *tar*, *tsr* double mutants, which have a very low tumbling frequency. Mutants that tumble constantly also exist; they could be altered in the flagellar signal reception proteins such that their flagellar control stem's shape was like the wild type "on" state. The methylation system may work in response to changes in membrane potential that occur when chemotaxic chemical are added to a responsive bacterial culture. The linkage between the system is not yet clarified, however.

Notice that this system, like the GS regulatory scheme using covalent modification, involves whole-organismic responses rather than control of individual pathways.

11

EUKARYOTIC GENE REGULATION

The regulation of gene expression in prokaryotes has been extensively studied. However, the regulation of genes has also been studied in eukaryotic cells. For many protein-coding genes, transcriptional control is the most frequent level of control and regulation at this level is quite strict. Gene control can also occur at a number of post transcriptional levels. The mechanisms and molecules that are involved in the various types of control are unknown.

Potential Sites for Regulation of Enzyme Synthesis

A number of steps are involved in producing a functional mRNA from a protein-coding gene and then having it translated by the ribosomes. That is, the transcription units for mRNAs are often longer than the mature mRNAs. These long pre-mRNAs are processed in the nucleus to produce the final mRNA product. This includes :

1. The addition of a 5' cap, usually before the rest of the RNA is completed. Essentially all RNA chains initiated by RNA polymerase II become 5' capped, so no control operates at this level.

2. The addition of a poly (A) tail at the 3' end.

3. The removal of specific spacer sequences (*introns*) and rejoining of the remaining RNA pieces (*exons*) to produce the mature mRNA.

RNA TRANSCRIPTION

The first level of control is the choice of RNA polymerases : *RNA polymerase I* transcribes rRNA genes, *RNA polymerase II* transcribes protein-coding genes, and *RNA polymerase III* transcribes

5S rRNA and tRNA genes. This specificity is clearly related to the nucleotide sequence of the promoter to which the appropriate RNA polymerase has affinity. Apart from the strongly conserved regions necessary for the initiation of transcription, other sequences in the vicinity are presumably important in regulating access of RNA polymerases to DNA. These latter sequences undoubtedly control the rate at which transcription initiation occurs and, therefore, the amount of pre-RNA produced.

Thus at least for RNA polymerase II, transcription initiation is believed to be the major controlling step in transcriptional control. However, relatively little is known about transcriptional termination and whether control is exerted at that level. For example, not all RNA polymerase II molecules that start a chain complete it.

RNA Processing

While transcriptional control is the predominant level of control, it is not the only one. Some regulation occurs during RNA processing.

Processing of RNA polymerase II-catalyzed transcripts commences by the addition of the 5' cap and 3' poly (A) tail. No control appears to occur with respect to the addition of the 5' cap. The situation regarding the poly (A) tail is less clear, however. Although the precision of transcription termination sites is not understood for RNA polymerase II transcription, the enzyme transcribes past the site for poly (A) addition in a number of well-studied genes. This means that poly (A) addition may need endonucleolytic cleavage and terminal addition of poly (A) to the cleaved 3' end. Poly (A) addition usually precedes the splicing steps of mRNA processing.

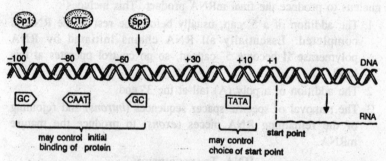

Fig. 11.1. A DNA segment in a eukaryote showing promoter sites and the enhancer site.

Splicing of pre-mRNA to mature mRNA for most transcripts may be an automatic event for some transcription units; however, the primary transcript can give rise to two more mRNAs that encode two or more different proteins. In these cases, differential processing occurs in response to particular regulatory signals.

Another regulatory choice at this level is whether a transcript will processed or discarded in the nucleus. The latter is what is called *nuclear RNA turnover*. For many years it has been known that only a portion of the heterogeneous nuclear RNA is ever processed and found as cytoplasmic mRNA. While all transcripts contain a cap and over 90% of newly capped mRNAs found in polyribosomes contain poly (A), poly (A) is added in the nucleus only to about 25% of all primary transcripts. Presumably the other 75% are discarded with time. What controls these events is unknown.

Cytoplasmic Control

Once the mature mRNA has been produced in the nucleus, at least a proportion of them are transported to the cytoplasm. The mechanism for this is unknown.

Once mRNA have entered the cytoplasm, the fates of the molecules differ. Specifically there is a wide range of half lives for different specific mRNA in the same cells and different half lives for the same mRNA in the same cell under different circumstances. These

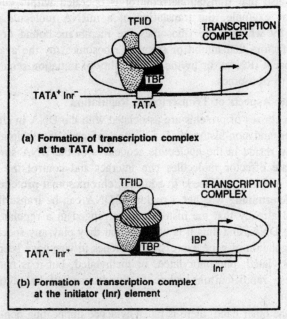

Fig. 11.2. Transcription complexes of TATA box and initiator (Inr) element.

have different consequences to the cell in terms of the relative accumulation of the gene products involved, but the regulatory events operating are here essentially unknown.

Translational Control

There is good evidence, for example, in embryonic development, for differential translation of completed mRNA molecules that are in the cytoplasm. It is also possible that tissue-specific preference for translation of specific mRNAs may occur.

EFFECTOR MOLECULES

Regulation of the transcriptional and post-transcriptional events in the nucleus may be related to the types and concentrations of effector molecules (*e.g.,* inducers, activators, repressors) that are transported into the nucleus from the cytoplasm. Controlling factors that alter the synthesis of these molecules and/or their transport into the nucleus can therefore affect the amount of enzyme ultimately synthesized.

In addition, other subtle control devices may be operating in the cell to regulate the amount of mRNA available for translation, and at present little is known about the regulatory signals for any of this. It is clear also that translational control is operated within eukaryotic cells. For example, the translation of a mRNA molecule may be affected by whether the ribosomes are membrane-bound or not by specific factors that inhibit or simulate ribosomes, by the availability of aminoacyl tRNAs, or by the accessibility of initiation sequences of mRNAs to ribosomes.

Molecular Aspects of Transcription Regulation

Two classes of proteins are associated with the DNA in chromatin : histones and non-histones. The control of gene transcription must ultimately reside in the nucleotide sequences of the DNA so that the appropriate effector molecules can interact and control the amount and type of RNA produced. In addition, chromosomal proteins play a role in determining whether a region of DNA can be transcribed. As discussed already that the histones are arranged in a regular fashion along the DNA, and thus it is unlikely that they play any specific role in the regulation of gene expression. Histones *in vivo* have been shown to be acetylated, phosphorylated, or methylated, but it is not known how these modifications relate to the transcriptional activity of chromatin.

On the other hand, there is much evidence implicating non-histones in the regulation of gene expression in eukaryotes. For example,

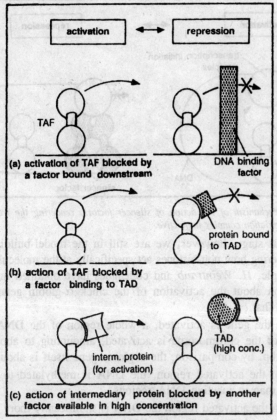

Fig. 11.3. Three ways in which activation (not binding on DNA) by TAF is blocked.

nonhistone proteins have tissue specificity and DNA binding specificity; they are present in higher amounts in transcriptionally active tissues as compared to inactive cell; they are much more diverse than histones; and certain specific classes of nonhistone proteins have, in fact, been linked with the induction of gene activity. In addition, if chromatin from transcriptionally active and inactive tissues is dissociated into DNA, histones, and non-histones, it can be determined by reconstitution experiments which component confers the capacity for transcription. These have shown that the non-histones are indeed the components that determine whether DNA can be transcribed. Thus it is currently believed that nonhistone proteins, presumably in response to specific signals, play a central role in the basic regulation of gene transcription in eukaryotes.

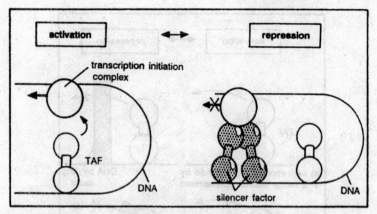

Fig. 11.4. Mechanism of the action of silencer factors, rendering the transcription initiation complex ineffective.

At this stage, however, we are still in the model-building stage for considering how non-histones act specifically at the molecular level. For example, *H. Weintraub* and colleagues have obtained interesting information about the activation of the chick α-globin genes. They concluded that :

1. When the gene is activated, a whole region of the DNA in that area of the chromosome is activated, amounting to about 50 to 100 kbp. by comparison, the α-globin gene itself is about 1 kbp.

2. Within the activated region, the DNA is methylated to a lower level than in inactive DNA regions.

3. Within the activated region the DNA is significantly more sensitive to DNase 1 than is inactive DNA.

4. Within the activated region, specific nonhistone proteins are bound to the chromatin. These are called *high-mobility group (HMG) proteins* because they migrate rapidly in electrophoresis.

In summary, gene activation must involve and unwinding of the highly compact nucleosome secondary and tertiary structure so that RNA polymerase and other regulatory molecules can access the DNA.

REGULATION OF GENE EXPRESSION IN
LOWER EUKARYOTES

The demonstration that gene regulation in prokaryotes often involves operons that are controlled in ways analogous to the lactose operon of *E. coli* prompted researchers to investigate whether operons existed in eukaryotes. Indeed much of the early model building concerning the regulation of enzyme synthesis in eukaryotes was influenced by the regulatory models of enzyme synthesis in bacteria. However, enzyme synthesis is regulated in different ways in eukaryotes.

Eukaryotes have many basic similarities to prokaryotes. For example, the processes of DNA replication, transcription, and translation are more or less the same. However, eukaryotes are vastly more complex, with discrete cellular compartments (nuclei, mitochondria, chloroplasts, etc.) that determine the organization of the process. In this regard the lower eukaryotes, and particularly the fungi, have proved to be useful model systems for the study of gene regulation since they are typically eukaryotic in their cellular structure and genetic organization, yet they are microorganisms that can be handled in ways very similar to bacteria. Further, these organisms are simple and live in environments that are subject to rapid changes. Like bacteria, lower eukaryotes must be able to adapt rapidly at the gene expression level when such changes occur.

Yeast and *Neurospora* will be discussed in this section. These organisms have a genome complexity of approximately ten times that of *E. coli*. Early studies concentrated on determining whether operons exist in these fungi. Since they are highly amenable to genetic and biochemical investigations, it is relatively easy to isolate mutants affecting enzyme function and also the regulation of enzyme synthesis. This of course parallels the approach of *Jacob* and *Monod* in their studies of the regulation of the *E. coli* lactose operon. In general the fungal studies showed that, contrary to the findings in prokaryotes, genes with related function are not closely linked but rather tend to be scattered over the chromosomes in the genome. Nonetheless, it has been shown in both lower and higher eukaryotes that there is coordinate synthesis of all the enzymes in a particular biochemical pathway. This presumably involves a regulatory system different from that of prokaryotes. Characteristically, then, the gene products in eukaryotes consist of monocistronic mRNAs and not polycistronic mRNAs.

In some cases, however, evidence was obtained for apparent clustering of genes in fungi, and this raised the possibility of the existence of operons in eukaryotes. Three representative cases will now be discussed, and while the early information was highly suggestive of an operon organization, all the evidence to date runs counter to that possibility.

Galactose Fermentation Genes of Yeast

The first three enzymes for galactose fermentation in yeast are *galactokinase, α-D-galactose 1-phosphate uridyl transferease* and *uridine diphosphoglucose 4-epimerase.* The genes for these enzymes, as defined by mutants, are GAL_1, GAL_7, and GAL_{10}, respectively, and these are apparently closely linked on chromosome II in the order GAL_7-GAL_{10}-GAL_1. The three genes are coordinately induced more than 5000-fold by the addition of galactose to the medium.

Regulatory mutants that affected the expression of the GAL genes were studied. Once class of such mutants maps at a locus distinct from the structural genes, and these mutants are characterized by constitutive synthesis of the three GAL enzymes. These mutants are recessive to the wild-type allele. By analogy with the lactose operon of *E. coli*, the locus involved was called i and the mutants were designated i^-. A second class of regulatory mutants carry mutations that map to a locus, GAL_4, which is linked to either the i locus or the GAL structural genes. These GAL_4 mutants are pleiotropically negative in that they are uninducible by galactose. A third class of regulatory mutants maps immediately adjacent to the GAL_4 locus at the gal_{81} region, and these result in a constitutive production of galactose-fermenting enzymes. The GAL_{81} mutants resemble o^c mutants of the lactose operon in that they behave as cis-dominants in diploids.

From the data *H. Douglas* and *D. Hawthorne* proposed a model for the regulation of expression of the GAL genes. Here the i gene produces a repressor that represses the expression of the GAL_4 gene by interacting with the adjacent gal_{81} region if galactose is absent. If galactose is added, the repressor is inactivated and the GAL_4 gene can then be transcribed. Since gal_4 mutants are pleiotropically negative, the GAL_4 product is presumably a positive effector molecule required for the expression of three GAL structural genes. How and where the GAL_4 effector interacts with the GAL gene cluster is not known. In other words, the i^--gal_{81} relationship resembles the repressor-operator

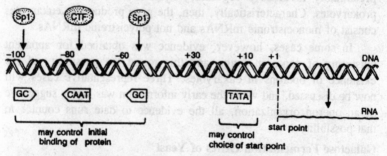

Fig. 11.5. *Different consensus sequences (boxex) in the promoter region for thymidine kinase gene.*

relationship of bacterial operons. Whether this is formally the case is a question for debate. The existence of i^s (super-repressible) mutations certainly supports the repressor concept in the model. Still unknown, however, is the exact nature of the i and GAL_4 gene products at the molecular level, how the i product interacts with the gal_{81} region, and whether a polycistronic mRNA is produced from the GAL structural genes.

Genes for Aromatic Amino Acid Biosynthesis is Neurospora

Another potential candidate for an operon in eukaryotes are the genes for the early steps of the pathway for aromatic amino acid (phenylalanine, tyrosine, and tryptophan) biosynthesis in *Neurospora crassa*. These have been studied by *N. Giles, M. Case* and their colleagues for many years.

Of particular significance was the discovery that a multienzyme aggregate (molecular weight 230,000 daltons) contained five different enzyme activities. These five activities are coded for by the so-called *arom* gene cluster of five adjacent genes, *aro 2, aro 4, aro 5, aro 9,* and *aro 1.* Genetic studies showed that mutations in a particular gene either affected the individual enzyme activity or caused the loss of two or more of the activities of the complex. These pleiotropic mutants were reminiscent of nonsense mutants in operons of bacteria where polar effects result during the translation of a single polycistronic mRNA. It was suggested, therefore, that the *arom* gene cluster coded for a polycistronic mRNA, and transcription commencing at the *aro*-2 gene. This supported the possibility that the *arom* gene cluster was an operon. However, *F. Gaerner* and *Giles'* group, working independently, have shown that to so-called *arom* gene cluster is actually a *single* structural gene that codes for a single polypeptide of molecular weight 115,000 daltons. This dimerizes to produce an enzyme that has the five enzyme activities just discussed. The separate polypeptides that were found in early investigations have been shown to be artifacts of the cellular fractionation techniques where the pentafunctional

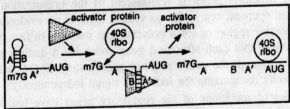

Fig. 11.6. Hypothetical mechanism for activation of translation in mammalian systems.

polypeptide is cleaved by endogenous protease activity. Thus the *arom* system is not an operon but a fusion of five ancestral genes into one. This cluster gene has one promoter region. This not the only example of a multifunctional polypeptide in eukaryotes; a number of other example are known, particularly in the lower eukaryotes. The point it illustrates is that when one breaks open the cell and examines the contents, the results one obtains do not necessarily reflect the situation in vivo.

Regulation of Quinic Acid Metabolism in Neurospora

N. Giles, M. Case, and their colleagues have also studied the regulation of expression of the *qa* genes of *Neurospora*, genes that are involved in the metabolism of quinic acid (QA) as a carbon source. From genetic and DNA-sequencing experiments, the *qa* genes have been shown to be clustered and to involve five structural genes and two regulatory genes.

Transcription of the structural genes is induced 300-to 1000-fold by the addition of QA to the medium. The structural genes qa-3, qa-2 and qa-4 code for the enzymes for the first three steps in the catabolism of QA (i.e., quinic acid dehydrogenase, catabolic dehydrogenase, and dehydroshikimic acid dehydrase, respectively). Note that both this catabolic pathway and the aromatic amino acid biosynthetic pathway just described have a dehydroquinase involved. There is no overlap between the pathways, however, since the multifunctional polypeptide of the biosynthetic pathway serves to channel the intermediates effectively.

The other two structural genes, *qa-x* and *qa-y*, were identified by analysis of the DNA sequence of the qa region. It is known that these two structural genes are transcribed and that they respond to QA induction, but the functions of their protein products are currently unknown. At the *qa-y* end of the *qa* structural gene cluster are two regulatory genes qa-1S and qa-1F. A regulatory gene adjacent to a cluster of structural genes is reminiscent of the organization of the prokaryotic operons, but in the *qa* system there is no evidence either for an operator region or for a polycistronic mRNA. In fact, there is solid evidence that each structural gene codes for a distinct mRNA. Thus, even though the genes respond coordinately to QA induction, they do so by recognizing the induction signal independently.

Studies of mutations of the regulatory genes have led to some understanding of the regulation of expression of the *qa* structural genes. The regulatory gene mutations were studied both in the normal haploid cells and also in heterokaryons involving nuclei with different genetic constitutions in order to study dominance relationships. Mutants of the qa-1S gene are either constitutive and recessive (qa-1S⁻alleles). Mutants of the qa-1F gene (qa-1F⁻ alleles) are noninducible and recessive even in the presence of a (constitutive) qa-1Sᶜ allele. The following model has been proposed: qa-1F codes for an activator protein needed for transcription of itself and for all the structural genes except qa-x. qa-1S codes for a repressor protein that interacts with QA, in which state it has no effect on qa-1F transcription. In the absence of QA, however, the qa-1S protein blocks transcription of the qa-1F activator protein so that most of the structural genes are repressed. The exact role of qa-x in the qa system remains to be defined.

Thus the qa gene cluster is not like the arom gene cluster, since the qa genes clone for individual mRNAs and distinct protein products. The absence of a polycistronic mRNA or of an operator-like region in the qa gene system also distinguishes the qa gene cluster from prokaryotic operons.

In summary, in most instances genes with related functions in eukaryotes tend to be unlinked, although coordinately regulated. In lower eukaryotes in particular, where more extensive genetics has been possible, there are a number of examples of clustered genes but no definitive example of a bacterial-like operon. At least in some instances the gene cluster may actually be a single gene that codes for a multifunctional polypeptide.

REGULATION OF GENE EXPRESSION IN HIGHER EUKARYOTES

Higher eukaryotes are characterized by the differentiation of cells into tissues, organs, etc., that have specific functions. In this they differ markedly from the comparatively undifferentiated lower eukaryotes. The following section will concentrate on animal systems, in particular the vertebrates.

With the great complexity of cell specialization in higher eukaryotes come different problems in terms of the regulation of gene expression. For example, the specialized cells in these organisms are not subjected to drastic changes in the environment as in the case for lower eukaryotes and prokaryotes, this results in the fact that animals have homeostatic mechanisms that maintain relatively constant extracellular and intracellular environments. This is mediated by the blood, which has a fairly constant composition that is maintained by a variety of mechanisms. In vertebrates, for example, this is controlled by hormones. Thus animal cells are generally not exposed to large changes in the concentration of metabolites or substrates and therefore is less need for rapid changes in the rates of enzyme synthesis. Characteristically, then such changes are less frequent and of less magnitude than in lower eukaryotes or bacterial cells. For example, the enzyme *ornithine decarboxylase*, one of the most rapidly responding enzymes, exhibits a maximum increase of only 10 to 20 fold in four hours when induced. Contrast this with the 1000-fold induction of β-*galactosidase* within minutes in *E. coli*.

Before discussing the role of hormones in the regulation of enzyme synthesis, it must be stated that there are indeed enzyme induction and repression mechanisms operating in higher eukaryotes that are similar to those in prokaryotes. Because of the low number of regulatory mutants available in animal cells, there are relatively few systems that have been investigated in this regard. By contrast, the action of hormones on gene expression have been studied extensively, and in the following section, some of the information that has been obtained will be considered.

Regulation of Enzyme Synthesis by Hormones

A *hormone* may be defined as an effector molecule produced in low concentrations by one cell that evokes a physiological response in another cell. In vertebrates, a large number of classes of molecules have been shown to have hormonal activity, including polypeptides, amino acids, fatty acid derivatives, and steroids. Some of the hormones act directly on the cell's genome whereas others act at the cell surface, thereby activating membrane-bound adenyl cyclase to produce cyclic AMP (cAMP ; 3' 5'-cyclic adenosine monophosphate) from ATP. The cAMP acts as a "second messenger" to evoke the intracellular effects observed following hormonal release.

Hormones act on specific target tissues that posses receptors capable of recognizing and binding to that particular hormone. For most of the polypeptide hormones, the receptors are on the cell surface, whereas the receptors for steroid hormones are in the cytoplasm.

Model for Steroid Hormone Action

Steroid hormones are biosynthetically derived from sterols, which occur only in eukaryotic cells. In general, each class of steroid hormones mediates its biological response by binding to an intracellular receptor protein that is confined to target tissues. The interaction of the hormone with its receptor protein brings about a change in the structure of the protein such that there is increased affinity of the steroid-receptor complex for DNA. While steroid-receptors complexes bind to all

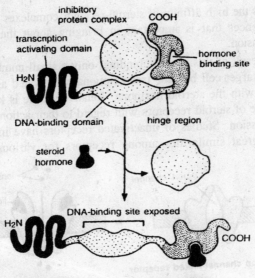

(a) a model for the function of intracellular receptor protein

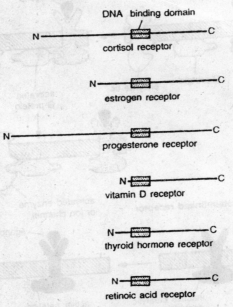

(b) six receptors, each having a DNA binding domain

Fig. 11.7. The intracellular receptor superfamily.

DNAs, it is the high affinity of steroid-receptor complexes with *specific DNA* sequences that is important in bringing about the changes in gene expression.

As a result of this specific binding, only a small number of genes within the target cell become transcriptionally activated as a result of interaction with the steroid hormone. Relatively little is known about the structure of steroid receptors with regard to their action in affecting gene expression. Studies of unactivated receptors have indicated that there are great similarities among receptors for various classes of

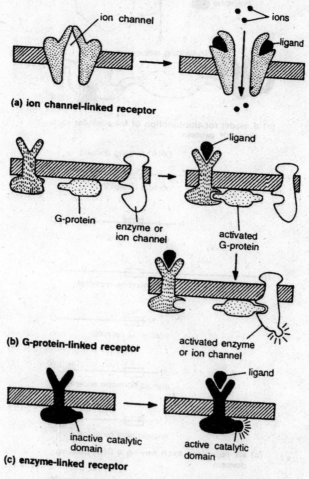

Fig. 11.8. Three classes of cell surface receptors.

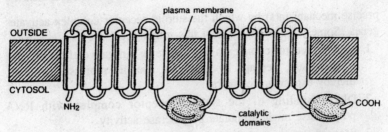

Fig. 11.9. Structure of adenyl cyclase enzyme, showing two clusters of six transmembrane segments, separating two similar cytoplasmic catalytic domains.

steroids. In all cases studied to date, the unactivated receptor exists as a multimer with a molecular weight of 200,000–300,000 daltons, and with sedimentation values of 8-10S. The activated form of steroid receptors always have lower S values than the unactivated forms. In the typical case, activation of an 8-10S receptor leads to the production of a 3-4S activated form, suggesting that the most stable activated form of steroid receptors in a monomeric structure. It should be pointed out, however, that there is evidence that a multimeric from is involved in gene activation. There is no question that a great deal of progress has been made in recent years in establishing the structure of steroid receptors and the nature of their interaction with the steroid molecule itself. Further, in some cases information is coming to hand about the nature of the DNA sequences involved in high-affinity binding of the steroid-receptor complexes in the nucleus. However, much more information is needed before we will have an understanding of the

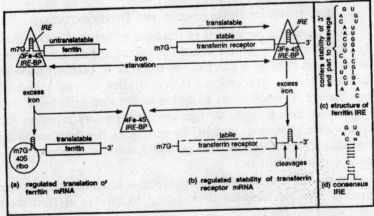

Fig. 11.10. Post-transcriptional regulation of two genes involved in the uptake and detoxification of iron in mammalian cells.

precise mechanism(s) by which the steroid-receptor complex activates genes. Some possibilities of how this might occur are :

1. Steroid-receptor complexes might reverse a negative effect on gene transcription, perhaps by removing specific repressor proteins, thereby exposing promoters.

2. Direct binding of the steroid-receptor complex with RNA polymerase might stimulate polymerase activity.

3. Steroid-receptor complexes might after the conformation of the chromatin (e.g., by removing nuclear proteins) in such a ways as to facilitate RNA polymerase binding to a promoter.

In summary, hormones act to integrate metabolism in higher eukaryotes. In some cases (e.g., in the liver) the coordination of metabolic activities involves the combined actions of several hormones. It is generally accepted that hormones act at the transcriptional level.

Long-term Genetic Regulation in Higher Eukaryotes

The examples of the previous section all show short-term regulation of gene expression in higher eukaryotes, that is, where adjustments are made in cellular activity in response to environmental changes (e.g., hormone release). There are, however, two properties of higher eukaryotes (and some lower eukaryotes) that reflect the long-term regulation of gene expression : development and differentiation. These processes are really outside the area of genetics and in the areas of developmental biology and embryology, and therefore only a very general discussion of them will be given in this text.

DEFINITIONS OF DEVELOPMENT AND DIFFERENTIATION

Development is the process of regulated growth that results from the interaction of the genome with the cytoplasm and the environment. Development involves a programmed sequence of phenotypic events that are usually irreversible. *Differentiation* is one aspect of development. It involves the formation of different cell, tissue, and organ types from a zygote through specific regulatory processes that control gene expression. In short, the genome carries the potential for the adult organism, but the final product results from complex gene-environment interactions.

In general, development is an irreversible or virtually irreversible process. We can consider development to involve at least three interacting processes :

1. The replication of the genetic material.

2. The growth of the organism as a result of cellular metabolic activity.

3. Cellular differentiation by which genetically identical cells diverge in their structure and function to give rise to organized tissues, which in turn associate to form organs.

Differentiation is the formation of different types of cells and tissues form a zygote by the specific regulation of gene activity in temporal and spatial ways.

General Aspects of Development and Differentiation

A number of general attributes of development and differentiation can be related to the genetic concepts that have been presented in the text.

Nuclear DNA remains constant

Early models for gene involvement in development included one where there was a programmed loss of nuclear DNA as the organism developed, or rather that the development processes that occurred were the result of losses of particular genes in an ordered sequence. That is not true. Rather, cells of differentiated tissues contain the same genomic content of DNA as the fertilized egg (although some differentiated cells may be polyploid). On elegant experiment that showed this to be the case was performed by *J. Gurdon*. He transplanted a nucleus from the gut cell of a tadpole of *Xenopus laevis*, the South African clawed toad, into an unfertilized egg of that organism from which the nucleus had been removed. The result was that the egg, once stimulated, developed into a normal adult toad. Thus the differentiated cells of the tadpole exhibited *totipotency*; that is, they contained all of the genetic information required for the egg to develop and differentiate into an adult organism.

DNA is transcribed in a programmed way

All of the available evidence shows that development and differentiation involve a detailed program of transcription of the DNA, which occurs in response to specific activator and repressor molecules. Two lines of evidence to support this will be considered here.

1. As mentioned previously, it is possible to quantify the extent to which RNA isolated from a cell hybridizes to the nuclear DNA. In general, the experiments involve RNA and DNA molecules that are radioactively labelled with different isotopes. A refinement of this technique is competitive DNA : RNA hybridization where

unlabelled RNA is first allowed to hybridize with the DNA before the radioactive RNA is added. If the RNAs are from the same tissue, the unlabelled RNA should effectively block all of the DNA sites to which the labelled RNA can bind, and this would be detected as 100% competition when the radioactivity is measured. If the RNAs are from two different tissues, however, the effect on the amount of radioactive RNA that will bind to the DNA will depend on how many of the RNA species were synthesized in common by both the tissues. One can do this experiment using mRNAs isolated from different tissues (e.g., lung, liver, kidney, muscle) of the same organism. Results of such an experiment show that there is limited competition between the mRNAs of the tissues in the hybridization and leads to the conclusion that differentiated cells reflect differences in the gene transcription activity. This correlates well with other studies showing different spectrums of enzymes and relative differences in enzyme amounts and activities in different tissues of the same organism. These differences must, of course, reflect differential gene activity.

2. In certain insects as *Drosophila*, the chromosomes of the larval salivary gland cells undergo *polytenization*. That is, the chromosomes replicate up to a thousand times but without there being cell division. The replicated chromosomes remain together as the *polytene chromosomes*, which show characteristic banding patterns. The bands are thought to represent the coding sequences of genes, while the function of the interband region is not known. The DNA is continuous along the length of these chromosomes. In *Drosophila*, there are three larval stages, each separated by a molting event. The last larval stage is followed by pupation. This is an interesting model system, therefore, for studying gene activity (since the genes are visible, if indeed the bands are genes) during development. In fact, specific bands "puff" in a particular pattern related to the time of larval development. The puffs are localized loosenings of the compact polytene chromosome that occurs so that RNA polymerase can initiate transcription. Indeed it can be shown that RNA is being actively synthesized in the puffs, and thus the puffs are visual evidence of gene activity. More importantly, the puffing patterns are reproducible, and, as has been stated, they are tissue and developmental stage specific.

Gene-cytoplasm Interactions

The gene activities of a cell are affected by the cytoplasm. Thus when certain genes are turned on during differentiation, particular proteins are synthesized, some of which have regulatory role in maintaining the differentiated state of the cell. For example, in Gurdon's transplantation experiment discussed earlier, we made the point that the nucleus carried all the genetic information necessary for the egg to develop into an adult. However, the fact that the egg cell behaved as an egg cell and not as a tadpole gut cell is an example of how the activity of the nuclear genome is controlled by the cytoplasmic state.

12

BIOCHEMICAL GENETICS

The cells is a very complex and its function depends upon the integration of the activities of many genes. The genes may interact within the organism. The genes control various traits is an organism through a control exercised on the developmental processes. Such a control is due to the synthesis of enzymes or proteins. It is a well-known fact that the synthesis of protein is under the direct control of gene or genes. Thus we see that the genes express themselves through the synthesis of enzymes and it was demonstrated for the first time 1941 by *G.W. Beadle* and *E.L. Tatum* while working on the biochemical mutations is Neurospora. Based on their this work, *Beadle* and *Tatum* proposed a concept called "one-gene-one-enzyme" hypothesis. This hypothesis means that all the steps which transform a precursor substance to its end product that is ultimately expressed into a structural and functional phenotypic trait, constitutes a *biosynthetic* or *metabolic* pathway, and each step of a biosynthetic pathway is catalyzed by a specific enzyme which in turn is synthesized under the control of a specific gene.

Biochemical genetics has been widely studied in haploid organisms whose growth requirement are known. Any error in the metabolic pathway is expressed in the form of disease as in human beings.

GENETIC CONTROL OF METABOLISM IN HUMANS

Early evidence for the relationship between genes and enzymes came from the work of the physician *Archibald Garrod* in 1909, the results of which were published as a book called *Inborn Errors* of Metabolism. Garrad was interested in human diseases that had an apparent genetic basis. He postulated and rightly so, that biosynthesis and degradation of a product takes place in several sequential steps and these steps are controlled by genes, one gene controlling one step. He suggested further that any of these genes mutates in the metabolic path, all the other reactions ahead of it, stop and there is accumulation of the substance which the intact gene preceding the mutant one, synthesizes as shown under the following subheads:

Phenylketinuria or Folling's Disease (PKU)

This disease is caused sue to the absence of enzyme which catalyses the conversion of phenylpyruvic acid into hydroxy-phenylpyuvic

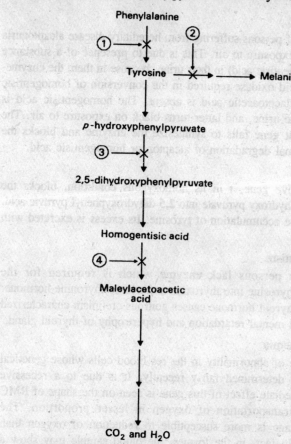

Fig. 12.1. Part of the biochemical pathway for the metabolism of phenylalanine and tyrosine. The sites of metabolic blocks associated with human diseases are indicated by crosses: (1) phenylketonuria; (2) albinism; (3) tyrosinosis; (4) alkaptonuria.

acid. As a result phenylpyruvic acid accumulates in the blood and causes impairment of brain tissue, pale skin and a tendency to epileptic seizure. Thus PKU child-ren are mentally retarded and are known as phenylpyruvic idiots. Such persons have recessive genotype pp that fails to produce enzyme phenyl-alanine hydroxylase.

Persons suffering from phenylketonuria also show mild symptoms of albination; this is because melanin pigment is not produced in such individuals in as much abundance as is necessary for normal colour development.

Alcaptonuria

The urine of persons suffering from hereditary disease alcaptonuria turns black on exposure to air. This is due to presence of a substance adoption (homogentisic acid) in their urine, because in them the enzyme-homogentisic acid oxidase required in the conversion of homogentisic acid into maleylacetoacetic acid is absent. The homogentisic acid is passed out in the urine, and latter turns black on exposure to air. The recessive mutant gene fails to synthesize the enzyme and blocks the step in the normal degradation of alcapton or homogentisic acid.

Tyrosionsis

The recessive gene, t in its homozygous condition, blocks the conversion of p-hydroxy pyruvate into 2,5 dihydroxyphenyl pyruvic acid. This leads to the accumulation of tyrosine. Its excess is excreted with the urine.

Goitrous Cretinism

Sometimes persons lack enzyme which is required for the conversion of thyrosine into thyroxine and trioido thyronine hormone. Deficiency of thyroid hormone causes goitrous cretinism characterized by physical and mental retardation and hypertrophy of thyroid gland.

Sickel Cell Anemia

It is a type of abnormality in the res blood cells whose genetical basis has been determined fairly recently. It is due to a recessive gens. The immediate effect of this gene is seen on the shape of RMC affecting the transportation of oxygen in lesser proportion. The homozygous stage is more susceptible to reduction of oxygen than heterozygous. In fact, in the former, the blood sample may show a few sickel-shaped cells before any substantial reduction of oxygen.

The homozygous recessive individuals rarely survive to leave any progeny because of secondary (*pleiotropic*) effect of the gene (the arms and legs are elongated and there are other physical deformities). The heterozygous individuals are indistinguishable from the normal except that the shape of their RBC changes consequently or lowered oxygen supply. These heterozygotes have been found to be superior over normal in respect of their immunity to the attack of malarial parasites. When the haemoglobin from normal and sickle cell anemic cells were analyzed, they were seen identical in all the fragments excepting for the number four. From the determination of amino acid sequence, it was seen that the fragment four of the abnormal haemoglobin contained valine in place of glutamic acid, other amino acids being identical. In other words, valine was seen to replace glutamic acid and the rest of the 285 amino acids remained undisturbed.

GENETIC CONTROL OF DROSOPHILA EYE PIGMENTS

Garrod's pioneering work provided the first clue to the link between Mendelian factors and proteins. In 1935 G. Beadle and B. Ephrussi obtained more evidence for gene enzyme relationships in a biochemical pathway in their studies of the synthesis of the eye pigments in the fly, *Drosophila melanogaster*.

There are two pigments in the eye of *Drosophila* the bright red pterins and the brown ommochromes. As we now know, these two pigments are made in two multistep biochemical pathway, each reaction of which is catalyzed by an enzyme. The bright red and brown pigments that are the end products of these pathways become attached to protein granules and are deposited in the eye cells. The combination of the two pigments results in the dull red eye colour characteristic of the wild type. Further, in *Drosophila*, the larval stages contain groups of cells called *discs*, each of which develops into a particular adult structure during metamorphosis. Two discs can be identified as the progenitors of eyes. In their initial experiments, Beadle and Ephrussi showed that an eye disc from a larva can be transplanted into the abdomen of a second larva and disc will develop into an identifiable eye structure that can be found in the abdomen of the adult following metamorphosis. This paved the way for a series of elegant experiments in which eye discs were transplanted between larvae of different genetic constitutions.

At the time if *Beadle* and *Ephrussi's* experiments, three gene lock were known that were implicated in the production of brown pigment; scarlet, cinnabar and vermilion. Mutations in any one these genes resulted in a bright orange eye (the shade of orange differs in each mutant type). *Beadle* and *Ephurssi* first addressed the question of whether embryonic eye tissue from the three mutant types *st* (scarlet), *cn*

Eye discs

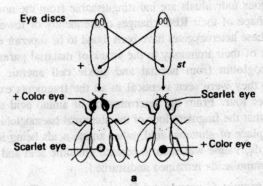

+ Color eye
Scarlet eye

Scarlet eye
+ Color eye

a

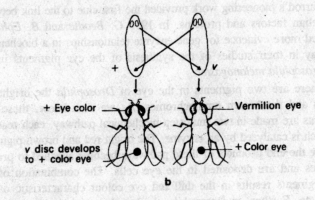

+ Eye color
Vermilion eye

v disc develops
to + color eye
+ Color eye

b

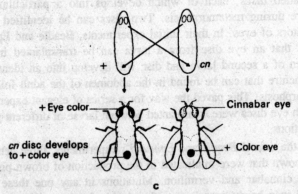

+ Eye color
Cinnabar eye

cn disc develops
to + color eye
+ Color eye

c

Fig. 12.2. Results of Beadle and Ephrussi's reciprocal transplant experiments with eye discs of Drosophila. (a) Reciprocal transplants between + and st (scarlet). (b) Reciprocal transplants between + and v (vermilion). (c) Reciprocal transplant between + and cn (cinnabar).

(cinnabar) or *v* (vermillion) transplanted into a wild type larval host would develop a wild type eye colour. In the case of the st mutant the transplanted disc developed into a scarlet-coloured eye and s an example of *autonomous development* in which the wild type host was unable to provide substances to the disc to enable the brown pigment to be produced. By contrast, transplanted discs from either *v* or *cn* developed into normal-coloured eyes in the wild type host and thus showed non-autonomous development. The conclusion in these cases was that the wild type provided a diffusible substance that the discs used to bypass the genetic block and to make brown pigment.

Of more importance historically were the result of reciprocal transplant experiments between *v* and *cn* larvae. The experiments showed that *cn* discs transplanted into v hosts produced cinnabar-coloured, eyes, whereas v discs transplanted into *cn* hosts developed into wild type coloured type. They concluded from these results that the production of the brown pigment involved a biochemical sequence with at least two precursors, the wild type having both, *cn* having one, and *v* having neither. Thus, the production of a wild type coloured eye when a *v* diffusible substance so that it becomes wild type. In the reciprocal experiment, the cn disc cannot convert the *v*+ substance to the *cn*+ substance and the *v* host is deficient in the production of *v*+ substance so no brown pigment can be produced.

At the time of these experiments, the relationships between genes and enzymes was known. *Beadle* and *Ephrussi's* work was important historically since it indicated a strong link between a phenotype (in this case eye colour) and genotype (*v* and *cn*) E. *Tatum* further investigated this system by making extracts of v and *cn* flies of homogenization and by injecting the extracts into host larvae. He found that the same results were obtained as for the eye disc transplantation experiments; the injection of a *cn* extract into v larvae resulted in the production of wild-type coloured eyes. This experiment was the first in a series designed to discover the nature of the *v*+ and *cn*+ substances. At that time, it was difficult to analyze the extracts he had prepared, and his limited analysis showed that the substances were water soluble and low molecular weight. He proposed that the substances were discs is implanted into a *cn* host follows logically. This is the *v* disc cannot make the *v*+ substance (the product of the wild type allele of v) whereas the *cn* host can. This *v*+ substance diffuses to the *v* discs where it converted to the brown pigment. In other words, the *cn* host makes up for the deficiency of the *v* disc by carries the wild type allele of *cn*, and this substance is then converted to the brown pigment. In other words, the *cn* host make sup for the deficiency of the *v* disc by supplying it with a relatives of amino acids and set about trying to supplement the fly food in a defined way to try to bypass the genetic blocks in the growth pigment pathway and therefore to identify the biochemical precursors in the pathway and therefore to identify the biochemical precursors in the pathway in this way. Several complex media such as peptone resulted in brown pigment formation in adult eyes when fed to *v* and *cn* larvae. One exception was gelatin, which is deficient in tryptophan and tyrosine. Tatum then injected tryptophan into *v* and *cn* larvae and no brown pigment was produced in most experiments. However, in one experiment, brown pigment was produced, and it turned out that this occurred as a result of a bacterial contamination, which resulted in the metabolism of tryptophan into chemical that are required by *v* and *cn* for the production of brown pigment. With the implication of tryptophan metabolism in the production of brown pigment, it was then a relatively simple matter to work out the biochemical pathway and to localize the steps catalyzed by the *v+* and *cn+* gene products. As can be seen the *v* mutants are unable to convert tryptophan to formylkynurenine and the *cn* mutants cannot convert formylkynurenine to 3-hydroxykynurenine because the enzymes they have for these respective steps are non-functional.

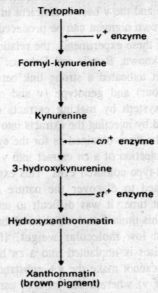

Fig. 12.3. *The pathway for the production of brown eye pigment of Drosophila from the amino acid tryptophan.*

The pathway can serve to illustrate a general point about the sequence of reactions and the consequences of genetic mutations. In the *v* mutations, for example, the flies accumulate high amounts of tryptophan since it is not converted to the brown pigment in this pathway. This is analogous to the accumulation of homogentisic acid in alkaptonuriacs. Here it provided further evidence that tryptophan metabolism is involved with eye pigment formation. Indeed, if one feeds wild-type larvae with radioactive tryptophan, the brown ommochrome pigment of the adult eye is found to be radioactive.

Biochemical Mutations in Neurospora

The unicellular fungus Neurospora has been most widely utilized in this study of biochemical mutations influencing or amino metabolic pathways, concerned with the synthesis of acids, molecules of nucleic acids and some of the vitamins.

The normal strain of Neurospora is able to grow in the minimal medium containing sucrose, inorganic salts and one of the vitamins-biotin. It can synthesize all other complex substances, like vitamins, proteins, nitrogenous bases and the nucleic acid from the simple substances of culture medium. Beadle and Tatum exposed some of the asexual spores (conidia) of Neurospora crassa to mutagen (X-rays or ultraviolet rays). These mutated ascospores were found unable to grow in minimal medium but required the addition of some supplement for the normal growth. The mutated strains of Neurospora are called *nutritional mutants* showing mutations in the nutritional genes.

Controlled experiments by *Beadle* and *Tatum* have shown that biosynthesis of each amino acid involves a number of sequential steps and each step is regulated by a specific enzymes. The end product of one reaction acts as a precursor for the next one. For example, synthesis of amino acid arginine involves the following steps.

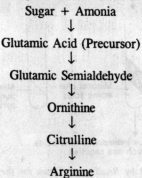

Sugar + Amonia
↓
Glutamic Acid (Precursor)
↓
Glutamic Semialdehyde
↓
Ornithine
↓
Citrulline
↓
Arginine

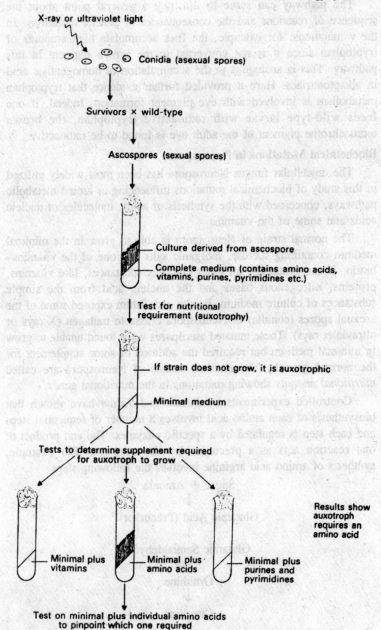

Fig. 12.4. Procedure used by Beadle and Tatum for the induction, isolation, and classification of nutritional mutants of Neurospora.

There are 12 different strains of *N. crassa* which are unable to synthesize arginine. These form three mutant categories.

(a) Mutants which grow only when either citrulline or arginine is supplied but not grow if ornithine or cutrulline.

(b) Mutants which grow when either citrulline or arginine is supplied but not grow if ornithrine is added to the medium.

(c) Mutants which can grow in the medium containing either ornithine, citrulline or arginine.

These mutants indicate that in first case (a) the mutants are incapable of utilizing intermediate products ornithine or citrulline. In them the gene responsible for the conversion of citrulline into arginine has undergone mutation and fails to synthesize the specific enzyme. (b) The mutants are incapable of utilizing ornithine. It means the enzyme responsible for transformation of ornithine into citrulline is lacking and the gene concerned with the synthesis of this enzyme has undergone mutation. In third case (c) the mutant can utilize intermediate products but not the precursor (i.e. glutamic acid).

Biochemical Mutants in Flowering Plants

Arabidopsis thaliana is a small rapidly growing crucifer with about a 28 day life cycle. It has a low chromosome number (2n=10). The number of seeds per fruit is quite large (150-300 seeds) and 25000 per plant. It cannot however tolerate a temperature higher than 25. Requirement of such low temperature therefore makes it extremely difficult to work with this material in the tropics except in winter. When grown under controlled condition, it is supplied with 20 hours photoperiod and high intensities of 10-12 thousand lux. Because of their small size and fast growth rate they can be grown continuously through their life cycle in the test tube on sterile nutrient medium +2 percent sucrose modified in suitable concentration of agar. The trace elements used in the culture solutionis chelated.

By means of various mutagenic agents e.g. X-rays EMS (1 per cent for two hours) etc. auxotrophs are easily obtained. Different types of lethal embryos (vanda, fusca, parwa, diffusa) can be picked up under the dissection microscope. The unripe fruits are opened and the undeveloped embryos can be seen without dissecting the seeds. Chlorophyll mutants appear in the form of albino, X antha, chlorine (yellow green). As in the case of biochemical mutants in *N. crassa*, supply of different growth requiring substances (amino-acids, vitamins) either individually as in combination in the culture medium enables the mutants grow to different lends of development. Some chlorophyll mutants die at the cotyledon stage some at the 3 rosette stage without turning green, still others at the bud stage. Some of the mutants which deserve special mention are leucine, tryptophan, thiamine anxotrophs. These, on supply of their specific requirements, turn green and grow to full length and produce seeds. One of the interesting observation in these studies 15 that in leucine auxotroph, addition of this amino acid by itself restores the normal growth but in combination with valine in different proportions inhibits growth.

GENE CONTROL OF PROTEIN STRUCTURE

So far we have learned that there is a direct relationship between genes and enzymes. Since an enzyme catalyzes one reaction in a biochemical pathway, a mutation in the gene for the organism depends on the nature of the pathway, the effects of the compound accumulated prior to the block, and the effects of a deficiency of the end product.

However, while all enzymes are proteins, not all proteins are enzymes. Nevertheless, the functions of proteins are also affected by changes in amino acid sequence and tertiary structure. For example, the human disease sickel cell anemia is characterized by a sickling of the red blood cells. This leads to problems with the red blood cells passing through the capillaries, hereby causing tissue and organ damage, anemia, and possibly death. The life of the red cells is also greatly shortened. Sickle cell anemia is caused by homozygosity for a mutation in the gene for the b-polypeptide of haemoglobin. (Haemoglobin consists of two copies each of a and b polypeptides). The mutation results in the substitution of the neutral amino acid valine for the normal acidic amino acid glutamic acid at the sixth position form the N-terminal end. This change is at an important part of the molecule, and the presence of a neutral amino acid instead of an acidic amino acid makes the region hydrophobic (water-hating) instead of hydrophilic (water-loving). As a result, the b-polypetide folds to place the altered region away from the aqueous environment, and this causes an unusual stacking of haemoglobin molecules and sickling of the red blood cells.

Colinearity

A more precise understanding of the relationships between a gene (cistron) and the sequence of amino acids in the polypeptide for which it codes came from the work of *C. Yanofsky* and his group in 1967. Their studies centered on the enzyme tryptophan synthetase from *E. coli*. This enzyme consists of two copies each of two distinct polypeptides A and B, which are coded for by two adjacent genes. Here is an example of where two genes code for one enzyme—a clear

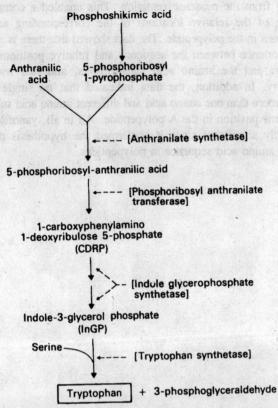

Fig. 12.5. The tryptophan biosynthetic pathway. The enzymes that catalyze the reaction steps are shown in square brackets. Tryptophan synthetase catalyzes the last step in the pathway.

exception to Beadle and Tatum's hypothesis. The reactions that the enzyme carries out are in the biosynthetic pathway for the amino acid tryptophan.

Tryptophan synthetase is easily isolated and the two polypeptide A and B can be purified. Further, the amino acid sequence of the 267-amino acids-long. A polypeptide was determined at the outset of their experiments. They then isolated a series of tryptophan auxotrophs and, with further tests, identified those that carried missense mutations in the tip A gene, which codes for the A polypeptide. The tip A mutants cannot carry out the production of tryptophan form indole glycerol phosphate and serine. Fine-structure mapping was used to locate the various mutations within the gene and amino acid sequencing was used to pinpoint the amino acid substitutions in the A polypeptide resulting from the missense mutation. This enabled a comparison to be made of the relative locations of the corresponding amino acid substitutions in the polypeptide. The data showed that there is a complete correspondence between the sequence and relative positioning of the mutations and the amino acid substitutions, and this was termed colinearity. In addition, the data indicated that no single mutation affected more than one amino acid and different amino acid substitutions at the same position in the A polypeptide. All in all, yanofsky's work was highly significant since it confirmed the hypothesis that genes code for amino acid sequence in polypeptides.

13

MANIPULATION OF GENES

The manipulation of gene is the called the genetic engineering. Genetics is also important in manipulating biological systems for scientific or economic reasons, an endeavor that has made possible the creation of organisms having new phenotypes or genotypes. The fundamental techniques for accomplishing this have been mutagenesis or recombination followed by selection for desired characteristics. When using such techniques, geneticists have been forced to work with the random nature of mutagenic and recombination events, which required selective procedures, often quite complex, to find an organism with the required genotype among the many types of organisms produced. Since the 1970s techniques have been developed by which the genotype of an organism can instead be modified in a *directed* and *predetermined* way. This is alternately called *recombinant DNA technology*, or *genetic engineering*.

Genetic engineering involves isolation of DNA fragments and recombination outside of a cell. Selection of a desired genotype is still necessary but the probability of success is usually many orders of magnitude greater than that with traditional procedures. The basic technique is quite simple: two DNA molecules are isolated and cut into fragments by one or more specialized enzymes and then the fragments are joined together *in a desired combination* and restored to a cell for replication and reproduction.

Current interest in genetic engineering centers on its many practical applications, a few examples of which are the following:

1. Isolation of a particular gene, part of a gene, or region of a genome.
2. Production of particular RNA and protein molecules in quantities formerly thought to be unobtainable.

3. Improvement in the production of biochemicals (such as enzymes and drugs) and commercially important organic chemicals.

4. Production of varieties of plants having particular desirable characteristics (for example, requiring less fertilizer or resistance to disease).

5. Correction of genetic defects in higher organisms, and

6. Creation of organisms with economically important features (for example, plants capable of maturing faster or having greater yield). Some of these examples will be considered later in the chapter.

Separation of Particular DNA Fragments

In genetic engineering the immediate goal of an experiment is usually to insert a *particular* fragment of chromosomal DNA into a plasmid or a viral DNA molecule. This is accomplished by techniques for breaking DNA molecules at specific sites and for isolating particular DNA fragments. DNA fragments are obtained by treatment of DNA samples with a specific class of nuclease. Many nucleases have been isolated from a variety of organisms, and most produce breaks at random sites within a DNA sequence. However, the class of nucleases called *restriction endonucleases*, or, more simply, *restriction enzymes*, consists of sequence-specific enzymes. Most restriction enzymes recognize only one short base sequence in a DNA molecule and make two single-strand breaks, one in each strand, generating 3´-OH and 5´-P groups at each position. Several hundred of these enzymes have been isolated from hundreds of species of microorganisms.

The sequences recognized by restriction enzymes are often *palindromes*—that is, the sequence has symmetry of the form:

A B C	C´ B´ A´		A B	B´ A´		A B	B´ A´
A´ B´ C´	C B A	or	A´ B´	B A	or	A´ B´	B A

in which the capital letter represent bases, a´ indicates a complementary base, X is any base, and the vertical line is the axis of symmetry. Most of these sequence have 4-6 bases.

One of the most exciting events in the study of restriction enzymes was the observation by electron microscopy that fragments produced by many restriction enzymes spontaneously circularize. These circles could be relinearized by heating, but if after circularization they were also treated with *E. coli* DNA ligase, which joins 3´-OH and 5´-P groups, circularization became permanent. This observation was the first evidence for three important features of restriction enzymes:

Table 13.1. Some restriction endonucleases, their sources, and their cleavage sites.

Name of enzyme	Microorganism	Target sequence and cleavage sites
Generates cohesive ends		
EcoRI	*E.coli*	G A A ┊ T T C C T T ┊ A A G
BamHI	*Bacillus amyloliquefaciens* H	G G A ┊ T C C C C T ┊ A G G
HaeII	*Haemophilus aegyptius*	Pu G C ┊ G C Py Py C G ┊ C G Pu
HindIII	*Haemophilus influenza*	A A G ┊ C T T T T C ┊ G A A
PstI	*Providencia stuartii*	C T G ┊ C A G G A C ┊ G T C
TaqI	*Thermus aquaticus*	T C ┊ G A A G ┊ C T
Generates blunt ends		
BalI	*Brevibacterium albium*	T G G ┊ C C A A C C ┊ G G T
SmaI	*Serratia marcescens*	C C C ┊ G G G G G G ┊ C C C

Note : The vertical dashed line indicates the axis of symmetry in each
sequence. Arrows indicate the sites of cutting. The enzyme TaqI
yields cohesive ends consisting of two nucleotides, whereas the
cohesive ends produced by the other enzymes contain four
nucleotides. Pu and Py refer to any purine and pyrimidine,
respectively.

1. Restriction enzymes make breaks in palindromic sequences.
2. The breaks are usually not directly opposite one another.
3. The enzymes generate DNA fragments with complementary ends.

Examination of a very large number of restriction enzymes showed
that the breaks are usually in one of two distinct arrangements: (1)

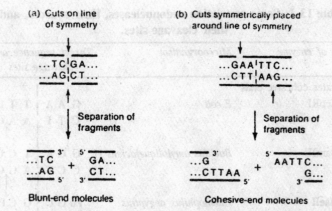

Fig. 13.1. *Two types of cuts made by restriction enzymes. The arrow indicate the cleavage
sites. The dashed line is the center of symmetry of the sequence.*

staggered, but symmetric around the line of symmetry (forming *cohesive
ends*) or (2) both at the center of symmetry (forming *blunt ends*). Two
types of enzymes produce cohesive ends—those yielding a single-stranded
extension with a 5´-P terminus and those yielding a 3´-OH extension.
Table 13.1. lists the sequences and cleavage sites for several restriction
enzymes, some of which generate cohesive sites and others of which
yield blunt ends.

Most restriction enzymes recognize one base sequence without
regard to the source of the DNA. Thus,

Fragments obtained from a DNA molecule from one organism
have the same cohesive ends as the fragments produced by the
same enzyme acting on DNA molecules from another organism.

Since most restriction enzymes recognize a unique sequence, *the
number of cuts made in the DNA from an organism by a particular
enzyme is limited.* A typical bacterial DNA molecule, which contains
roughly 3×10^6 base pairs, is cut into several hundred to several
thousand fragments, and nuclear DNA of mammals is cut into more
than a million fragments. These numbers are large but still small
compared to the number of sugar-phosphate bonds in an organism. Of
special interest are the smaller DNA molecules, such as viral or
plasmid DNA, which may have only 1-10 sites of cutting (or even
none) for particular enzymes.

Plasmids having a single site for a particular enzyme are especially
valuable. Because of the sequence specificity, *a particular restriction
enzyme generates a unique set of fragments for a particular DNA
molecule.* Another enzyme will generate a different set of fragments

from the same DNA molecule. Figure (given below) shows the sites of cutting of *E. coli* phage λ DNA by the enzymes EcoRI and BamHI. A map showing the unique sites of cutting of the DNA of a particular organism by a single enzyme is called a *restriction map*.

The family of fragments generated by a single enzyme can be detected easily by gel electrophoresis of enzyme-treated DNA, and particular DNA fragments can be isolated by cutting out the portion of the gel containing the fragment and removing the DNA from the gel. Several techniques enable one to locate particular genes on fragments of a restriction map. One of the most generally applicable procedures is *Southern blotting*. In this procedure a gel in which DNA molecules have been separated by electrophoresis is treated with alkali to render the DNA single-stranded (denature the DNA) and then the DNA is transferred to a sheet of nitrocellulose in a way that the relative positions of the DNA bands are maintained. The nitrocellulose, to which the single-stranded DNA tightly binds, is then exposed to radioactive RNA or DNA in a way that leads to renaturation.

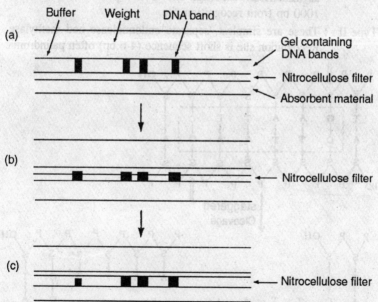

Fig. 13.2. *Southern blotting. (a) A weight is placed on a stack consisting of the gel, a nitrocellulose filter, and absorbent material. (b) At a later time the weight has forced the buffer, which carries the DNA, into the nitrocellulose. (c) The lowest layer has absorbed the buffer but the DNA, which remains bound to the nitrocellulose.*

Radioactivity becomes stably bound (resistant to removal by washing) to the DNA only at positions at which base sequences complementary to the radioactive molecules are present. The radioactivity is located by placing the paper in contact with x-ray film; after development of the film, blackened regions indicate positions of radioactivity. If a radioactive mRNA species transcribed from a particular gene is used (for example, mRNA isolated from a specialized cell that predominantly makes one type of mRNA), it will hybridize only with the restriction fragment containing that gene.

Restriction Endonucleases

Restriction enzymes are nucleases and as they cut at an internal position of DNA strand (and not at end) they are known as endonucleases. Restriction enzymes fall into following categories:

Type I : These are most complex, bi-functional (i.e. same enzyme possesses both restriction and modification activity) and are made up of 3 subunits. Recognition site is bipartite and asymmetrical. Cleavage site is nonspecific and is atleast 1000 bp from recognition site.

Type II : These are simplest, separate endonuclease and methylase. Recognition site is short sequence (4-6 bp) often palindromic

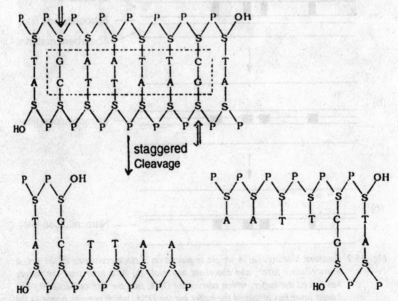

Fig. 13.3. *Symmetrical staggered cleavage by Eco RI arrows indicate sites of cleavage.*

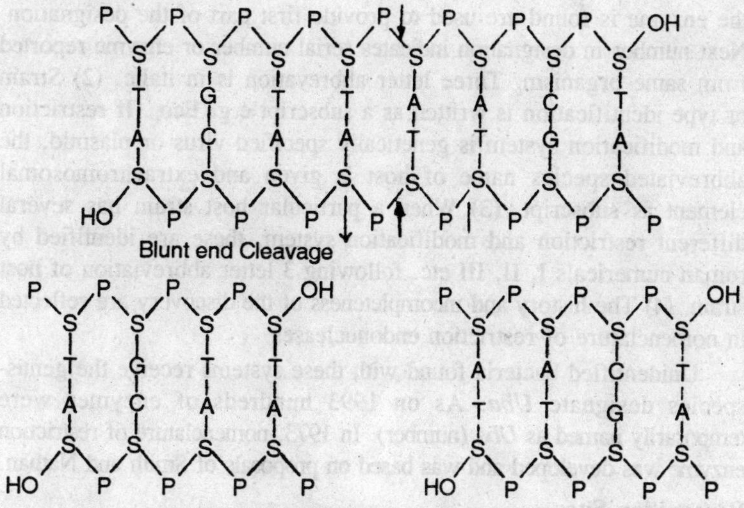

Fig. 13.4. Blunt end cleavage by hind III.

(with symmetry). Cleavage site is same as or close to recognition site.

Type III : These are moderate complex, bi-functional, have two subunits. Recognition site is asymmetrical sequence of 5-7 bp. Cleavage site is 24-26 bp downstream from recognition site.

Type II restriction endonucleases are most important tools in gene manipulation techniques. Most of the restriction enzymes cleave DNA at unmethylated target site. Discovery of restriction enzymes (restriction endonucleases) has been useful in most of the modern genetic manipulations. Restriction endonucleases are indispensable tools for recombinant DNA research. They recognize specific oligonucleotide sequence and make double stranded cleavage to generate unique fragment of DNA molecule. Restriction endonucleases are used for dissecting, analysing and re-configuring genetic information at molecular level. Restriction endonucleases are used in: (1) cleavage mapping, (2) preparation of DNA probes, (3) gene cloning etc.

Nomenclature

There are over 2400 type II restriction endonucleases known so far (since 1968) and they recognize more than 188 different restriction sites. These enzymes have been well characterized.

The nomenclature of restriction enzyme is based on various conventions: (1) The generic and specific name of organism in which the enzyme is found are used to provide first part of the designation. Next number in designation indicates serial number or enzyme reported from same organism. Three letter abbrevation is in italic. (2) Strain or type identification is written as a subscript e.g. Eco_k. If restriction and modification system is genetically specified virus or plasmid, the abbreviated species name of host is given and extrachromosomal element as subscript. (3) When a particular host strain has several different restriction and modification system, these are identified by roman numericals I, II, III etc. following 3 letter abbreviation of host strain. (4) The history and incompleteness of the discovery are reflected in nomenclature of restriction endonucleases.

Unidentified bacteria found with these systems receive the genus-species designate *Uba*. As on 1993 hundreds of enzymes were temporarily named as *Uba* (number). In 1973, nomenclature of restriction enzyme was developed and was based on proposals of Smith and Nathan.

Recognition Sites

Restriction enzymes usually recognize a specific DNA sequence of 4, 5 or 6 nucleotides in length and cleave the DNA within this restriction site. There are 4 bases in DNA, randomly distributed. The expected frequency of any particular sequence can be calculated as 4^n where n is the length of recognition sequence. Thus, tetranucleotide sites will occur every 256 basepair, pentanucleotide sites will occur every 1025 basepairs and hexanucleotide sites will occur every 4096 basepairs. Restriction enzymes either cut (1) Straight across the DNA to give blunt ends, or (2) Straight single strand cuts producing short, single stranded projections at each end of the cleaved DNA to produce cohesive or sticky ends.

Table 13.2. Classification of restriction endonucleases based on recognition site.

(i) Tetranucleotides recognizing	— *Alu I, Hae III, Hpa II, Mbo I, Taq I, Msp I* etc.
(II) Pentanucleotides recognizing	— *Ava II, Dde I, Eco R II, Hinf I* etc.
(III) Hexanucleotides recognizing	— *Kpn I, Xma I, Pst I, Hpal, Bam HI, Hind III* etc.
(IV) Heptanucleotides recognizing	— *Me II* etc.

One unit of enzyme (Restriction endonuclease) is defined as the amount of enzyme required to produce a complete digest of 1 μg of substrate DNA in a reaction volume of 0.05 ml in 1 hour under optimal conditions of salt, pH and temperature. All digestions are performed at 37°C and substrate used is lambda DNA. Optimum temperature for most of the restriction enzymes is 37°C. However, in some cases like *Tha I, Taq I, Bcl I, Bst NI* optimum temperature is 60-65°C. Recognition sequences of *Eco RI* are *palindromic*. Sometimes within a same strand sequence may be palindromic.

Table 13.3. Restriction endonucleases.

	Enzyme	Source	5´ Recognition site 3´
1.	Kpn II	Klebsiella pneumoniae	GGTAC↓C
2.	Bam HI	Bacillus amyloliquifaciens	G↓GATCC
3.	Sma I	Serratia marcesecens	CCC↓GGG
4.	Stu I	Streptomyces tubercidicus	AGG↓CCT
5.	AVA II	Anabenia variabilis	G↓G(A/T) CC
6.	Pva I	Proteus vulgaris	CGAT↓CG
7.	Hind III	Hemophilus influenzae Rd	A↓AGCTT
8.	Rsa I	Rhodopseudomonas sphaeroids	GT↓AC
9.	Hin C II	Hemophilus influenzae C1161	GTPyPvAC
10.	ECORI	E.coli RY 13	G↓AATTC
11.	Xma I	Xanthomonas malvacearum	C↓CCGGG
12.	Pst I	Providencia stuartii	CTGCA↓G
13.	Bgl II	Bacillus globigii	A↓GATCT
14.	Hpa II	Hemophilus parainfluenzae	C↓CGG
15.	Alu I	Arthrobacter luteus	AG↓CT
16.	Hae III	Hemophilus aegyptius	CG↓CC
17.	Hpa I	Hemophilus parainfluenzae	GTT↓AAC
18.	Mbo I	Moraxella bovis	N↓GATC
19.	NCo I	Nocardia corallina	G↓CATGG
20.	Sac I	Streptomyces achromogenes	GAGCT↓C
21.	Sal I	Streptomyces albus G	G↓TCGAC
22.	Sau 3AI	Staphylococcus aureus 3AI	N↓GATC
23.	Taq I	Thermus squatius YTI	T↓CGA
24.	Hinc II	Haemphilus influenzae Rc	GTPyPuAC
25.	Acc I	Acinetobacter calcoaceticus	GT↓(AC)(GT)AC
26.	Dde I	Desulfovibrio desulfuricans	C↓GNAG
27.	Eco RII	E.coli R-245	↓CC(A/T)GG
28.	Hinf I	Haemophilus influenzae Rf	G↓ANTC
29.	Mst II	Microcoleus species	CC↓TNAGG

If cut is not shown it means exact cutting size is not known. Parentheses indicate that either bracketed base will suffice recognition.

Note : Py, Pu indicate non-specific pyrimidines or purines. N indicates any nucleotide base.

Complementary DNA (cDNA)

A second method for obtaining a gene of interest is to create a *complementary DNA (cDNA)* strand from a strand of messenger RNA (mRNA). This procedure is used when specific mRNA molecules can be isolated from cells that produce high levels of a certain protein. For example, a protein called *factor VIII* is necessary for proper blood clotting. It is the protein that most hemophiliacs are missing because

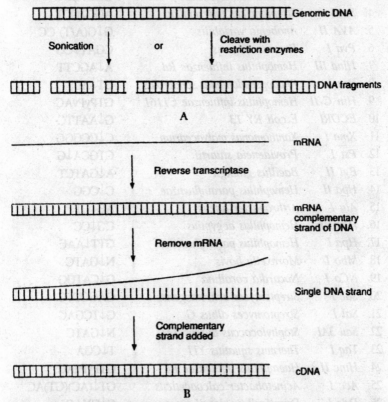

Fig. 13.5. A—To obtain DNA for cloning, large molecules are first broken into smaller segments by sonication or by cleaving them with restriction enzymes. The DNA fragments can then be separated and analyzed to determine which contain a gene of interest. B—If the mRNA encoding a gene of interest can be isolated, a DNA strand that is complementary to this mRNA can be synthesized.

of a mutation in the relevant encoding gene. From several cleaver studies, high levels of this protein were found to be produced in the liver along with the key mRNA molecules directing its synthesis

By separating the factor VIII protein and the affiliated mRNA from other proteins and other mRNAs that were also present, it was possible to identify the gene encoding factor VIII. The major advantage of this method is that a "pure" DNA sequence can be produced that does not contain the extraneous DNA sequences (introns) that occur in genomic DNA. Once the mRNA is isolated and purified, it is used as a template to construct a cDNA strand using the unique enzyme *reverse transcriptase*, which synthesizes DNA from RNA. When the cDNA has been formed, the mRNA strand is removed, and a DNA strand that is complementary to the cDNA is then added, resulting in a typical double-stranded molecule. Once DNA has been obtained, the next step in gene cloning is to create an rDNA molecule that can be used for cloning cDNA or any of the thousands of fragments that can be obtained from genomic DNA.

VECTORS

Vectors are the carrier DNAs into which 'foreign' DNAs or genes of interest are spliced to make a recombinant DNA. Vectors along with this 'foreign' DNAs (i.e., recombinant DNA) are then introduced into appropriate host cell and are maintained for study or expression.

Vectors are essentially expected to replicate inside the host cell along with the inserted DNA. The complete technique of isolating a gene of interest and inserting it into a vector and then replicating and maintaining it into a host cell is called as *Gene cloning*.

Types of Vectors

There are two types of vectors:

(a) Cloning vectors.

(b) Expression Vectors.

(a) Cloning vectors

Cloning vectors are used for obtaining millions of copies of cloned DNA segment. The cloned genes in these vectors are not expected to express themselves, at transcription or translation level. Cloning vectors are used for creating genomic library or preparing, the probes or genetic engineering experiments or other basic studies.

(b) Expression vectors

Expression vectors allow the expression of cloned gene, to give the product (protein). This can be achieved through the use of promoters and expression cassettes and regulatory genes (sequences). Expression vectors are used for transformation to generate transgenic plant, animal or microbe where cloned gene expresses to give the product (protein). Commercial production of product of cloned gene may also be achieved by high level expression using the expression vectors.

Promoters in Vectors

Routine manipulations in gene cloning experiments do not require expression of the cloned DNA. But when required, selection of host/ vector system plays important role. If cDNA molecule is used for cloning eukaryotic gene in prokaryotic system then problem of post transcriptional modification is obviated. For given host cell, there may be several types of expression vectors, then in addition of other consideration, a key feature of selection of expression vector is the type of promoter used to direct expression of the cloned sequence.

A vector with very efficient promoter is chosen to maximise the expression. Promoters are referred to as strong or weak depending on their efficiency of expression. Weak promoters are used if overexpression and excess product formation is likely to be toxic to host cell. Promoters are regions with a specific base sequence, to which RNA polymerase will bind. In addition to the strength of promoter, it is also desirable to regulate expression. This is done by using promoters that are either inducible or repressible. This exerts some control.

Arrangement of restriction sites immediately downstream from the promoter is critical. Thus expression vector will have following essential features:

(a) Origin of replication that is functional in target host cell.

(b) Antibiotic resistance genes or other genetic selection mechanism.

(c) Promoter (strong or weak as per suitability) along with regulatory control.

(d) Restriction sites immediately downstream form the promoter.

(e) Unique restriction site for cloning located in a position where the inserted cDNA sequence can be expressed effectively.

For expression of cloned gene in plants or animals only plant specific or animal specific promoters work. Promoters can confer the transferred gene a specific pattern of expression.

Expression Cassettes

These are gene constructs which allow the insertion of foreign genes, either as transcriptional or transnational fusions, behind specific promoters. PRT series of plasmids which have been derived from pUC 18/19 are the examples.

Organism	Gene promoter	Induction by
1. *E.coli*	lac operon, trp operon, λ P$_L$	IPTG, β-indolylacetic acid, temperature sensitive λ cl protein resp.
2. *A. nidulans*	Glucoamylase	Starch.
3. *S. cerevisiae*	Acid phosphatase	Phosphate depletion
	Alcohol	glucose depletion
	dehydrogenase	galactose heavy
	galactose utilization	metals.
	Metallothionein	
4. *T. reesei*	Cellobiohydrolase	Cellulose
5. Mouse	Metallothionein	heavy metals
6. Human	Heat shock protein	Temperature 740°C
7. Plants (in basal region)	Nopaline synthase (Nos) Mannopine synthase (Mas)	
8. Plants (in leaf tissue)	35 S promoter of Ca MV [high expression (10 fold) at distance of 2 kbp]	
9.	Polyhedrin promoter from baculovirus (used for developing biopesticides or for production of specific chemicals in industry)	

Expression Vectors

Expression vectors are simply designed to express detectable levels of foreign proteins usually at the bench-scale level (i.e. in shake flask cultures).

Production Vectors

Production level vectors are designed for stable large scale production of gene products at economically significant levels. This means production level vectors have additional genetic elements such as *par* sequences, transcription terminators downstream from the cloned genes etc. This is only artificial distinction. Efficients expression vectors are used successfully to express wide variety of proteins. Plasmids like *pASI* are attractive for production purposes as they have strong *pL* transcriptional unit and also a strong transnational unit.

Cloning in *E.coli*

Plasmid DNA used as vector can be cleaved at a site with restriction endonuclease enzyme and foreign DNA segments can be inserted here. Generally, plasmids with two genes for different antibiotic resistance are used—one to identify bacteria that carry plasmid and second to distinguish chimeric plasmid from the parental vector. Insertion of foreign DNA segment is done in site at one antibiotic resistance gene, therefore resistance is lost to one antibiotic.

The chimeric plasmid is resistant to only one antibiotic while the parental plasmid is resistant to two antibiotics. Multicopy plasmids are more suitable since 10-30 copies of one plasmid in a cell along with the inserted gene will give an amplified response. Addition of chloramphenicol often affects new rounds of chromosome replication while plasmid replication is unaffected. This makes isolation of plasmid easier. A common method for cloning DNA is to cleave both plasmid and insert DNA with the same restriction endonuclease. Most of the plasmids which are used as cloning vectors are plasmids derived from natural plasmids so as to posses desirable features.

pBR 322

This is derived from *E. coli* plasmid Col E1. Bolivar and Rodriguez prepared this vector hence the name and 322 are numericals which were significant to these scientists. Alternations and restructuring is done while deriving these plasmids from original natural plasmids. Genes for relaxed replication and genes for antibiotic resistance are inserted in them. pBR 322 is 4362 bp long DNA with genes for resistance to tetracycline and ampicillin. pBR 322 possesses on origin of replication and restriction sites for cleavage by variety of restriction enzymes.

Characteristics of pBR 322

1. It is much smaller in size than natural plasmid. Advantages of small size are : (i) easier to handle, (ii) less susceptible to physical damage, (iii) simpler restriction man, (iv) easy uptake by bacteria during transformation, (v) higher copy number therefore easy detection.

2. Bacterial origin of replication is present and this ensures that plasmid will be replicated in host.

3. Origin of replication is relaxed here, hence activity is not tightly linked to cell division. Resultantly plasmid replication will be initiated for more frequently than chromosomal replication. So more copy number of plasmid per cell is possible.

4. Two genes for different antibiotic resistance.

5. There are single restriction sites for number of enzymes, scattered on plasmid and can be used for cleavage and insertion. Presence

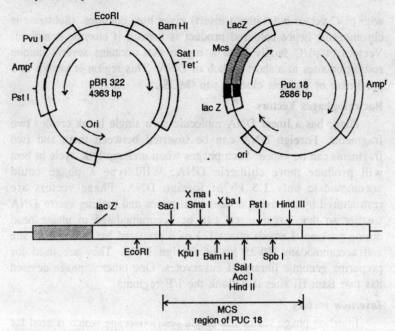

Fig. 13.6. Plasmids pBR 322 and pUC 18.

of such sites within antibiotic resistance gene are important, as they cause respective loss of resistance.

pAT 153 and *pXf 3* are two derivatives of pBR 322 having smaller size and higher copy number.

pBR 327

This is derived from pBR 322, by deletion of nucleotides between 1427 and 2516. These nucleotides are deleted to reduce size of vector and reduce interference. pBR 327 still has genes for resistance against tetracycline and ampicillin.

pUC Vectors

The name is derived from the place of their initial preparation (i.e., University of California). These vectors have 2700 base pairs and ampicillin resistance gene and lac Z gene. Insertion of foreign DNA in lac Z gene causes inactivation of lac Z gene. *E. coli* which is lactose –ve is used for transformation. When culture is grown in presence of IPTG (Isopropyl thiogalactoside) which induces the synthesis of β galactosidase) and X-gal substrate, *E. coli* (transformed with pUC vector with insert) gives white colonies while *E. coli* (transformed with pUC vector but without insert) gives blue colonies. (Substrate is chromogenic hence coloured product is formed if enzyme is active). Vectors of pUC family have a region that contains several unique restriction sites in a short stretch of DNA. This region is known as a polylinker or multiple cloning site (MCS).

Bacteriophages Vectors

Phage has a linear DNA molecule so a single break creates two fragments. Foreign DNA can be inserted between them and two fragments can be joined. Such phages when undergo lytic cycle in host will produce more chimeric DNA. Wild type λ phage could accommodate only 2.5 kb of foreign DNA. Phage vectors are restructured by removing nonessential genes and making vector DNA smaller so that larger insert can be accommodated in phage head during packing. Lambda phage (λ) such prepared has one Eco Rl site and accommodates 20-25 kb of foreign DNA. They are used for preparing genomic library of eukaryotes. One other λ phage devised has two Bam HI sites that flank the I/E region.

Insertion vectors

Insertion phage vector has single restriction site which is used for insertion of foreign DNA. Smaller foreign DNA can be packed here.

Replacement vectors

Replacement vector has two restriction sites which flank a region known as stuffer fragment. Larger fragment of foreign DNA can be replaced between these two sites.

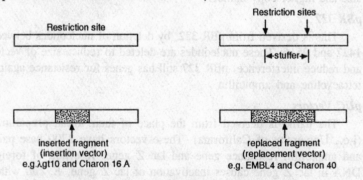

Fig. 13.7. Insertion and replacement vectors.

Cosmids

Cosmids are the novel cloning vectors which possess properties of both plasmid and λ phage. Cosmids first were developed in 1978 by

Barbara Hohn and John Collins. Cosmids contain a cos site of λ phage (which is essential for packaging of nucleic acid into protein coat) plus essential features of plasmid and several unique restriction sites for insertion of DNA to be cloned. Cosmids can be perpetuated in bacteria in plasmid form, but can be purified by packaging *in vitro* into phages. When viral DNA is injected into the cell as a linear molecule it's both ends are cohesive and complementary to each other, 12 base in length.

Once inside the cell, these ends base pair and become permanently joined by ligation to form a region which is known as *cos site* and give rise to circular DNA molecule. Replication of DNA by rolling circle mechanism results into a concatemer which is a long molecule made up of many copies of viral DNA linked end to end through cos sites. DNA is packaged by looping regions between cos sites into precursor of the viral head. When head is full, the cos sites should be at the mouth of the head, where they will be cleaved to generate a linear molecule with cohesive ends. Subsequently tail proteins are added to give infective particle. Thus only requirement for length of DNA to be packaged into viral heads is that it should contain cos sites spaced at correct distance. This distance ranges from 37 to 52 kb. Cos sites of λ possess 280 bp flanking sequence.

For cloning foreign DNA into cosmid vector, cosmid DNA is first linearised by cutting it with appropriate restriction enzyme. Then it is treated with the calf intestinal phosphatase to remove phosphate groups (5´) at its ends so as to prevent recircularisation of cosmid DNA. Foreign DNA which is to be cloned is also treated with the same restriction enzyme which was used for treating cosmid DNA. Subsequently cosmid DNA and foreign DNA fragments are mixed in presence of T4 DNA ligase. Many different products generate in the mixture.

A product may form where foreign DNA binds to cos site of cosmid in same orientation. This on *in vitro* incubation with phage head and tail proteins, cleavage of cos sites takes place and intervening DNA is packed into phage particles. When susceptible bacteria are infected by such phage, hybrid DNA is injected into cell. Then it functions like plasmid and expresses antibiotic resistance gene. The infected cells can be selected and isolated on basis of antibiotic resistance gene expressed. Foreign DNA presence can be detected in antibiotic resistant bacterial colonies. Inserts of 40-50 kb length can be easily placed between cos sites and to get packageble forms of cosmids.

Advantage of using cosmid vector is that larger DNA can be cloned than what is possible with phage or plasmid. As larger inserts are possible genomic library can be created which is composed of fewer clones to be screened. Efficiency of cosmids is high enough to produce a complete genomic library of 10^6-10^7 clones from a mere $1\mu g$ of insert. Genomic libraries of Drosophila, mouse and several other organisations has been produced with cosmid vectors. Cosmid PLFR-5 has two cos sites, 6 restriction enzymes target sites, origin of replication and tetracycline resistance marker. It can insert 50 kb of DNA. Cosmid system in case of P_1 bacteriophage of *E. coli* can carry 85 kb of inserted DNA.

For *in vitro* packaging of recombinant DNA containing cosmid *packaging extract* is used. This is nothing but two strains of bacteria. These two strains when mixed with concatameric recombinant DNA under suitable conditions head, tail and DNA with proper cos site distance is available and phage particles are produced. These infective phages then can be used to infect *E. coli* cells.

Phasmid Vectors

Here combination of plasmid and λ phage is produced. Plasmid is inserted into phage λ genome by means of site specific recombination mechanism of the phage that is normally used by phage for insertion into bacterial chromosome during lysogen formation. This process is called 'lifting' the plasmid and combination is called phasmid.

Phasmid contain functional origins of replications of the plasmids and of λ and may be propagated as plasmid or phage in appropriate *E. coli* host strains. Plasmids can be released by several of lifting. Phage particles are easy to store, have infinitive shelf life and their screening as plaques by hybridization gives better results than screening of bacterial colonies. So plasmid with cloned gene can be lifted by phages and conveniently handled. Release of recombinant plasmid is easier. λ ZAP is highly developed phasmid containing λ, M_{13} and T_7 phages. λ ZAP is suitable for cloning cDNAs. λ ZAP has multiple unique cloning sites, can hold 10 kb of inserts, easy excision of cloned DNA possible. Insertional inactivation of β galactosidase gives blue/white screening on X gal plates. Expression of hybrid polypeptides is analogous to that in λ gt 11.

Shuttle Vectors

Transfer of genes between unrelated species is one of the requirements of molecular biotechnology. Broad host range vectors exist in Gram negative bacteria and *Streptomyces* naturally. A shuttle vector however may be required having necessary replicon for maintenance in different combinations of unrelated hosts. Shuttle vectors have potential importance in the genetic manipulations of industrially important species. Shuttle vectors can exploit gene manipulative procedures of different hosts for example when *E. coli* amplification will be possible. Shuttle vectors exist for *E. coli* yeast cells combination. *E. coli—Agrobacterium* combination and *E. coli—B. subtilis. E. coli—Streptomyces lividans* and *E. coli—mammalian* cells combinations.

VEHICLES

A DNA molecule needs to display several features to be able to act as a vehicle for gene cloning. Most important, it must be able to replicate within the host cell, so that numerous copies of the recombinant DNA molecule can be produced and passed to the daughter cells. A cloning vehicle also needs to be relatively small, ideally less than 10 kilobases (kb) in size, as large molecules tend to break down during purification, and are also more difficult to manipulate. Two kinds of DNA molecule that satisfy these criteria can be found in bacterial cells: plasmids and bacteriophage chromosomes. Although plasmids are frequently employed as cloning vehicles, two of the most important types of vector in use today are derived from bacteriophages.

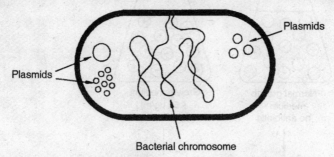

Fig. 13.8. Plasmids independent genetic elements found in bacterial cells.

Plasmids

Basic features of plasmids

Plasmids are circular molecules of DNA that lead an independent existence in the bacterial cell. Plasmids almost always carry one or more genes, and often these genes are responsible for a useful characteristic displayed by the host bacterium. For example, the ability to survive in normally toxic concentrations of antibiotics such as

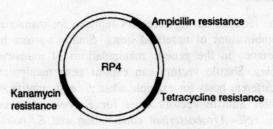

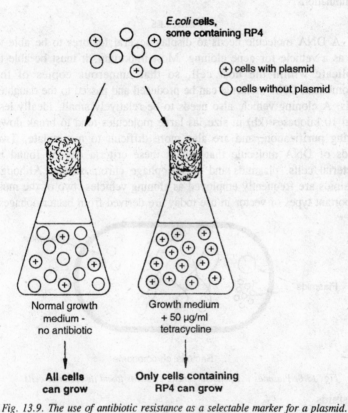

Fig. 13.9. The use of antibiotic resistance as a selectable marker for a plasmid.

chloramphenicol or ampicillin is often due to the presence in the bacterium of a plasmid carrying antibiotic resistance genes. In the laboratory antibiotic resistance is often used as a *selectable marker* to ensure that bacteria in a culture contain a particular plasmid.

All plasmids possess at least one DNA sequence that can act as an *origin of replication*, so they are able to multiply within the cell

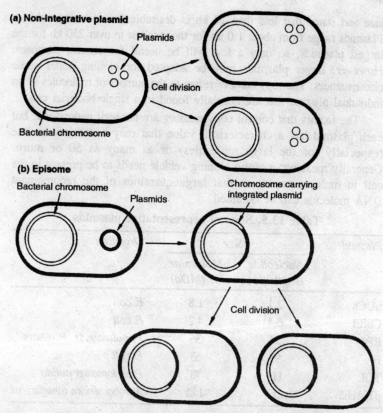

Fig. 13.10. Replication strategies for (a) a non-integrative plasmid, and (b) an episome.

quite independently of the main bacterial chromosome. The smaller plasmids make use of the host cell's own DNA replicative enzymes in order to make copies of themselves, whereas some of the larger ones carry genes that code for special enzymes that are specific for plasmid replication. A few types of plasmid are also able to replicate by inserting themselves into the bacterial chromosome. These integrative plasmids or *episomes* may be stably maintained in this form through numerous cell divisions, but will at same stage exist as independent elements. Integration is also an important feature of some bacteriophage chromosomes and will be described in more detail when these are considered.

Size and copy number

These two features of plasmid are particularly important as far as cloning is concerned. We have already mentioned the relevance of plasmid size and stated that less than 10 kb is desirable for a cloning vehicle. Plasmids range from about 1.0 kb for the smallest to over 250 kb for the largest plasmids, so only a few will be useful for cloning purposes. However, larger plasmids may be adapted for cloning under some circumstances. The *copy number* refers to the number of molecules of an individual plasmid that are normally found in a single bacterial cell.

The factors that control copy number are not well understood, but each plasmid has a characteristic value that may be as low as one (especially for the large molecules) or as many as 50 or more. Generally speaking, a useful cloning vehicle needs to be present in the cell in multiple copies so that large quantities of the recombinant DNA molecule can be obtained.

Table 13.5. Sizes of representative plasmids

Plasmid	Size		Organism
	Nucleotide length (kb)	*Molecular wt (MDa)*	
pUC8	2.1	1.8	*E.coli*
ColEI	6.4	4.2	*E.coli*
RP4	54	36	*Pseudomonas* + others
F	95	63	*E.coli*
TOL	117	78	*Pseudomonas putida*
pTiAch5	213	142	*Agrobacterium tumefaciens*

Conjugation and compatibility

Plasmids fall into two groups conjugative and non-conjugative. Conjugative plasmids are characterized by the ability to promote sexual *conjugation* between bacterial cell, a process that can result in a conjugative plasmid spreading from one cell to all the other cells in a bacterial culture. Conjugation and plasmid transfer are controlled by a set of transfer or *tra* genes, which are present on conjugative plasmids but absent from the non-conjugative type.

A non-conjugative plasmid may, under some circumstance, be cotransferred along with a conjugative plasmid when both are present in the same cell. Several different kinds of plasmid may be found in a single cell, including more than one different conjugative plasmid at any one time. In fact, cells of *E. coli* have been known to contain up to seven different plasmids at once. To be able to coexist in the same cell, different plasmids must be *compatible*. If two plasmids are incompatible then one or the other will be quite rapidly lost from the

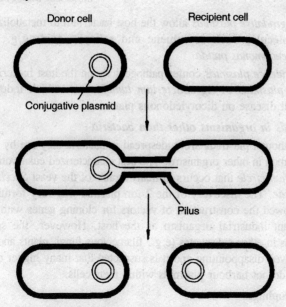

Fig. 13.11. Plasmid transfer by conjugation between bacterial cells.

cell. Different types of plasmid can therefore be assigned to different *incompatibility groups* on the basis of whether or not they can coexist, and plasmids from a single incompatibility groups are often related to each other in various ways. The basis of incompatibility is not well understood, but events during plasmid replication are thought to underlie the phenomenon.

Plasmid classification

There are five main types of plasmid which are as follows:

1. *Fertility* or *'F' plasmids* carry only *tra* genes and have no characteristic beyond the ability to promote conjugal transfer of plasmids, e.g., F plasmid of *E. coli*.

2. *Resistance* or *'R' plasmids* carry genes conferring on the host bacterium resistance to one or more antibacterial agents, such as chloramphenicol, ampicillin and mercury, R plasmids are very important in clinical microbiology as their spread through natural populations can have profound consequences in the treatment of bacterial infections; e.g., RP4, commonly found in *Pseudomonas*, but also occurring in many other bacteria.

3. *Col plasmids* code for colicins—proteins that kill other bacteria; e.g., ColE1 of *E. coli*.

4. *Degradative plasmids* allow the host bacterium to metabolize unusual molecules such as toluene and salicylic acid; e.g., TOL of *Pseudomonas putida*.

5. *Virulence plasmids* confer pathogenicity on the host bacterium; e.g., *Ti plasmids* of *Agrobacterium tumefaciens*, which induce crown gall disease on dicotyledonous plants.

Plasmids in organisms other than bacteria

Although plasmids are widespread in bacteria they are by no means so common in other organisms. The best characterized eukaryotic plasmid is the *2μm circle* that occurs in many strains of the yeast *Saccharomyces cerevisiae*. The discovery of the 2 μm plasmid was very fortuitous as it has allowed the construction of vectors for cloning genes with this very important industrial organism as the host. However, the search for plasmids in other eukaryotes (e.g., filamentous fungi, plants and animals) has proved disappointing and it is suspected that many higher organisms simply do not harbour plasmids within their cells.

Bacteriophages

Basic features of bacteriophages

Bacteriophages, or phages as they are commonly known, are viruses that specifically infect bacteria. Like all viruses, phages are very simple in structure, consisting merely of a DNA (or occasionally RNA) molecule carrying a number of genes, including several for replication of the phage, surrounded by a protective coat or *capsid* made up of protein molecules.

The general pattern of infection, which is the same for all types of phage, is a three-step process.

1. The phage particle attaches to the outside of the bacterium and injects its DNA chromosome into the cell.

2. The phage DNA molecule is replicated, usually by specific phage enzymes coded by genes on the phage chromosome.

3. Other phage genes direct synthesis of the protein components of the capsid, and new phage particles are assembled and released from the bacterium.

With some phage types the entire infection cycle is completed very quickly, possibly in less than 20 minutes. This type of rapid infection is called a *lytic cycle*, as release of the new phage particles is associated with lysis of the bacterial cell. The characteristic feature of a lytic infection cycle is that phage DNA replication is immediately

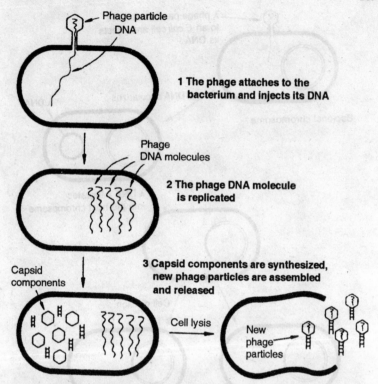

Fig. 13.12. The general pattern of infection of a bacterial cell by a bacteriophage.

followed by synthesis of capsid proteins, and the phage DNA molecule is never maintained in a stable condition in the host cell.

Lysogenic phages

In contrast to a lytic cycle, *lysogenic* infection is characterized by retention of the phage DNA molecule in the host bacterium, possibly for many thousands of cell divisions. With many lysogenic phages the phage DNA is inserted into the bacterial genome, in a manner similar to episomal insertion. The integrated form of the phage DNA (called the *prophage*) is quiescent, and a bacterium (referred to as a *lysogen*) which carries a prophage is usually physiologically indistinguishable from an uninfected cell.

The prophage is eventually released from the host genome and the phage reverts to the lytic mode and lyses the cell. The infection cycle of λ, a typical lysogenic phage is of this type. A limited number of lysogenic phages follow a rather different infection cycle. When M13, or a related phage, infects *E. coli*, new phage particles are continuously

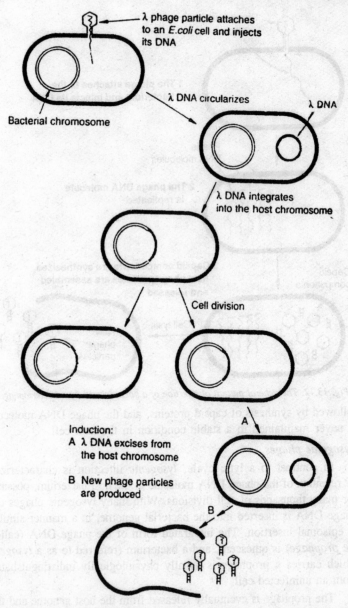

λ phage particle attaches
to an *E.coli* cell and injects
its DNA

Bacterial chromosome

λ DNA circularizes

λ DNA

λ DNA integrates
into the host chromosome

Cell division

Induction:

A λ DNA excises from
   the host chromosome

B New phage particles
   are produced

Fig. 13.13. The lysogenic infection cycle of bacteriophage λ.

assembled and released from the cell. The M13 DNA is not integrated
into the bacterial genome and does not become quiescent. With these

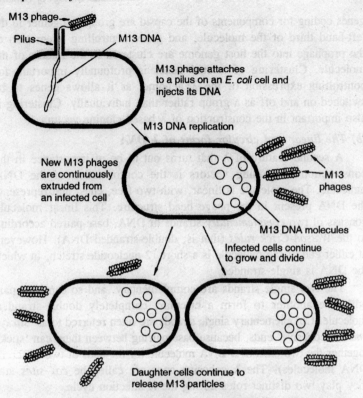

M13 phage

Pilus

M13 DNA

M13 phage attaches to a pilus on an *E. coli* cell and injects its DNA

M13 DNA replication

New M13 phages are continuously extruded from an infected cell

M13 phages

M13 DNA molecules

Infected cells continue to grow and divide

Daughter cells continue to release M13 particles

Fig. 13.14. *The infection cycle of bacteriophage M13.*

phages, cell lysis never occurs, and the infected bacterium can continue to grow and divide, albeit at a slower rate than uninfected cells. Although there are many different varieties of bacteriophage, only λ and M13 have found any real role as cloning vectors. The properties of these two phages will now be considered in more detail.

(a) Gene organization in the λ DNA molecule

λ is a typical example of a head-and-tail phage. The DNA is contained in the polyhedral head structure and the tail serves to attach the phage to the bacterial surface and to inject the DNA into the cell. The λ DNA molecule is 49 kb in size and has been intensively studied by the techniques of gene mapping and *DNA sequencing*. As a result the positions and identities of most of the genes on the l DNA molecule are known.

A feature of the λ genetic map is that genes related in terms of function are clustered together on the genome. For example, all of the genes coding for components of the capsid are grouped together in the left-hand third of the molecule, and genes controlling integration of the prophage into the host genome are clustered in the middle of the molecule. Clustering of related genes is profoundly important for controlling expression of the λ genome, as it allows genes to be switched on and off as a group rather than individually. Clustering is also important in the construction of λ-based cloning vectors.

(b) The linear and circular forms of λ DNA

A second feature of λ that turns out to be of importance in the construction of cloning vectors is the conformation of the DNA molecule. The molecule is linear, with two free, ends, and represents the DNA present in the phage head structure. This linear molecule consists of two *complementary* strands of DNA, base-paired according to the *Watson-Crick rules* (that is, double-stranded DNA). However, at either end of the molecule is a short 12-nucleotide stretch, in which the DNA is single-stranded.

The two single strands are complementary, and so can base-pair with one another to form a circular, completely double-stranded molecule. Complementary single strands are often referred to as *'sticky'* *end* or 'cohesive' ends, because base-pairing between them can 'stick' together the two ends of a DNA molecule (or the ends of two different DNA molecules). The λ cohesive ends are called he *cos sites* and they play two distinct roles during the λ infection cycle.

First of all, they allow the linear DNA molecule that is injected into the cell to be circularized, which is a necessary prerequisite for insertion into the bacterial genome. The second role of the *cos* sites is rather different, and comes into play after the prophage has excised from the host genome. At this stage a large number of new λ DNA molecules are produced by the rolling circle mechanism of replication in which a continuous DNA strand is 'rolled off' of the template molecule. The result is a catenane consisting of a series of linear λ genomes joined together as the *cos* sites. The role of the *cos* sites is now to act as recognition sequences for an *endonuclease* which cleaves the catenane at the *cos* sites producing individual λ genomes.

The endonuclease (which is the product of gene A on the λ DNA molecule) creates the single-stranded sticky ends, and also acts in conjunction with other proteins to package each λ genome into a phage head structure. The cleavage and packaging processes recognize just the *cos* sites and the DNA sequences to either side of them. Changing the structure of the internal regions of the λ genome, for example by inserting new genes, has no effect on these events so long as the overall length of the λ genome is not altered too greatly.

(c) M13—a filamentous phage

M13 is an example of a filamentous phage and is completely different in structure from λ. Furthermore, the M13 DNA molecule is much smaller than the λ genome, being only 6407 nucleotides in length. It is circular, and is unusual in that it consists entirely of single-stranded DNA. The smaller size of the M13 DNA molecule means that it has room for fewer genes than the λ genome. This is possible because the M13 capsid is constructed from multiple copies of just three proteins, whereas synthesis of the λ head-and-tail structure involves over 15 different proteins. In addition, M13 follows a simpler infection cycle than λ and does not need genes for insertion into the host genome. Injection of an M13 DNA molecule into an *E. coli* cell occurs via the *pilus*, the structure that connects two cells during sexual conjugation.

Once inside the cell the single-stranded molecule acts as the template for synthesis of a complementary strand, resulting in normal double-stranded DNA. This molecule is not inserted into the bacterial genome, but instead replicates until over 100 copies are present in the cell. When the bacterium divides, each daughter receives copies of the phage genome, which continues to replicate, thereby maintaining its overall numbers per cell. New phage particles are continuously assembled and released, about 1000 new phages being produced during each generation of an infected cell.

(d) The attraction of M13 as a cloning vehicle

Several features of M13 make this phage attractive as the basis for a cloning vehicle. The genome is less than 10 kb in size, well within the range that we stated was desirable for a potential vector. In addition, the double-stranded *replicative form* of the M13 genome behaves very much like a plasmid and can be treated as such for experimental purposes. It is easily prepared from a culture of infected *E. coli* cells and can be reintroduced by *transfection*.

Most importantly, genes cloned with an M13-based vector can be obtained in the form of single-stranded DNA. Single-stranded versions of cloned genes are useful for several techniques, notably DNA sequencing and *in vitro* mutagenesis. Using an M13 vector is an easy and reliable way of obtaining single-stranded DNA for this type of work.

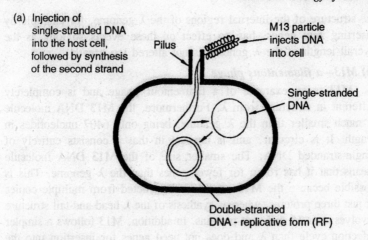

(a) Injection of
single-stranded DNA
into the host cell,
followed by synthesis
of the second strand

Pilus

M13 particle
injects DNA
into cell

Single-stranded
DNA

Double-stranded
DNA - replicative form (RF)

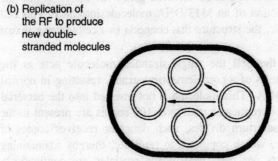

(b) Replication of
the RF to produce
new double-
stranded molecules

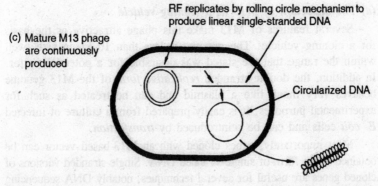

RF replicates by rolling circle mechanism to
produce linear single-stranded DNA

(c) Mature M13 phage
are continuously
produced

Circularized DNA

Mature phage particles

Fig. 13.15. The M13 infection cycle showing the different types of DNA replication.

Viruses as cloning vehicles for other organisms

Most living organisms are infected by viruses and it is not surprising that great interest has been shown in the possibility that viruses might be used as cloning vehicles for higher organisms. This is especially important when it is remembered that plasmids are not commonly found in organisms other than bacteria and yeast. In fact viruses have considerable potential as cloning vehicles for animal cells. Mammalian viruses such as *simian virus 40 (SV40)* and *adenoviruses*, and the insect *baculoviruses*, are the ones that have received most attention so far, but others are also being studied.

THE ROLE OF BACTERIA

Bacteria are one-celled organisms that reproduce very rapidly by binary fission (dividing into two cells) after a brief growth period. They live in practically every environment, but the species of greatest use to molecular biologists are those that can be easily cultivated in the laboratory by placing them on a suitable culture medium contained in a small dish. A single bacterial cell can give rise to tens or hundreds of thousands of identical cells (clones) in a single day. When a vector containing rDNA is inserted successfully into a bacterial cell, it is replicated, and hence the DNA fragment of interest is cloned.

Much of the earliest information about cell biology and molecular biology came from studies of bacteria. Today, they play a critical role in gene-cloning technologies. The most popular bacterium in all of this work has been *E. coli*, a normally harmless inhabitant of mammalian digestive tracts. More is known about the molecular biology of *E. coli* than about any other species on Earth. *E. coli* and some other bacteria are used to perform two functions in rDNA technology. First, they are used to clone genomic DNA or cDNA to obtain unlimited numbers of genes that can be used in further studies. Second, pure cultures, in which every bacterium contains a gene encoding a desired protein, can be created and put to work manufacturing huge quantities of that protein. Plasmids that contain specific sequences to direct protein synthesis are called *expression vectors*.

GENE LIBRARIES

One of the major uses of rDNA technology is to create *gene libraries* for different species. In accordance with the procedure used to obtain the DNA, there are libraries of both genomic clones and cDNA clones. The number of "volumes" (DNA fragments or genes) required in the library to ensure that all gene sequences are represented is generally related to the size and complexity of the species. For *E. coli*, 1,500 fragments are necessary; for yeast, 4,600; fruit flies, 48,000; and humans, 800,000.

Researchers create a *gene library* for a particular species in the following sequence of events:

1. Genomic DNA is cut into thousands of fragments with appropriate restriction enzymes.
2. Each fragment, representing approximately one gene, is spliced into a phage-cloning vector.
3. The phages are replicated by the "host" bacteria, thus replicating (cloning) the inserted gene fragments.

Such a library is a repository of the entire genome where every gene of a species is represented. The space required for a typical gene library is a test tube or a set of small culture dishes that can be conveniently kept in a refrigerator pending further analysis. Molecular biologists have developed specialized techniques to "screen" gene libraries, that is, to determine where specific genes are located in the pieces of DNA. This involves isolating a gene and identifying the protein it encodes. Once a gene has been isolated and cloned, it is possible quickly to determine its entire base sequence. As you might expect, the greatest emphasis is currently on research related to the human gene library, and remarkable progress has been made in isolating human genes of medical importance. Nevertheless, the human gene library is so immense, and many genes are so difficult to locate, that a complete reading of our library probably lies one or more decades in the future.

APPLICATIONS OF GENETIC ENGINEERING

Recombinant DNA technology has revolutionized biology in the past decade. At present, its main uses are (1) facilitating the production of useful proteins, (2) creating bacteria capable of synthesizing economically important molecules, (3) supplying DNA and RNA sequences as a research tool, (4) altering the genotype of organisms such as plants, and (5) potentially correcting genetic defects in animals (gene therapy). Some examples of these applications follows:

Commercial Possibilities

Bacteria with novel phenotypes can be produced by genetic engineering sometimes by combining the features of several other bacteria. For example, several genes from different bacteria have been inserted into a single plasmid that has then been placed in a marine bacterium, yielding an organism capable of metabolizing petroleum; this organism has been used to clean up oil spills in the oceans.

Many biotechnology companies are at work designing bacteria that can synthesize industrially important chemicals. Bacteria have been designed that are able to compost waste more efficiently and to fix nitrogen (to improve the fertility of soil), and an enormous effort is currently being expended to create organisms that can convert biological waste to alcohol. A human insulin, synthesized in *E. coli*, is already commercially available. Altering the genotype of plants is an important application of recombinant DNA technology. Of great use is the bacterium *Agrobacterium tumefaciens* and its plasmid Ti, which produces crown gall tumors in dicotyledonous plants. These tumor result from disruption of the bacterium inside plant cells, release of bacterial DNA, and integration of a segment of the plasmid DNA into the plant chromosome.

It is possible by genetic engineering to introduce genes from one plant into this plasmid and then, by infecting a second plant with the bacterium, transfer the genes of the first plant to the second plant. (Actually genes are first cloned in an *E. coli* plasmid and then recloned in Ti). Attempts are being made to perform plant breeding in this way. An example is the attempted alteration of the surface structure of the roots of grains such as wheat, by introducing certain genes from legumes (peas, beans), in order to give grains the ability of the legumes to establish root nodules of nitrogen-fixing bacteria. If successful, this would eliminate the need for the addition of nitrogenous fertilizers to grain-growing soils.

The first engineered recombinant plant of commercial value was developed in 1985. An economically important herbicide (weed killer) is glyphosate, which inhibits a particular essential enzyme in many plants. However, most herbicides cannot be applied to fields growing crops because both the crop and the weeds would be killed.

The target gene of glyphosate is also present in the bacterium *Salmonella typhimurium*. A resistant form of the gene was obtained by mutagenesis and growth of *Salmonella* in the presence of glyphosate; the gene was cloned in *E. coli*, and then recloned in *Agrobacterium*. Infection of plants with purified Ti containing the glyphosate-resistance gene has yielded varieties of maize, cotton, and tobacco that are resistant to glyphosate. Thus, fields of these crops can be sprayed with glyphosate at any stage of growth of the crop. All weeds are killed, and the crop is totally unharmed. An interesting bacterium is a strain of *Pseudomonas fluorescens*, which lives in association with maize and soybean roots. A lethal gene from *Bacillus thuriengis*, a bacterium pathogenic to the back cutworm, has been engineered into this bacterium. The black cutworm causes extensive crop damage and is usually combatted with noxious insecticides. In preliminary studies inoculation of soil with the engineered *Ps. fluorescens* resulted in death of the cutworm.

Uses in Research

Recombinant DNA technology is extraordinarily useful in basic research. Several examples were already given in mutant bacteria in which particular genetic systems have been altered in an effort to make them more amenable to study (for example, the numerous mutants in the *lac* operon). Such mutants have usually been derived through standard genetic techniques. For simple mutants this procedure is straightforward, but for mutants required to have many genetic markers (which may be very closely linked) the frequency oi production of mutants can be so low that their isolation becomes very tedious.

Recombinant DNA techniques can simplify mutant construction, since fragments containing desired genetic markers can be purified, altered, and combined in test tube, and then introduced into another cell. This saves time and labour, and often enables mutants to be constructed that cannot in practice be formed in any other way. An example is the formation of double mutants of animal viruses, which undergo crossing over at such a low frequency that mutations can rarely be recombined by genetic crosses.

The greatest impact of the new technology on basic research has been in the study of eukaryotes, in particular, of eukaryotic regulation. Experiments of the type, which study the regulation of operons in bacteria, have been made possible by the use of mutations in promoters, operators, and structural genes. However, this approach has not been feasible with eukaryotes, because eukaryotes are diploid and, hence, mutants are difficult to isolate.

Furthermore, except for the unicellular eukaryotes such as yeast, there is no simple and rapid way to do multiple genetic manipulations with eukaryotic cells. Cloning techniques have made it possible to study regulation of gene expression in eukaryotes by direct assays of mRNA molecules produced by particular genes. The approach is based on the success with which it has become possible to understand gene activity in bacteria by studying the synthesis of mRNA in a variety of conditions.

An excellent assay is DNA-RNA hybridization, in which either a primary transcript or mRNA is detected by hybridization to a DNA sample that has been enriched for the gene being studied. In microbial experiments specialized transducing particles would be the source of the DNA—for example, *E. coli* gal mRNA is assayed by hybridization of radioactivity labeled intracellular RNA with DNA of *l gal* transducing particles. However, transducing particles do not exist for eukaryotic systems, so recombinant DNA techniques have been used to clone a gene whose regulation is to be studied.

The usual procedure is to clone the gene first in a plasmid (or a phage) vector and then allow the cell containing the plasmid to multiply. Purified plasmid DNA provides the researcher with a large supply of the DNA of that gene. The vector containing that DNA sequence is called a DNA *probe*, because its DNA, in denatured form, can be added to a cell extract containing mRNA, to probe for a particular mRNA by renaturation. Since no natural genes of the vector are present in eukaryotic cells, the vector DNA can be regarded as a source of pure DNA copies of a particular eukaryotic gene because no other genes in the vector will participate in the renaturation.

A further useful technique is to apply denatured probe DNA to a nitrocellulose filter and then to use a filter-binding assay for the specific RNA species. DNA but not RNA binds to these filters. Radioactive mRNA can then be incubated with a filter containing the DNA, using conditions such that renaturation will result. Except where the mRNA has renatured to the denatured DNA, the RNA can be removed by washing the filter. Thus, presence of radioactivity in the filter after washing indicates that complementary mRNA has been bound to the DNA on the filter. This simple technique and variations such as Southern blotting have revolutionized the study of eukaryotic gene regulation.

Production of Eukaryotic Proteins

One of the most valuable applications of genetic engineering is the production of large quantities of particular proteins that are otherwise difficult to obtain. The method is simple in principle. The gene encoding the desired protein is cloned in a vector adjacent to a bacterial promoter, and tests are performed to ensure that the gene is oriented such that its coding strand is linked to the strand containing the promoter. A plasmid for which many copies are present in each cell, or occasionally an actively replicating phage (such as λ), is used as a vector; in both cases, cells can be prepared that contain several hundred copies of the gene, and this can result in synthesis of a gene product to reach a concentration of about 1 to 5 percent of the cellular protein. In practice, production of large quantities of a prokaryotic protein in a bacterium is straightforward. However, if the gene is from a eukaryote, special problems exist:

1. Eukaryotic promoters are not usually recognized by bacterial RNA polymerases.
2. The mRNA transcribed from eukaryotic genes may not be translatable on bacterial ribosomes.
3. Introns may be present, and bacteria are unable to excise eukaryotic introns.
4. The protein itself often must be processed (for example, insulin); and bacteria cannot recognize processing signals from eukaryotes.
5. Eukaryotic proteins are often recognized as foreign material by bacterial protein-digesting enzyme and are broken down.

Several approaches to solving these problems have been taken with some degree of success. One procedure uses a genetically engineered plasmid, called a *shuttle vector*, that consists of both *E. coli* and yeast DNA and replicates in both organisms.

Cloning is done in *E. coli*, which for a variety of technical reasons is easier than cloning in yeast, and then the plasmid is isolated and transferred to yeast for expression of the cloned gene. In yeast the five problems just stated are avoided, or at least substantially reduced. Another approach uses a plasmid containing the *E. coli lac* region, cleaved in the *lacZ* gene by a restriction enzyme making blunt ends. Either c-DNA or a synthetic DNA molecule whose sequence is known from the amino acid sequence of the protein product is inserted into the *lacZ* gene, so that the eukaryotic protein is synthesized as the terminal region of β-galactosidase, from which it can be cleaved.

The first example of this approach resulted in a synthetic gene capable of yielding a 14-residue polypeptide hormone—somatostatin—which is synthesized *in vivo* in the mammalian hypothalamus. The procedure, applicable to most short polypeptides, was the following.

By chemical techniques, a double-stranded DNA molecule was synthesized containing 51 base pair; the base sequence of the coding strand was

TAC-(42 base encoding somatostatin)-ACTATC

The base sequence of the corresponding mRNA molecule was

AUG-(42 bases encoding somatostatin)-UGAUAG

The AUG codon of the mRNA was not used for initiation, but specified methionine. The mRNA terminated with two stop codons UGA and UAG.

The vector was the plasmid pBR322 modified to contain the *lac* promoter-operator region and a portion of the *lacZ* gene encoding the amino-terminal segment of β-galactosidase. The vector was cleaved at a site in the *lacZ* segment by a restriction enzyme that leaves blunt ends; the synthetic DNA molecule was then blunt-end-ligated to the cleaved plasmid. When the *lac* operon was induced, a protein was made consisting of the amino-terminal segment of β-galactosidase *coupled by methionine* to somatostatin, and terminated at the repeated stop codons of the synthetic DNA. This protein was purified and treated with cyanogen bromide, a reagent that cleaves proteins only at the

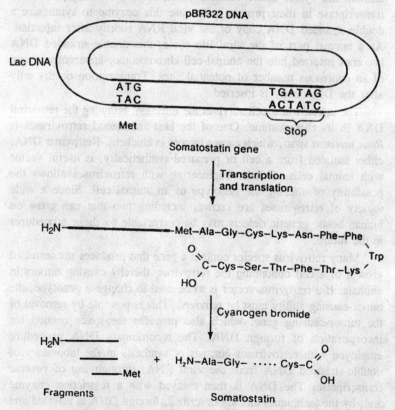

Fig. 13.16. Synthesis of somatostatin from a chemically synthesized gene joined to the plasmid pBR22 lac.

carboxyl side of methionine. In this way, the methionine linker remains attached to a β-galactosidase fragment and somatostatin is released. Use of methionine-coupling followed by cleavage with cyanogen bromide is a useful technique for separating any polypeptide from a bacterial protein to which it is fused, as long as the polypeptide itself does not contain methionine. Another more generally useful linker is $(Asp)_4$-Lys. In a sequence (Asp_4)-Lys-X, in which X is another amino acid, the enzyme enterokinase cleaves between lysine and X. Since such a sequence is not common, this linker is of more value than methionine.

Genetic Engineering with Animal Viruses

Retroviruses are RNA-containing animal viruses that have an unusual life cycle. These viruses, which contain the enzyme reverse transcriptase in their protein coats, use this enzyme to synthesize a double-stranded DNA copy of the viral RNA shortly after infection. As a normal part of the viral life cycle, this double-stranded DNA becomes inserted into the animal-cell chromosome, apparently at one of an enormous number of potential sites. Transcription occurs only after the DNA copy is inserted.

The infected host cell survives the infection, retaining the retroviral DNA in its chromosome. One of the best-understood retroviruses is *Rous sarcoma virus*, which causes tumors in chickens. Retrovirus DNA, either isolated from a cell or prepared synthetically, is useful vector with animal cells. Genetic engineering with retroviruses allows the possibility of altering the genotype of an animal cell. Since a wide variety of retroviruses are known, including two that can grow on human hosts, genetic defects may be correctable by these procedures in the future.

Many retrovirus species contain a gene that produces uncontrolled growth of a cell containing the retrovirus, thereby causing tumors in animals. If a retrovirus vector is to be used to change a genotype, the tumor-causing ability must be removed. This is possible by removal of the tumor-causing gene, which also provides the space needed for incorporation of foreign DNA. The recombinant DNA procedure employed with retroviruses consists of synthesis in the laboratory of double-stranded DNA from the viral RNA, through use of reverse transcriptase. The DNA is then cleaved with a restriction enzyme and, by the techniques already described, foreign DNA is inserted and selected.

Treatment of mutant cells in culture with the recombinant DNA, and application of a transformation procedure suitable for animal cells, yields cells in which recombinant retroviral DNA has been permanently inserted into an animal-cell chromosome. In this way, the genotype of the cell can be altered. Experiments have been done in which human cells deficient in the synthesis of purines have been obtained from patients with Lesch-Nyhan syndrome and grown in culture; these cells have been converted to normal cells by transformation with recombinant DNA. The exciting potential of this technique lies in the possibility of correcting genetic defects—for example, restoring the ability of a diabetic individual to make insulin or correcting immunological deficiencies. This technique has been termed *gene therapy*. However, it must be recognized that retroviruses are not well understood and are potentially dangerous. Gene therapy is not yet a practical technique, for major problems exist; for example, there is no reliable way to ensure that a gene is inserted in the appropriate target cell or target tissue. In addition, some means is needed to regulate the expression of the inserted genes. A major breakthrough in disease prevention has been the development of synthetic vaccines. Production of certain vaccines such as anti-hepatitis B has been difficult because of the extreme hazards of working with large quantities of the hepatitis B virus. The danger would be avoided if the viral antigen could be cloned and purified in *E. coli* or yeast, because the pure antigen could be given as a vaccine.

Several viral antigens have been cloned, but because of either thermal instability or poor antigenicity when pure, attempts to make vaccines in this way have generally been unsuccessful. However, the use of vaccinia virus (the anti-smallpox agent) as a carrier has been fruitful. The procedure makes use of the fact that viral antigens are on the surface of virus particles and that some of these antigens can be engineered into the coat of vaccinia. By 1985 vaccinia hybrids with surface antigens of hepatitis B, influenza virus, and vesicular stomatitis virus (which kills cattle, horses, and pigs) have been prepared and shown to be useful vaccines in animal tests. A surface antigens of *Plasmodium falciparum*, the parasite that causes malaria, has also been placed in the vaccinia coat; this may lead to an antimalaria vaccine.

Diagnosis of Hereditary Diseases

Restriction mapping has also been used in prenatal diagnosis—for example, in detecting sickle-cell anemia. This disease is caused by possession of an altered hemoglobin. The base change causing the mutation generates a cleavage site for a particular restriction enzyme. Cleavage of DNA from a sickle-cell patient produces a restriction map that differs from that of the DNA of a normal patient. The different restriction pattern can be detected by using Southern blotting and, as a probe, radioactive RNA prepared by transcribing cloned globin genes. The technique is so sensitive that the sickle-cell mutation can be detected in a small sample of cells obtained from the amniotic fluid surrounding a fetus, and detection is possible at a very early stage of development. Possibly in the future, gene therapy might be used to produce a normal child.

14

TREATMENT OF GENETIC DISORDERS

Therapy, by definition, is the treatment of an individual. Therefore, the term *genetic therapy* (or *gene therapy*) is used within this chapter to mean any procedure that has as its purpose the prevention, reduction, or cure of a genetic disease. Although dramatic gains are being made in the areas of screening and counseling, lasting genetic therapy is still unavailable for most of the human hereditary diseases. However, in most cases a good diagnosis and discussion of available therapy will at least eliminate the agony that parents go through while looking for answers to What is it and can it be treated? Just knowing "what it is" can be of great relief to many parents.

There are no treatments or therapies currently available to *cure* any genetic disease, but in many cases, therapy will increase the affected person's life span and improve the quality of his or her life.

Genetic therapy for genetic-disease expression is called *euphenics*. Euphenics can be divided into three classes based on the type of therapy administered.

CLASS-I GENETIC THERAPY

Procedures and techniques are designed to offset the symptoms of the disease. The therapy involves organ transplantation, drugs, surgery, dietary manipulation, and the avoidance of substances that elicit symptoms. Brief summaries of the different uses of class-I genetic therapy follows:

Organ Transplantation

Organ and tissue transplants are possible ways of installing normal genes into genetically affected patients. The cells of the transplanted tissue contain the genes necessary to produce the required gene product for normal health. The human pancreas has been transplanted in cases of diabetes, and the kidney has been used in transplants for patients who demonstrated the inherited form of polycystic renal disease. Kidney transplants have been unsuccessful in the treatment of patients with Fabry's disease and cystinosis. Bone marrow transplants have also been performed on patients with thalassemia and various forms of immune deficiency diseases and in several lysosomal storage diseases, including Gaucher's and the Maroteaux-Lamy syndromes. However, bone marrow transplants are limited to diseases that do not affect the central nervous system because transplanted bone marrow cells do not cross the blood-brain barrier. Liver transplantation has been used in cases of severe familial hypercholesterolemia.

A major problem in transplantation therapy, even where it is successful, is obtaining scarce organs. In addition, there are problems with continued suppression of the immune system to hold the graft. "Successful" genetic transplants may lead to unforeseen complications later in life. In general, tissue transplantation has not made a major impact on patients demonstrating genetic diseases.

Drugs

Drugs are used in many cases where the genetic disease affects the central nervous system. In many cases, drugs have produced excellent results in normalizing mood and behavioural changes in inherited depressive disorders, in reducing excessive cholesterol in hypercholesterolemics, and in reducing pain and discomfort resulting from gout, migraine headache, and hereditary jaundice. Drugs may also be used to induce or increase the production of certain enzymes. It has been demonstrated, for example, that the drugs danazol and tamoxifen cause an increase in serum levels of alpha-antitrypsin. With respect to enzyme induction, in some types of hereditary jaundice, phenobarbital stimulates the production of a missing enzyme and relieves the symptoms of the disease. The drug 5-azacytidine, when administered to adult beta-thalassemia and sickle-cell anemia patients, turned on dormant genes to produce foetal hemoglobin, which boosted the patients' hemoglobin and red blood cell production. A search is underway to find other drugs that can also turn on normal, but silent, foetal genes to replace abnormal or missing adult gene products.

One inherited recessive disorder, *acrodermatitis enteropathica*, is effectively treated with the drugs diiodohydroxyquinoline and zinc sulfate. This disease is very striking in that the symptoms are scaling and blistering around the body orifices, the eyes, genitals, and anal areas. If left untreated, the affected person loses his or her hair, eyebrows, and eyelashes and passes bulky, putrid-smelling stools. Patients become withdrawn and die at an early age. The administration of diiodohydroxy-quinoline brings about a dramatic improvement, hair grows, weight increases, and skin lesions heal. The action of the drug is not understood, but it has been suggested that there is an enzyme defect in the intestinal lining of such people. Because of the lack of enzyme activity in the intestinal lining, a "toxic" substance is not properly detoxified. The drug, binding to this substance, neutralizes the toxic effect, and normal body activities resume.

A wide variety of cytotoxic drugs are also used in cancer chemotherapy. Selected drugs preferentially kill tumor cell. Theoretically, with the use of these drugs a cancer should be disposed of before the host is damaged. However, cancer cells develop a drug resistance. Recent evidence suggests that this drug resistance is associated with a change in the chromosomes of tumor cells. It has been demonstrated that tumor-cell resistance to drug therapy is associated with irregular chromosome morphology and with the presence of extraneous small, paired chromosome fragments called *double minutes*. Some of the change in chromosome morphology is associated with the amplification of certain chromosome regions called *homogeneously staining regions* (HSRs). The presence of extra chromosomal material, double minutes, and HSRs, indicate that such tumor cells contain multiple copies of certain genes. Logically, protein products of these gene play a role in the cell's resistance.

A gene that codes for *multiple drug resistance* (mdr) has now been assigned to human chromosome 7. The gene codes for the production of P-glycoprotein, which is found in relatively large concentrations in human drug-resistant tumor cells. Because P-glycoprotein spans the cell membrane and was found to be structurally similar to some bacterial "pump" proteins (pump unwanted molecules outside the cell), it is speculated that drug-resistance genes—and mdr in particular—circulate the cytotoxic drugs out of the cancer cells before the drugs can kill. It is now believed that gene amplification produces an excess of the *glutathione peptide* that is present in drug-resistant colon-cancer cells. Glutathione neutralizes cell-damaging peroxides and hydroxyl radicals, which are agents that normally kill tumor cells. In cases where a drug or radiation is used to stop DNA replication, thereby stopping cell division of cancer cells, the cancer cell produces gaining an even better understanding of how cancer cells become resistant to different forms of therapy, more effective forms of therapy will be introduced.

Table 14.1. Inherited diseases and class-I genetic therapy

Disease	Therapy	Results
Acrodermatitis enteropathica	Diiodohydroxyquinoline plus zinc (e.g., zinc, sulfate)	Excellent
Adrenal congenital hyperplasia	Corticosteroids	Excellent
Adrenogenital syndrome	Cortisone induce salt loss	Good
Alpha₁-antitrypsin emphysema	No smoking (clean air)	Good
Apert's syndrome	Surgery	Poor to fair
Cystic fibrosis	Diet, antibiotics, mist	Good short-term life expectancy
Cystinosis	Diet (restricted methionine and cystine plus increase ascorbic acid)	Questionable
Cystinuria	High-fluid intake, alkaline, penicillamine	Fair to good for urolithiasis
Diabetes, type I	Insulin	Good
Diabetes, type II	Diet, insulin	Good
Diabetes insipidus	High-fluid intake, low salt	Fair
Familial goiter	Levothyroxine	Questionable
Familial hyperlipo-proteinemia	Diet (restricted to short-chain fatty acid)	Fair
Familial xantho-matosis	Cholesterol diet plus drugs	Poor to fair
Favism (G-6-PD dificiency)	Avoidance of specific drugs and fava beans	Excellent
Fructosemia	Fructose-free diet	Good
Galactosemia	Galactose-free diet	Good
Glycinemia	Protein-restricted diet	Poor to fair
Gout (hyperuricemia)	Low-uric acid diet, colchicine plus allopunnol	Good for pain
Gynecomastia	Surgery	Cosmetically excellent

Hartnup disease	Nicotinamide	Fair to good
Hemochromatosis	Iron-restricted diet; venesections	Fair to poor
Hemophilia	Blood factor VIII injections	Good to excellent
Hereditary jaundice	Phenobarbital	Good
Hirschsprung's disease	Surgery	Good
Histidinemia	Histidine-restricted diet	Questionable
Huntington's disease	Drugs for behaviour control	Good
Hydrocephaly	Cranial shunt; head wrap	Good
Hypercholesterolemia	Low-cholesterol diet plus drugs	Fair to good
Hyperlipidemia	Low-fat diet	Fair to questionable
Hyperuricemia	Low-uric acid diet	Poor to fair
Hypospadias	Surgery	Cosmetically good
Ichthyosis vulgaris (alligator skin)	Retinoic acid	Fair to good
Intestinal polyposis	Surgery	Good if early
Lactose intolerance	Avoidance of milk and other dairy products	Excellent
Manic depression	Drugs	Fair to good
Maple syrup urine disease	Diet (restricted leucine, isoleucine, valine and methionine)	Poor to good
Marfan's syndrome	Surgery	Fair to excellent
Meningomyelocele	Surgery	Poor to fair
Methylmelonic acidemia	Vitamin B_{12}	Good
Migraine headache	Drugs	Fair to excellent
Mucopolysaccharidosis VI	Bone marrow transplant	Under evaluation
Multiple carboxylase deficiency	Biotin	Good
Oroticaciduria	Uridine	Good
Osteogenesis imperfecta	Calcitonin	Fair
Osteoporosis	Calcitonin	Good
Pernicious anemia	Vitamin B_{12}	Excellent
Phenylketonuria	Phenylalanine-free diet	Good
Polycystic renal kidney disease (late)	Kidney dialysis; kidney transplant	Life saving

Prophyria, acute intermittent	IV 3 mg hermatin/kg body weight (experimental status)	Good (initial reports)
Pyridoxine dependency	High intake of pyridoxine	Fair to good
Ragweed hay fever	Desensitization	Fair to good
Renal tubular acidosis	Alkali	Good
Retinoblastoma	Surgery, radiation therapy plus cryotherapy	Life saving
Scurvy	Vitamin C (ascorbic acid)	Excellent
Short stature	Human growth hormone	Fair to good
Sickle-cell anemia	Cyanate injection; vitamin B_6 Nitrilosides	Fair to good in crisis Under study
Some solid tumors	Interferon	Poor to good
Spina bifida	Surgery	Poor
Tyrosinemia	Diet (restricted phenylalanine and tyrosine)	Questionable
Urea cycle disorders Argininosuccini-caciduria Ornithinuria Citrullinura	Moderate protein-intake restriction; diet supplemented by arginine	Under evaluation
Usher's syndrome (progressive deafness and blindness)	Vitamin A	Poor
Wilson's disease	Penicillamine restricted copper	Fair
Xeroderma pigmentosum	Avoidance of direct sunlight; use of medicated creams	Fair

Table 14.2. Inherited diseases and Class-II genetic therapy

Disease	Therapy	Results
Crigler-Naijar syndrome	Blood transfusions; phenobarbital	Fair; short-term life expectancy
Fabry's disease	Enzyme replacement	Questionable
Homocyastinuria	Methionine-restricted diet plus vitamin $B_6{}^2$	Questionable
Rh incompatibilty	Gamma globulin injection	Good to excellent
Von Willebrand's disease	Blood factor VIII injections	Good to excellent
Wiskott-Aldrich syndrome	Blood platelet transfusion	Good

General Surgery

Surgery is most often used for the removal of an organ or an undesirable growth. In effect, surgery helps to relieve the patient's symptoms. For example, splenectomy (removal of the spleen) is quite effective in correcting the disorder of hereditary spherocytosis, a type of anemia. Removal of part or most of the large intestine also eliminates colon polyps that may become malignant. For achondroplasia, leg lengthening operations now lead to, on average, 30 cm of growth in the lower limbs.

Constructive cosmetic surgery has been very helpful in inherited disorders. It is frequently used in cases of cleft lip and palate, Apert's syndrome, gynecomastia (breast enlargement in males). Hypospadias (urethra opening on the underside of the penis), retinoblastoma (cancer of the eye), and some polygenic central nervous system disorders, such as spina bifida and various myeloceles.

Foetal Surgery

Foetal surgery has been developed for urinary-tract obstruction and hydrocephalus (water on the brain). The most successful surgical procedure has been the treatment of urinary-tract obstruction. The obstructed bladder or ureters are drained by temporary nephrostomy tubes implanted in the foetus. *In utero* drainage of foetal hydrocephaly to date has shown less long-term success. The decision to perform a surgical procedure on the foetus must be based on analysis of the total situation. A decision not to undertake foetal surgery may be made when the presence of other equally severe or noncorrectable anomalies are present.

Dietary Manipulation: Ingestion and Avoidance

The most successful treatment of inherited disorders to date appears to be diet regulation. This is not to say that diet therapy alone is adequate; rather, it reflects the present limitations in the treatment of inherited disease. Diet modifications may call for one of the following:

1. Low-level intake of dietary metals, such as low iron for patients with hemochromatosis (excess iron in the liver, heart, and pancreas) or low-copper intake for patients with Wilson's disease.

2. High-level intake of dietary metals, such as copper in patients with Menkes' disease (kinky-hair syndrome).

3. Low-level intake of various dietary amino acids. In phenylketonuria, a minimal level of phenylalanine has been established; in homocystinuria, cystine is kept low.

4. Elimination of dietary factors. In galactosemia and lactose sensitivity, milk sugars galactose and lactose, respectively, are eliminated from the diet; for glucose-6-phosphate. dehydrogenase deficiency, fava beans are eliminated from the diet and various drugs, especially barbiturates, are eliminated from medications.

5. High-level intake of dietary vitamins. For the treatment of scurvy, vitamin C is used; for refractory rickets, vitamin D is used; and for pernicious anemia, vitamin B12 is recommended.

The success of dietary manipulation in treating a number of genetic disease suggests a close relationship between the gene and its environment and, more specifically, between the gene and nutrition. The administration of large doses of vitamins sometimes restores enzyme function, perhaps through establishing the lost affinity or association between an enzyme and its vitamin cofactor. For example, administration of vitamin B_6 offers some relief in homocystinuria and sickle-cell anemia. The most successful vitamin therapies to date are vitamin D for inherited refractory rickets and vitamin B_{12} for pernicious anemia and methylmelonic acidemia, although over twenty-five inherited diseases can now be treated with megadose vitamin therapy.

For many of the recessive metabolic inherited diseases, diet restriction is an effective treatment. For example, all six genetic disorders of the urea cycle respond to restricted protein ingestion and arginine supplementation. In phenylketonuria, the patient builds up phenylalanine, which causes brain damage. This patient is placed on a diet low in phenylalanine. In contrast to PKU is the disease oroticaciduria where, because of the lack of the enzyme orotic decarboxylase, orotic acid is not converted into uridine. High levels of orotic acid do not appear to be harmful, as is the case in high levels of phenylalanine, but the deficiency of uridine, which is a precursor to the synthesis of nucleic acids, is disastrous. In this case, adding uridine to the diet is an effective therapy.

For those defects (galactosemia, phenylketonuria, maple syrup urine disease, and tyrosinemia) that may be treated with some success, dietary management should begin as soon after birth as possible. Because early diet therapy in these disorders may be of significant help to the individual patient, it is important that the physician, who may only see one or two cases in his or her career, be able to obtain the information on both patient management and special diets. To this end, food and drug manufactures in the United States and Europe produce specially formulated diets for the treatment of particular inherited diseases, and a number of genetic centers provide assistance in diagnosis and management of patients, or in admission to a center if required. One specially formulated diet food is Lofenalac, a compound that is low in the amino acid phenylalanine, for use in treating phenylketonuria.

CLASS-II GENETIC THERAPY

Class-II genetic therapy involves the administration of human gene products—an enzyme or other proteins—to patients who demonstrate an enzyme or protein-factor deficiency.

Enzyme Therapy

Regardless of route of entry, enzymes, which are protein in nature, are quickly inactivated by the body's immune defense mechanisms. Because of this inactivation, enzyme therapy has not been successful and to date is not considered to be a practical means of genetic-disease therapy. Enzyme therapy has been tried with minimum success in the treatment of Fabry's disease, a glycolipid metabolic disease. With Hurler's and Hunter's syndromes (mucopolysaccharide diseases), unsuccessful attempts have been made to infuse patients with plasma from normal persons. It was hoped that in such treatment, the enzyme of the normal plasma would degrade the accumulated mucopolysaccharides in the patients. Hexosaminidase A enzyme therapy has also been tried in Tay-Sachs disease and Sandhoff's disease patients with similar lack of success. Arylsulfatase A therapy in metachromatic leukodystrophy patients is also unsuccessful. Children with argininemia (high levels of arginine) have been infected with Shope papilloma virus on the theory that a viral gene might allow for the production of the enzyme arginase, which would degrade the accumulated arginine. To date, these experiments have been unsuccessful. The administration of glucocerebrosidase to some Gaucher's disease patients (a recessive glycolipid metabolic disease) resulted in a temporary reduction in accumulated glycolipid levels. Recently, a capsule form of a fungus lactase enzyme has been marketed. The enzyme temporarily restores deficient human intestinal lactase enzyme activity in person who are lactase deficient. Ingestion of the enzyme allows these people to consume milk and milk-related products like ice cream, cheese, pizza, and many other popular foods.

There is at least one other bright spot in the investigations on enzyme therapy for genetic diseases. It is the use of alpha 1-antitrypsin.

Alpha 1-antitrypsin

Alpha 1-antitrypsin is an enzyme secreted by the liver and macrophages. It protects lung connective tissue from degradation by *proteases* (enzymes that break down proteins), particularly the enzyme elastase. An excess of elastase in the lungs leads to *emphysema* (severe breathlessness). Weekly administration of alpha 1-antitrypsin brings the level of this enzyme in the blood and lungs of emphysema patients to normal.

The alpha 1-antitrypsin gene is codominant, and at least twenty-five variants in the glycoprotein structure of the gene have been described. The more common variants of the gene are listed in table 14.3. The most common, or "normal," genetic variant is called Pi M (Pi stands for protease inhibitor). About 90 percent of the U.S. population is homozygous Pi MM and have the highest level of the serum enzyme. Heterozygous variants of this gene produce at least 30 percent of the normal level and the phenotype is basically unaffected. However, the homozygous Pi ZZ produces a very low level of the enzyme and the phenotype suffers from emphysema and other liver and pulmonary disorders. There are over 100,000 Pi ZZ patient in the United States who may benefit when broad-based enzyme therapy begins. Currently, the major problem is widespread administration is obtaining a sufficient supply of the enzyme. This problem should soon be overcome as researchers have sequenced the 324 amino acids making up the enzyme and have produced the enzyme via recombinant DNA techniques. An associated problem, however, is that the genetically engineered enzyme, for reasons not yet understood, is too quickly removed from the serum. Attempts are being made to deliver the enzyme into the lungs in an aerosol form. Until such time that the enzyme can be successfully maintained in the serum, the very best therapy is to stop smoking. The deleterious effects of cigarette smoking in alpha 1-antitrypsin-deficient individuals has been extensively documented. Unlike smokers with normal enzyme levels who run a 20 percent risk of developing lung disease, the risk of lung disease in smokers with the enzyme deficiency is over 70 percent and probably approaches 100 percent over time.

Protein Factors

Various factors required by the body, but missing because of a genetic error, can be successful replaced. Examples are blood factor VIII, the antihemophilic globulin required for blood clotting; calcitonin, a hormone necessary for the retention of bone calcium in such hereditary

Table 14.3. Alpha 1-antitrypsin deficiency phenotypes

Genotype	Affected U.S. population (%)	(%) Serum alpha 1-antitrypsin concentration (% relative to concentration in subjects with the MM phenotype)
Pi MM	89.5	100
Pi MS	7.1	75
Pi MZ	3.0	57
Pi SZ	0.2	37
Pi ZZ	0.1	16

disorders as osteogenesis imperfectal the insulin hormone for diabetes; and anti-Rh globulin for prevention of Rh disease.

In both class-I and class-II genetic therapies, the procedures and treatment are compensatory and palliative rather than curative. That is, the use of class-I and class-II genetic therapies is aimed at modifying the consequences of a defective gene; such therapy does not cure the diseases. Class-I and class-II therapies do not alter the gene, only the environment. Class-III genetic therapy is gene therapy; it is a molecular attempt to cure genetic disease. Researchers are working to provide a means of curing genetic defects by manipulating the DNA of the gene.

CLASS-III GENETIC THERAPY

Class-III genetic therapy is the addition to a normal gene to cells carrying a defective gene. In theory, this third type of gene therapy is simple: insert a "good" gene into a somatic cell to compensate for a "bad" gene. In reality, somatic-cell gene therapy is biologically complex and raises many ethical questions. To begin with, the defective gene must be found from among the 100,000 or so other genes. The gene must then be cloned, placed into the cells of the proper tissue type, and finally induced to express normal function. The task is difficult, but not impossible. For example, in 1982 Wilson and colleagues established the amino acid sequence of normal *hypoxanthine-guanine phosphoribosyl transferase* (HPRT) enzyme from human RBCs. The enzyme consists of four protein subunits, each of which consists of 217 amino acids. Establishing the normal amino acid sequence of HPRT enzyme protein enabled Wilson and colleagues to identify the specific amino acid substitutions in mutant forms of the HPRT enzyme and to infer alterations that must have occurred in the DNA. They compared the amino acid data from three HPRT enzyme-deficient patients with missense mutations (one amino acid substituted for by another) who demonstrated gout with a missense mutation that did not affect the level of the HPRT enzyme in a Lesch-Nyhan patient. The substitution of asparagine for arginine at position 193 in the fourth individual resulted in a normal HPRT enzyme level, but the person developed the Lesch-Nyhan syndrome. While this method of mutant analysis has proved valuable in the description of pathogenic mutations, it is limited to those that result in the production of a protein product. In a study by Stout and Wilson, eleven of fifteen Lesch-Nyhan patients did not produce a protein.

Jolly and colleagues (1983) established the DNA sequence of the HPRT gene. The gene consists of nine exons and eight introns. Miller and colleagues have cloned the normal HPRT gene and inserted the

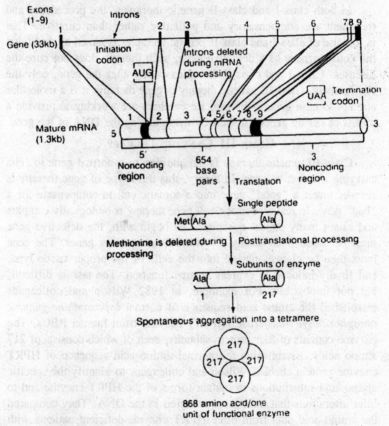

Fig. 14.1. Molecular reproduction of the HPRT gene.

DNA into murine retroviral vectors. The virus carrying the HPRT gene was used to infect HPRT-negative human cells in culture. The infected cells were cured of the genetic defect. The produced the HPRT enzyme at levels found in normal cells. Next, bone marrow cells of mice were infected with the virus carrying the HPRT gene and replaced in the mice whose bone marrow cells were killed by radiation. The engineered bone marrow cells successfully populated the mouse bone marrow and produced the HPRT enzyme. The next step is an attempt to engineer human bone marrow cells. The plan is to remove bone marrow from the hip of a Lesch-Nyhan patient, infect it *in vitro* with the virus, and then transplant it back into the patient. There is some evidence from animal experiments that an injection of the engineered virus may be effective. However, at this time there is no way of controlling or knowing where in the human system the virus will or will not locate. The purpose of the initial experiment is to create a model by which gene transplantation or genetic engineering can be routinely accomplished. After it is accomplished, a gene transplant into a defective newborn may be an effective treatment.

In parallel experiments to those of Jolly and colleagues, the normal human HPRT gene was isolated, cloned, and made ready for the first human genetic engineering experiment. In the meantime, the DNA probes made to hybridize with the HPRT gene have made possible accurate prenatal diagnosis and carrier testing for the male foetus or adult suspected of having the defective HPRT gene.

TYPES OF GENE THERAPY

Studies in preparation for human gene therapy engage a variety of technologies, the latest being recombinant DNA technology. The different technologies to actually be used depend on how the physician wishes to correct the defective gene. Currently following forms of genetic therapy are envisioned.

Genes and Gene Regulation

Researchers developing gene therapy approaches face two main obstacles: identifying key genes and their mode of regulation and inserting genes into appropriate chromosomal sites. For each single-gene disorder, all of the following will be necessary:

1. Identification of the normal gene site and nucleotide sequence that has been altered and the protein it encodes.
2. Understanding of how the gene's expression is regulated.
3. Creation of vectors or physical methods that can be used to transport the normal gene into cells where the gene can be expressed.

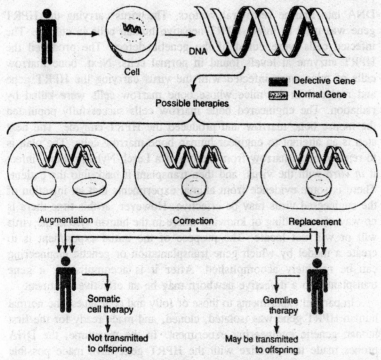

Fig. 14.2. Gene therapy consists of different strategies designed to modify the effects of a defective gene.

4. Ensuring that the gene becomes stably integrated and expressed so that the protein product is present at levels sufficient to reduce or eliminate effects of the disorder.

Gene Insertion

Since the early 1970s, the use of mouse and bird retroviruses as vectors for transferring normal human genes has been carefully investigated. *Retroviruses* are unusual viruses because their genetic material is RNA, not DNA. Once they infect a host cell, retroviruses are replicated through a mechanism that translates their RNA into DNA. This, of course, is the opposite of the normal translation of genetic information, DNA into RNA, hence the prefix *retro-*. Human retroviruses cause several important diseases, including some cancers and AIDS.

In the laboratory, retroviruses have several advantages as vectors compared to others that have been studied. They are easy to manipulate and have a demonstrated ability to transfer foreign genes into cells and have the genes expressed. However, retroviruses are sometimes unstable, it is impossible to control where the genes they carry are inserted, and even if they do become integrated, the genes are not always expressed. Recipient human cells must be dividing before the gene carried by a retrovirus can be integrated in their chromosomes. For example, bone marrow cells divided rapidly and constantly to produce blood cells and may be good candidates for retroviral vectors, depending on the purpose of the gene insertion. Because of the cell division requirement, these vectors cannot be used for introducing genes into the mature cells—brain, nerve, muscle, or other cells—that make up most human tissues.

Despite these problems, it is evident that retrovirus vectors will play a prominent role in future developments. Other viral vectors are now receiving increased attention. For example, *herpesviruses*, which normally live inside nerve cells (and cause such problems as cold sores and genital herpes in humans) can perhaps be modified to serve as vectors for inserting genes into nervous tissue, physical methods, such as microinjection and high-velocity microprojectiles, are also being studied.

Through all of the difficulties have not yet been overcome, impressive progress has been made since the mid-1980s. Some forms of gene therapy now appear to offer great promise for ameliorating the effects of certain human genetic disorders.

Ethical Issues

The policy of the U.S. National Institutes of Health Recombinant DNA Advisory Committee (RAC) currently prohibits germline therapy experiments, but human somatic cell therapy research is taking place in laboratories throughout the country and the world. Most scientists and physicians view the projected uses of somatic cell therapies as extensions of accepted medical procedures, comparable to blood and marrow transfusions used for treating diseases. Also, few disagree with the justification that the use of somatic cell therapy is appropriate for treating a genetic disorders when no other treatment is available. Consequently, few specific objections have been raised based on ethical considerations.

In sharp contrast, many people, including ordinary citizens, scientists, politicians and others, have questioned the wisdom of creating genetic alterations that can be transmitted to future generations Is it acceptable or unacceptable to attempt to alter the germinal cells of an individual with a genetic disorder in such a way that the person

can have children who will not have the disorder? Perhaps there would
be general agreement that germline therapy might be allowed for single-
gene disorders. However, most human traits are controlled by more
than one gene, and little is known about the genetics of such traits.

With respect to humans, no clear consensus about germline
therapies has yet emerged, in part because the research has not
progressed to the point where serious concerns have arisen. However,
because of the severe technical problems and a clear indication from
most groups that they are not yet ready to accept experiments centered
on human germline alterations, it seems unlikely that any research in
this area will be approved in the near future.

Somatic Cell Gene Therapy

There are two general categories of somatic cell gene therapy,
gene substitution and *gene augmentation*. As originally conceived, it
was thought that *gene substitution* could be used to remove and replace
mutant genes responsible for genetic disorders. However, there have
been no successes in creating such substitution therapies. Alternatively,
would it be possible to "correct" the abnormal DNA sequences of
mutant genes? This might be accomplished by using established gene
transfer methods to introduce a normal DNA sequence that would
recombine, through complementary base pairing, with the mutant
sequence. If the normal gene were then expressed, the needed protein
would be available and the effects of the disorder would be reduced or
eliminated. Some progress has been made in gene correction techniques
and their application to research on animals such as mice.

Gene augmentation involves techniques that will equip cells with
added genes that can produce the missing protein associated with the
genetic disorder. Two basic methods are being developed; (1) a
"standard" technique in which competent genes are inserted into cells
of an afflicted individual, followed by introduction of the altered cells
into the appropriate tissue where they are normally expressed, and (2)
the insertion of the needed gene into "donor" cells that are then placed
back into the body, where they produce the protein. This latter approach
has been referred to as a "drug delivery system," and it offers exciting
prospects. How does the donor cell system work? Vectors containing
a normal gene encoding a missing protein—an enzyme produced by
the liver, for example—are inserted into nonliver cells such as bone
marrow cells, which produce white blood cells, or endothelial cells,
which line the inside of blood vessels. These donor cells are then
transferred into the body, where they become established, express the

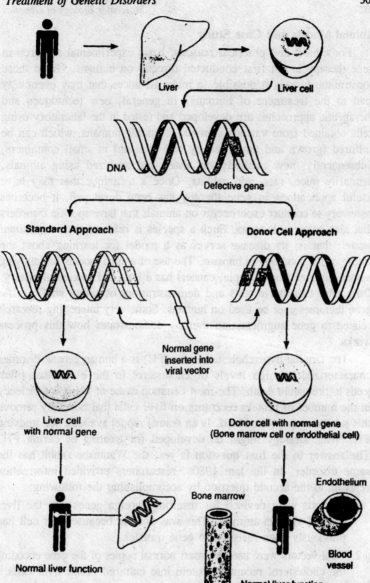

Liver

Liver cell

DNA

Defective gene

Standard Approach

Donor Cell Approach

Normal gene
inserted into
viral vector

Liver cell
with normal gene

Donor cell with normal gene
(Bone marrow cell or endothelial cell)

Bone marrow

Endothelium

Normal liver function

Blood
vessel

Normal liver function

Fig. 14.3. Two gene augmentation approaches have been developed.

gene, and pump out useful quantities of the missing enzyme into the bloodstream. There have been notable accomplishments using both the standard and donor cell types of gene therapy.

Animal Models and Case Study

For ethical and practical reasons, basic experimental research in gene therapy is not first conducted directly on humans. Given these constraints, how is it possible to make advances that may eventually lead to the treatment of humans? In general, new techniques and therapeutic approaches are developed and tested in the laboratory using cells obtained from various animals, including humans, which can be cultured (grown and amplified by cell division) in small containers. Subsequently, new methods are tested and analyzed using animals, primarily mice, rats, and rabbits. Once a technique that may have useful applications in gene therapy has been developed, it becomes necessary to conduct experiments on animals that have specific disorders that also occur in humans. Such a species is referred to as an *animal model*; that is, its disease serves as a model for learning about the nature of the condition in humans. The use of animal models for studying human diseases (for example, cancer) has a long and successful history. Only after exhaustive tests and demonstrations of safety will specific gene therapies ever be used on humans. Some very interesting research related to gene augmentation therapy demonstrates how this process works.

The familial hypercholesterolemia (FH) is a human genetic disorder characterized by high levels of cholesterol in the blood that often leads to premature death. The most common cause of FH is a deficiency in the number of protein receptors on liver cells that normally remove this substance from the blood. Is an animal model available for studying FH? What strategy might be developed for treating or curing FH? The answer to the first question is yes; the Watanabe rabbit has the same disorder. In the late 1980s, researchers provided information relevant to the second question by accomplishing the following:

1. Methods were devised for inserting foreign genes into the liver cells of various animals. This was notable because liver cell had previously been resistant to gene transfer.

2. Viral vectors were used to insert normal copies of the gene encoding the cholesterol receptor protein into cultured rabbit liver cells.

3. Once inside the rabbit cells, the cholesterol receptor gene produced functional receptor protein that removed cholesterol from the experimental system.

The next step will be to place the cells back into Watanabe rabbit in an attempt to cure the disease. For that to happen, the altered cells will have to become permanently established in the rabbit's body and continue to produce the receptor protein. Though these very exciting results have obvious implications for the treatment of FH, they represent only the first step in a long path leading to human clinical applications. What is required before similar types of gene therapy tests can be conducted on humans?

Authorization Procedures for Studies on Humans

Before conducting any experiments related to human gene therapy, scientists must obtain legal approval from several regulatory agencies. Research plans must first be reviewed by local institutional review boards and institutional biosafety committees. At the national level, approval is required from the RAC and the director of the NIH. In addition, the proposed experiment must be described in nonscientific language and published in the *Federal Register* so that members of the public can, if they wish, offer comments to the RAC and the NIH. The purposes of this review are to ensure that only qualified research teams conduct such tests, that all safety and ethical issues are fully considered and evaluated, and that the public has an opportunity to express its feelings.

The first experiment

How does the authorization process work in real life? Early in 1988, a request to conduct the first human gene therapy experiment in the United States was submitted by W. French Anderson of the National Heart, Blood, and Lung Institute and Steven Rosenberg and R. Michael Blaese of the National Cancer Institute. Their proposal stemmed from earlier investigations on a promising new approach for treating cancer. Specific immune cells—white blood cells called *lymphocytes*—that kill "foreign" cells, including cancer cells, normally exist in the body. In early studies, lymphocytes that had infiltrated the tumor (*tumor-infiltrating lymphocytes*, or TIL cells) of seriously ill patients were removed surgically and induced to grow and multiply in the laboratory. When sufficient numbers of cultured TIL cells had been generated, they were reinfused into the patient. TIL therapy caused significant tumor regression in about 50 percent of the 25 patients tested who had advanced cancers and had failed to respond to other treatments.

Why was TIL therapy effective only in some of he patients? To try to answer this question, Anderson, Rosenberg, and Blaese wanted to insert a single-gene "marker" (for resistance to the antibiotic neomycin) into TIL cells using a retrovirus vector and follow their progress once placed back into a patient. The marker would allow researchers to identify TIL cells with the gene by collecting blood samples periodically during treatment and then exposing all blood cells removed to neomycin; those with the marker would survive, while those without the resistance gene would perish. The marker would have no effect on either the TIL cells or their capacity for attacking cancer cells.

In accordance with the procedures described earlier, the proposal was approved by the various committees, but not without delays related to procedure (not all of the relevant preliminary data were made available to RAC members) and a large number of public hearings. A lawsuit alleging that the review process was not open to the public was eventually dismissed.

Finally, on May 22, 1989, a severely ill cancer patient received the first infusion of TIL cells that had been genetically altered to contain the foreign neomycin gene. Additional patients were treated during the following weeks. Results from the experiment were similar to those from earlier studies—some patients showed dramatic regression of their tumors, and others did not. The significance of the research lies in what was learned about the marker TIL cells introduced into the patient. They survived in the body, apparently attacked and killed tumor cells, and were unchanged by the inserted gene. The next step in this research was to seek approval to insert a gene for an active antitumor agent (a natural protein produced by the immune system) into TIL cells. Approval for such an experiment was granted in 1990, and results from new experiments may be available in 1991.

Though perhaps not technically a gene therapy experiment (the gene inserted into TIL was neutral, not therapeutic), this is considered the first such study in the United States. The TIL experiment opened the doors to further studies involving gene therapy. For example, the same group of researchers received approval to test the effects of a *tumor necrosis factor* (TNF) gene inserted into lymphocytes. TNF is a protein that shrinks tumors by cutting off their blood supply. The first patients were treated in 1990, and further tests are now under way. In 1990 and 1991, children with a rare, lethal immune deficiency known as ADA (because of a defective enzyme called *adenosine deaminase*) received transfusion of their own lymphocytes, which contained foreign ADA genes. One child, a 4-year-old girl, received cells on September 14, 1990. This is considered the first test of human gene therapy. Finally, in 1991, scientists succeeded in synthesizing normal dystrophin genes. Gene therapy trials involving this gene are expected to begin soon. Clearly, an increasing number of human gene therapy experiments can be expected in the next five years.

HUMAN GENOME PROJECT

What is known about the location of genes on human chromosomes? In a monumental achievement, the first partial map of the human genome was published in the journal *Cell* in 1987. This *genetic linkage map* is based on the location of gene loci on each chromosome relative to the positions of specific markers. Each marker provides a distinct reference point on the chromosome, and together they serve as a primitive map for identifying the approximate location of various genes

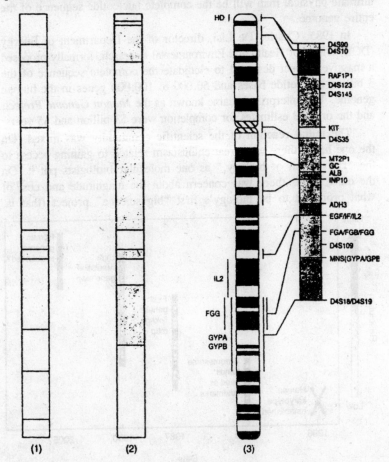

Fig. 14.4. Figure showing human genome map.

of interest. The blanks continued to be filled in and in October 1990, an undated human genome map was published in the journal *Science*.

A question on an even grander scale was raised during the mid-1980s: Could a high-resolution physical map consisting of the exact sequence of nucleotides in the entire human genome be drawn? A *physical map* shows the actual location of genes and also the distances between genes as determined by constant, identifiable landmarks. Figure shows the progression of human chromosome mapping. The crudest physical map uses chromosomal bands as landmarks. A map based on linkage markers represents a higher degree of resolution, and the ultimate physical map will be the complete nucleotide sequence of the entire genome.

In 1985, Charles De Lisi, director of the Department of Energy (DOE) Office of Health and Environmental Research, formally proposed a massive project designed to elucidate the complete sequence of the 3 billion nucleotide bases and 50,000 to 100,000 genes in the human genome. The enterprise became known as the *Human Genome Project*, and the original estimates for completion were $3 billion and 15 years.

The initial reaction of the scientific community was mixed. On the one hand, there was great enthusiasm related to gaining access to the "Holy Grail of biology," as one molecular biologists put it. On the other hand, there was concern about the magnitude and cost of what promised to be biology's first "big science" project (that is,

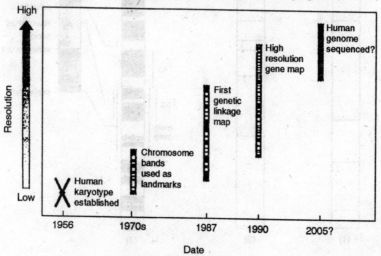

Fig. 14.5. Human genome map.

costing billions of dollars and involving large, organized, inter-disciplinary teams of scientists) and the possible effects on traditional "small science." These concerns have not yet been completely dissipated, and funding of the project remains contentious. In 1989, the proposal was approved under NIH control (although the DOE will still play a research role). The official starting date was October 1, 1990, large-scale sequencing trials began in 1991, and the projected completion date is September 30, 2005, approximately 50 years after James Watson and Francis Crick published their seminal paper on the structure of DNA. The project is centered in the new Office of Human Genome Research at the NIH, and the same James Watson was named director in 1988. Thus, as he put it, he will now complete his journey "starting with the double helix and going up to the double helical structure of man."

Project Research

How will the Human Genome Project proceed? From 1990 to 1995, emphasis will be on developing new technologies required to complete a physical map. Model organisms such as *E. coli*, yeast, *Drosophila*, and mice will be "sequenced" (that is, the exact sequence of the nucleotide bases in their DNA will be determined). Interesting regions of the human genome—for example, those known to be near genes that cause important genetic disorders such as Huntington disease—will also be sequenced. During the next five years, technology for large-scale mapping will be developed, and some of the smaller human chromosomes will be sequenced. Finally, during the last five years of he project, sequencing of the entire genome will be completed.

Mapping the human genome will be the centerpiece of the project, but maps for other organisms, including economically important plants, will also be produced. The current human genome map contains the equivalent of one street marker for each 10 to 50 miles of DNA; a higher-resolution physical map, perhaps achievable as early as the mid-1990s, will reduce that distance between markers to 1 mile. The ultimate DNA sequence map will consist of the nucleotide sequences for each chromosome.

The precise timetable for the project will remain quite fluid since new technical advances can arise quickly and create opportunities for accelerating progress. One such development has already occurred. In December 1989, the prestigious journal *Science* named DNA polymerase the "molecule of the year" because of its role in a powerful new technique called the *polymerase chain reaction* (PCR). PCR came into widespread use in the late 1980s and early 1990s and was selected as the "major scientific development of 1989" in the same issue. Using PCR, short unique pieces of DNA can be amplified, their squences determined, and their precise chromosomal location established. In other words, single-copy DNA sequences—those that occur only once in the human genome—rather than linkage markers or other identifiers, can be used to define the basic landmark on the physical map. These sequence-tagged sites (STS) represent a common language and a new approach that may move the timetable for the physical map forward at least five years and perhaps more.

Importance of the Project

The knowledge gained from the Human Genome Project will be of immediate importance in diagnosing single-gene disorders that affect our species. Progress can also be expected in learning about the underlying nature of enormously complex polygenic (or suspected polygenic) disorders—such as alcoholism, mental illnesses, certain cancers, and heart disease—that affect millions of people but are poorly understood at present. When the project is completed, genes associated with polygenic traits may become apparent as well as the underlying mechanisms that regulat their activities. As with single-gene defects, a basic understanding of the geneitc defect should direct research toward methods for the treatment of various disordes. Certainly, many questions exist about the regulation of such genes, which seem to operate in some coordinated fashion to produce a given trait or genetic disorder. Farther down the road, the new information will also contribute to a greater understanding of gene control mechanisms in eukaryotes, human genome organization, normal and abnormal cellular growth and development, and evolutionary biology.

Besides being vital to the applied sciences, the project is of considerable importance to basic science. The genetic information in the genome repesents the fundamental instructions for the origin, development, maintenance, and eventual demise of an organism. All questions related to these topics can conceivably be addressed from the conceptual framework provided by knowledge of the genome. However, deep knowledge of the genome does not guarantee that we will be able to understand complex processes such as the development of an organism from a fertilized egg. All the genes and their locations may be known, but key details for understanding how all of this information is processed may not be available. Nevertheless, the 1990s should be as fruitful for biological research as the previous decade, and almost certainly more spectacular.

The Future

With respect to humans, the future applications of some new genetic technologies offer exciting prospects for benefiting humankind. For other technologies the future remains uncertain. The molecular technologies we have described throughout this unit have revolutionized our understanding of many human diseases. This field of *DNA diagnostics*—the analysis of disease at the nucleic acid level—has progressed so rapidly that the time may be near when many genetic disorders, cancers, and viral diseases will be analyzed using rapid, automated, and inexpensive procedures. For some disorders, new technologies have already been used to determine the exact disease mechanism causing the phenotypic effect, and others will be identified shortly. Thus it may soon become possible to treat numerous disorders that diminish the quality of life or lead to premature death.

INDEX